T0373164

# Screen Dynamics
# Mapping the Borders of Cinema

Edited by
Gertrud Koch, Volker Pantenburg, Simon Rothöhler

**Österreichisches Filmmuseum**
**SYNEMA – Gesellschaft für Film und Medien**

A book by SYNEMA ≣ Publikationen
Screen Dynamics
Volume 15 of FilmmuseumSynemaPublikationen

This volume was initiated by members of the Collaborative Research Center "Aesthetic Experience and the Dissolution of Artistic Limits" of the *Free University Berlin* and was published with the financial support of the *Deutsche Forschungsgemeinschaft*.

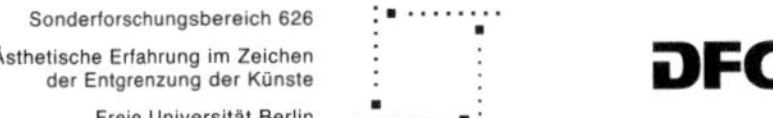




Copy editing: Alexander Horwath, Kellie Rife
Design and layout: Gabi Adébisi-Schuster, Wien
Printed by: REMAprint
Printed and published in Vienna, Austria.
Printed on paper certified in accordance with the rules of the Forest Stewardship Council.

ISBN 978-3-901644-39-9

Österreichisches Filmmuseum (Austrian Film Museum) and SYNEMA – Gesellschaft für Film & Medien are supported by Bundesministerium für Unterricht, Kunst und Kultur – Abteilung V/3 FILM and by Kulturabteilung der Stadt Wien.

# Contents

*In memory of Miriam Bratu Hansen*
*(1949–2011)*

# Preface

The screen shown on the cover of this book is part of the *Sun Cinema*, located above the city of Mardin in southern Turkey, not far from the borders of Syria and Iraq. Asked to participate in a cultural exchange program, the Berlin based artist Clemens von Wedemeyer proposed to build a communal outdoor movie theater. He discussed his plans with architecture students in Istanbul, and finally realized it onsite with the architect Gürden Gür. By day, the screen allows for shadow play; at night, during the film projections, its mirroring flipside reflects both the setting sun and the city lights. *Sun Cinema* was inaugurated in October 2010, halfway between the municipal area of Mardin and the Mesopotamian plains.

A collection of material that Wedemeyer gathered during his research discloses some of the heterogeneous backgrounds of the project: Images of a sun window found in 505 B.C. in the Mardin area; a fortress that sheltered Assyrian sun worshippers around 333 B.C.; sketches of a Persian sundial; a drawing by Robert Smithson that shows his sketches for an underground "Cinema Cavern;" photographs of an American drive-in and the open-air screen of a cinema in Mardin; various documents from the history of optical experiments with light and projection.[1]

Wedemeyer's project positions itself at the intersection of these local and cosmic, optophysical and political utopias and phantasms. It loosely refers to archaic cultural and religious customs, and at the same time it is meant to provide a present-day social space for the local community, which gathers at the annual film festival or at periodic screenings.

*Sun Cinema* is a case in point where the cultural technique of "cinema," with its basic setting of projector, screen and spectator, a communal and social space, is being (re-)enacted at the periphery of the Occidental world. Significantly, this movie theater is not only a "cinema without walls" (Timothy Corrigan) in the most literal sense, but also the result of a project in the tradition of Land Art, conceived and realized by a contemporary artist—an indication that, for more than two decades, a considerable amount of moving images along with the discourse around them has expanded from cinema and film theory to other institutional and discursive spaces.

~

1) See Clemens von Wedemeyer, "Sun Cinema," in *RES. Art World/World Art*, no. 6 (October 2010), pp. 50–57.

A discussion of "screen dynamics" in 2011 therefore implies an emphasis on the fact that "cinema"—more than ever before—is only one of countless media in which moving images are produced, circulated, watched and consumed. In recent years, it has become increasingly clear that the historically close relationship between "cinema" and the aesthetic practice of "film" is being supplemented by an array of different media configurations. From moving images on the Internet to giant IMAX displays, the number of screens in the public and private sphere has risen significantly. While this is often taken to indicate the "death of cinema," this volume attempts to reconsider the limits and specifics of film and the traditional movie theater. Rather than cultivating a narrative of decline and focusing exclusively on the dissolution of the film-celluloid-cinema-nexus, we are interested in the parallel process by which an extended and hugely productive field is opened up. It encompasses, for instance, new tendencies in digital film aesthetics, the exchanges taking place between web-based practices, and the relationship between film and its erstwhile competitor, television, or its old rival, the theater.

The high degree of complexity which characterizes the present constellation as well as the ubiquitous nature of the moving image seems like an apt starting point for our enquiry – an enquiry not only into the ways in which film has entered new aesthetic, technical and institutional spaces, but also into older film theoretical positions and arguments that are inevitably affected by such developments. In line with this approach, this book aims at exploring some of the terrain mapped out by the term "cinema" today.

~

In a volatile situation marked by the coexistence of very large and very small screens, low-resolution web-images and High Definition state-of-the-art cameras, movie theaters and home viewing, the spectrum of positions is wide and doesn't add up to a coherent picture. On the level of production, distribution and spectatorship, things are in flux. This calls for a multiplicity of viewpoints that stem from different convictions and both biographical and intellectual trajectories. It is from his classical cinephile background and a rereading of canonical theories of spectatorship that Raymond Bellour outlines the unique form of spectatorship and memory embedded in the institutional and aesthetic dispositif called "cinema." Focusing on present, web-based forms of sharing films and building communities, Ekkehard Knörer and Jonathan Rosenbaum, albeit from different perspectives, share a belief in the social and discursive power catalyzed by these new forms of spectatorship. While the shift from analog to digital images is often considered a radical rupture as far as the ontological status of film is concerned, a number of essays in this volume attempt to assess the phenomena that have evolved through digitization and the web from a different angle. What seems like a loss of indexicality, Tom Gunning argues, might as well point to a different kind of index, based in movement rather than in photographic realism.

What could easily be mourned as the fragmentation of movies into distractive clips on *YouTube* might be described more accurately with the tools of a "newer psychology," as Ute Holl suggests in her confrontation of classical phenomenology with current forms of watching web-based films. Digitization is a protean entity. More than just the catalyst of a rapid circulation of sound, image and text, it also entails a different aesthetic of the image; an aesthetic that owes more to the specific qualities of High Definition capture than to its digital condition per se, as Simon Rothöhler demonstrates in his chapter on Michael Mann's HD films.

There can be no doubt that the Internet has dislocated massive parts of the present and past film archive. At the same time, other sites of "Relocation" (Francesco Casetti) have begun to attract more and more moving images. Contemporary theater uses film and video projection to confront its specific mode of illusion and fiction with those proper to the moving image (see Gertrud Koch's contribution), museums and art spaces reclaim parts of the experimental cinema heritage (see Volker Pantenburg's essay), television series provide the highly self-reflexive grounds to harbor experiments in narrativity, turning it, as Thomas Morsch argues, into the site of a "permanent metalepsis." Vinzenz Hediger explores the dynamics of the current "cinema without walls" quite literally from a topographical point of view by looking at the "inherent spatiality of film theory."

Where are the edges and borders of cinema? Victor Burgin, both theoretician and visual artist, proposes the term "uncinematic" in order to characterize his own gallery work in its relation to and differences from other forms of "artists' cinema." Structurally different from movies shown in theaters, "uncinematic" moving image work relies on loop and reprise, on paratactical elements rather than on continuous temporal progress.

~

*Screen Dynamics—Mapping the Borders of Cinema* is largely based on talks that were given at a conference in the spring of 2010. Perturbed, as it were, by flight cancellations due to volcanic ashes, the event brought to mind Jean Epstein's inspiring reflections on the energies shared by cinematography and volcanism.[2] As the title of the conference, "Cinema without Walls—Borderlands of Film" suggests, its aim was to explore, based on the general diagnosis of a deepened "multi-medialization" of film, the specific ways in which new forms of interaction between film and adjoining visual worlds come about. Miriam Hansen had been willing to attend, but her health did not permit her to take the long flight. As her presence at the confer-

2) Accompanied by his cameraman Paul Guichard, Epstein was at the flanks of Mount Etna in June 1923 to document the volcano's giant eruption. The breathtaking and perilous spectacle of light and movement made Epstein reflect on animism, violence and the tremendousness of both nature and cinema, which he came to baptize "the most beloved of the living machines." See his *Le cinématographe vu de l'Etna* (1926), reprinted in Epstein, *Écrits sur le cinéma*, vol. 1 (Paris: Cinéma club/Seghers, 1974); German translation in Epstein, *Bonjour Cinéma und andere Schriften zum Kino* (Trans. Ralph Eue, eds. Nicole Brenez and Ralph Eue, Vienna: FilmmuseumSynemaPublikationen, 2008), pp. 43–54.

ence was sorely missed, we are all the more thankful to be able to posthumously include an essay of hers in this volume. It touches on the core issues of the book by combining thoughts about cinema's current situation with a careful reflection on Max Ophuls's sensitivity to "the dynamics between old and new media, as between traditional and technologically mediated arts, and the conflicted cohabitation of different forms of publicness and spectatorship."

None of the fields discussed here are easy to assess. As usual, the technological, cultural and aesthetic changes elicit hopes, doubts, anxieties, ideologies and uncertainties. Cinema, however narrow or expanded you define its scope, still provides a fertile ground and an exciting vantage point for thinking about these (and other) contemporary "screen dynamics."

*Gertrud Koch, Volker Pantenburg,*
*Simon Rothöhler, November 2011*

Raymond Bellour

# The Cinema Spectator: A Special Memory

I begin from a simple hypothesis, but one involving infinite detours: *the lived, more or less collective experience of a film projected in a cinema, in the dark, according to an unalterably precise screening procedure, remains the condition for a special memory experience, one from which every other viewing situation more or less departs*. This supposes a certain rule of faith of which the spectator would be the incarnation, in the unfolding of a liturgy associated with film, with cinema, and with film in the cinema situation.

I wrote "remains the condition," because the distinctive reality of this experience—more or less felt over the entire history of cinema's development from its very beginning, through the so-called silent era and the first years of the talkie—comes essentially to be formulated in the after-war period, alongside what we usually call modern cinema, including all the thinking (critical and theoretical) that accompanies it. And that experience has stayed in place until today, when we are aware of an ever-greater loss, since cinema's centenary and the century's end, to the extent that a conviction concerning the possible death of cinema (or at least its irremediable decline) has been formed and formulated—a situation extending far beyond the already ancient war openly won by television, into the more pressing, fundamental mutation belonging to the digital image, with everything it brings along concerning both the very nature of images and their modes of distribution and consumption.

There are at least two ways of approaching such a topic. The first would be historical, reviewing the specific norms defining the spectator, norms corresponding to this or that moment in the already long history of cinema—without forgetting all the variations according to the times, as well as places, social formations, countries and audiences. But I am not a historian and, anyhow, it would be crazy to open up such a vast framework here. The second way, which I have chosen, is to retain those elements from the past that may illuminate our present-day condition.

In order to encapsulate what is essential in reflection on cinema from its beginnings up to the mid 1950s, I have read or re-read three anthologies (in French, for convenience): Marcel Lapierre's *Anthologie du cinéma* (La Nouvelle Edition, 1946), Pierre Lherminier's *L'Art du cinéma* (Editions Seghers, 1960) and Daniel Banda & José Moure's *Le Cinéma: naissance d'un art 1895–1920* (Flammarion, 2008).

One striking trait in the writings on silent cinema: how little they rely on the notion of the *shot*, preferring instead, most often, to speak of images, scraps, pieces, fragments, framings. A sole exception stands out: Carl Dreyer who, in extremely modern language, situates the relationships between the different shot-scales. Apart from that, it is usually the close-up that catalyses specific attention (in Béla Balázs, for instance), as if every other type of shot against which the close-up defines itself did not really exist, or only exists for the sake of imparting value to the close-up. Soviet filmmakers—particularly Eisenstein and Vertov—are obviously a special case, with their notions of *fragment* and *interval*, implying the intensive multiplication of minimal space-time unities geared to produce an influencing effect on the spectator.

At the same time, another striking notion appears—clearly in some (like Eisenstein or Abel Gance), more vaguely in others: *shock*. A general shock, first of all, before the projection *dispositif*; then, above all, in a later phase, a shock when confronted with particular arrangements of images and the shots required to provoke that emotion—an experience handled in the light of whichever belief or ideology. This term, shock, is (as we know) the word used by Walter Benjamin when he describes cinema as the main site of the *destruction of the aura* that had for so long been associated with the work of art. It is also the word used to describe an art that affects the masses. We need to re-read the texts from this period to recollect to what extent cinema was felt to be the *art of the crowd and the mass*, at this very point when its social reality, as well as the obsession it elicited, exploded. Re-read Louis Delluc, for instance, in 1920: "Cinema is the only spectacle where all crowds meet and unite [...] It draws not the people, but the crowd."[1]

I can now propose a tripartite division that will eventually lead us to the uncertain spectator of our time.

In a *first phase*, thus, the spectator is the *mass subject*, belonging to the era of the development of the big studios, the art of revolutionary propaganda, and the rise of various forms of Fascism.

In a *second phase*, post World War II and prepared by sound cinema before the war, the *subject of the people*—let us call this the *citizen*—appears. It is with this subject that—at least virtually—a more open, constructive, critical relation to cinema is instituted. This phase significantly corresponds to the theoretical extension of the notion of the *shot*. Its charter would be the famous 1939 text by André Malraux, "Sketch for a Psychology of the Moving Pictures," which posited the division into and succession of shots as the fundamental condition for cinema art.[2] This regard for the shot would be taken up by Roger Leenhardt and, above all, André Bazin—to the point of excess in the latter's considerations of the long take and sequence-shot—and then embraced by French criticism and cinephilia, before the coming of theory. (This is equally true of Italy, where the cinema was re-inventing itself via neo-realism, so powerfully received by Bazin—so thoroughly connected are these two countries in relation to both cinematic modernity and the thought linked to it.) The spectator who finds himself imagined and solicited in this way is henceforth the type of viewer that Serge

Daney, in 1989, will retrospectively label "a high-level popular spectator."[3] Such a spectator is linked with the existence of a cinema of art and culture, propped up by institutional forces, and recognized in each country in relation to their own national situation.

This spectator was even able to imagine, at one point, that television, as it had just started to develop, would be the natural extension of cinema, its ally—rather than the shadowy partner who would end up relegating cinema to a lower level in the social system of images, completely opposite to the reason it was invented; even leading, as in Italy, to cinema's near-dissolution.

The *third phase* is the one we are in now. It is the exponential reality prompted, from the end of the 20th century, by the information revolution and the logics of the digital image. So much so that, right inside the cinema situation, there are now, more than ever, at two stark extremes, two kinds of cinema (and not just, like always, better, not-so-good and bad films). On one side, a globally dominant, commercial cinema that is ruled by its own by-products, a falsely spectacular art still supposed to attract a large audience—above all, those young spectators enamored of technological mutations, especially the video games with which film must compete: a cinema based on a degraded aesthetic of stereotypical shock and the unspecific violence of images. On the other side, a cinema that one can describe as *subtly shocking* still develops: a cinema that is increasingly local, diversified, at the same time as it becomes ever more international, seeking everywhere to gain spectators' attentions—avowedly or not, an *art of resistance*. This type of cinema spectator is no longer either the mass subject or the subject of a people (if the latter, it would have to be of those "missing people" invoked by Gilles Deleuze).[4] He has now become the *member of a limited community, but a community henceforth extended to the dimensions of the entire world* (recall the famous *limited action* dear to Stéphane Mallarmé in his 1897 essay of that title). It was on the basis of belief in such a community that Serge Daney felt the desire to create his film magazine *Trafic*, which we have continued since his death in 1992.

(Obviously, at one edge or other of this double cinema, ambiguous and complex bridges come into being. I am thinking, for example, not so much of *The Matrix*—which is above all a symptomatic film for voracious theorists—but rather James Cameron's *Avatar*, in which we find, through the very excess of its spectacle, a new perceptual sensibility emerging.)

Whoever would presume to include such a genesis of the cinema spectator within a logic and a history would have to follow these twin terms of *shock* and *distraction* down all their

1) Daniel Banda and José Moure (eds.), *Le Cinéma: naissance d'un art 1895–1920* (Paris: Flammarion, 2008), p. 507.

2) André Malraux, "Sketch for a Psychology of the Moving Pictures," in Susanne K. Langer (ed.), *Reflections on Art: A Source Book of Writings by Artists, Critics, and Philosophers* (New York: Oxford University Press, 1958).

3) Serge Daney, *L'Exercise a été profitable, Monsieur* (Paris: P.O.L., 1993), p. 234.

4) See Gilles Deleuze, "What is the Creative Act?" in *Two Regimes of Madness: Texts and Interviews 1975–1995* (New York: Semiotext(e), 2006), pp. 317–329.

paths. Shock is rightly that which can grab the attention or, equally, distract it—an attention which, born of shock, also, at the outset, both goes beyond and falls short of it. Attention is the term chosen by Jonathan Crary in his most recent great book *Suspensions of Perception* to define the ever-livelier concentration on the image during the 19th century, a phenomenon which finds one of its fulfillments in the invention of cinema.[5] Attention is also a key word in the first genuine book of cinema theory, which has long been a kind of aerolite, Hugo Münsterberg's *The Photoplay: A Psychological Study* (1916)—the chapter titles of which invoke, for the inner world of the spectator aroused by the forms of the exterior world on film, the four major processes of *attention*, *memory* and *imagination*, and *emotion*.[6] And these are the four processes that belong to any deep experience of cinema. Attention is, moreover, the word used by Benjamin in his "The Work of Art in the Age of its Mechanical Reproducibility" essay. We know how risky it is to try to pinpoint Benjamin's use of the term, particularly in relation to this essay, with its multiple versions and their changing inflections.[7] By sticking with the final 1939 version, however, we can grasp exactly how attention—which we will henceforth render as *attentiveness*—is articulated between distraction and shock. On one side, adopting—according to the ambiguous goal of politically redeeming the aura—the viewpoint of an art connected to the masses (with cinema as his example), Benjamin associates distraction with tactility, "being based on changes of scene and focus which have a percussive effect on the spectator."[8] He adds, a few lines on, that "the shock effect of the film, [...] like all shocks, seeks to induce heightened attention."[9] But this same effect also denies the spectator—this hero of "tactile reception"—such a mode of attention. Transforming him into an "examiner" or expert through his connection to technology, Benjamin can conclude (this is the end of the text before its epilogue) that "at the movies, the evaluating attitude requires no attention."[10]

Later, it would take—in the context of a cinema in the process of post-war renewal—the new type of consideration brought to film by a spectator and film critic like Bazin to turn attentiveness (regardless of whether Bazin used this word) into the process which at once grasps, bends to one's own purpose and renders in all their subtlety all those shocks (ever more diversified as mini-shocks mixed with consciousness effects) which accompany what can be called, from this point on, the reading of film. (Later, we will find in Deleuze this image of an image made readable.) It is moving to follow this work of reading in Bazin, which often tries to be terribly precise at a time when there existed no other means of study than to see the film again in a theater—so much so that the numerous (sometimes excessive) factual errors that dot his texts must be credited to the passion associated with this new type of attentiveness.

But it would also happen that, much later still, this adult, critical citizen-spectator finds himself, on the one hand, equipped with new means to support his reading and, on the other hand, threatened in this same historical reality by social and technological mutations that evoke the intuition of a possible death of cinema as art—in order that he may fully recognize his true condition, in a way that is at once retrospective and prospective, within the perspective of art as resistant thought (in the sense that Deleuze gives to these words, for example in his conference "What is the Creative Act?").[11]

This work of recognition was undertaken especially by Serge Daney across the totality of his critical work, from *Ciné journal* (prefaced by Deleuze in 1986) to the collection *Devant la recrudescence des vols de sacs à main* (1991) which is devoted to the conflicted relations between cinema and television. But it is above all in the posthumously published diary, *L'Exercice a été profitable, Monsieur* (1993), that Daney offered his most striking formulations on the difficult transition from the second to the third phase of spectatorship, and its consequently altered nature (in an eloquent parallel with the *Histoire(s) de cinéma* project [1988-1998] by Jean-Luc Godard—who tagged Daney the *ciné-fils* or cine-son).

So here, briefly, are some formulations that can be wielded to illuminate the renewed conception of the spectator, from the opening pages of this book by Daney that counts among the most precious moments in all reflection on cinema. Straight off we have the question: what is in crisis in cinema? And the dual response: on the one hand it is the dark theater and, on the other, cinema's means of recording. What they have in common is "a certain 'passivity' of the celluloid and/or the spectator. Things are imprinted twice over: first upon the film strip, then upon the spectator. [...] This *dispositif* is all of a piece." In relation to the temporality which is determined in this fashion, Daney is clear: it is a "time of the 'maturing' of a film within the body and nervous system of a spectator in the darkness." He adds that this relation to time allows us to "pass from the passivity of he who looks to the activity of he who writes. [...] To write is to recognize what is already written. Written in the film (the film as an organized depository of signs) and in me (the self organized as a depository of mnemic traces that, over time, comprise my his-

5) Jonathan Crary, *Suspensions of Perception: Attention, Spectacle, and Modern Culture* (Cambridge: MIT Press, 1999).

6) American edition: Hugo Münsterberg, *The Film: A Psychological Study—The Silent Photoplay in 1916* (New York: Dover, 1970).

7) I merely point any reader curious to explore this infinite mobility of terms in the direction of two crucial essays by Miriam Hansen: "Benjamin, Cinema and Experience," in *New German Critique*, no. 40 (Winter 1987), pp. 179–224; and "Room-for-Play: Benjamin's Gamble with Cinema," in *October*, no. 109 (Summer 2004), pp. 3–46 (bearing particularly on Benjamin's second, French version in which the positions are less clear-cut). See also, on distraction, the eloquent fragment published as "Theory of Distraction" in Benjamin, *Selected Writings Vol. 3, 1935–1938* (Cambridge: Harvard University Press, 2002), pp. 141–142.

8) Walter Benjamin, "The Work of Art in the Age of Its Technological Reproducibility: Third Version," in *Selected Writings Vol. 4, 1938–1940* (Cambridge: Harvard University Press, 2003), p. 267.

9) *Ibid.*

10) *Ibid.*, p. 269.

11) Deleuze, *op. cit.*

tory)."[12] Later, he elaborates: "Filling up time presumes a spectator who is capable of *memorizing the film as a sum of information*, thus a high-level popular spectator. As distinct from the spectator today who no longer waits around for this experience."[13] From which derives, ultimately, the optimistic reversal of obligatory pessimism, the temptation that led Daney to conceive a chronicle he never started, which would have had the title *The Cinema, Alone*—devoted to "what cinema alone has the mission to pursue."[14] Clearly, it would have tackled—according to the ever-renewed inventiveness of films themselves—the responsibility, as much psychic as ethical and political, of an attentiveness to and memory of shots, their unfolding and phrasing, their rhythm, about which none spoke better than Daney, across his texts and particularly his diary entries. "The shot is an indivisible block of image and time. [...] The shot is musical. [...] Breath, rhythm. There is 'cinema' whenever, inexplicably, something breathes between the images. [...] In cinema, the only thing I care about is the shots."[15]

We must thus inquire into the possible conditions of this spectator as he is today—twenty years after Daney's lines—definitively in the minority, but still and always waiting for the experience, even if it has necessarily become rather dissimilar.

The only truly inviolate element is the *dispositif*. The theater. The darkness. The fixed time of the screening, whatever form it takes (even those private sessions that bored Roland Barthes so much), as long as it preserves the experience of a projection in time and its inscription on the memory-screen, so that a special kind of work can occur. This is what was expressed very well, in 1912, by an author whose identity remains unknown, hidden under the pseudonym of Yhcam: "The darkness of the theater constitutes an important factor contributing, via the contemplation [*recueillement*] it produces, far more than one might imagine, to the impression created: the spectator's attention is solicited and concentrated on the luminous projection without any possible distraction emanating from the theater space."[16] Let us note that contemplation (*recueillement* in French, *Sammlung* in German) is the word that described for Benjamin the necessary relation to the artwork, menaced —for better and worse—by the 'distraction' which was, in his eyes, inherent to cinema. Listen, too, to Alfonso Reyes, three years after Yhcam: "The perfect film spectator demands silence, isolation and darkness: he is working, collaborating in the spectacle."[17] To which we can add, four years on again, some words from the Danish filmmaker Urban Gad, describing the screen by

12) Serge Daney, *L'Exercice a été profitable, Monsieur* (Paris: P.O.L., 1993), pp. 19–20.

13) *Ibid.*, p. 235.

14) *Ibid.*, p. 157.

15) *Ibid.*, p. 22.

16) Banda and Moure, *op. cit.*, p. 238.

17) *Ibid.*, p. 342.

18) *Ibid.*, p. 418.

19) No one, I believe, has evoked this feeling better than Federico Fellini in the course of his interviews with Giovanni Grazzini. I could quote two whole pages, but here are at least a few key lines: "The cinema has lost its authority, mystery, prestige, magic; this gigantic

invoking the superior reality of "a mirror [...] suspended above us, obliging us to lift our eyes."[18] Here we recall Godard's famous words cited by Chris Marker, who extends them in his CD-ROM *Immemory* (1997): "Cinema is what's bigger than us, to which we have to lift our eyes [...] What we see on TV is the shadow of a film, regret for a film, its nostalgia, its echo—never a real film."[19] That means neither television nor computers, not the Internet, mobile phones or a giant personal screen can take the place of cinema—whatever their respective advantages (which can sometimes be enormous).[20] For what is essential is always missing, everything that makes the *dispositif* 'all of a piece': silence, darkness, distance, projection for an audience, in the obligatory time of a session that nothing can suspend or interrupt. Daney wrote: "A film on TV belongs neither to cinema nor TV—it is a 'reproduction' or, better yet, a piece of 'information' on a prior state of coexistence between men and their images, those they feed on and those that help them live."[21]

By a fascinating reversal, we can thus attribute to the cinema screen, at the centre of its true *dispositif*, the 'distant' quality that Benjamin thought of as the guarantee of the aura traditionally associated with the artwork. We can re-read, in this paradoxical sense, the passage in which he described the relation between distance and nearness, while thinking of the effect that passes from one to the other—that instant when, rather than lifting our eyes toward the image, we can even touch it.

The definition of the aura as the "unique apparition of a distance, however near it may be," represents nothing more than a formulation of the cult value of the work of art in categories of spatiotemporal perception. Distance is the opposite of nearness. The *essentially* distant is the unapproachable. Unapproachability is, indeed, a primary quality of the cult image; true to its nature, the cult image remains "distant, however near it may be." The nearness one may gain from its substance [*Materie*] does not impair the distance it retains in its apparition.[22]

All of which amounts to: one can rewatch a

screen which dominates an audience lovingly gathered in front of it, filled with very small people who look, enchanted, at huge faces, huge lips, huge eyes, living and breathing in another unattainable dimension, at once fantastic and real, like that of a dream, this large magic screen no longer fascinates us. We have now learnt to dominate it. We are larger than it. Look what we have done with it: a tiny screen, no larger than a cushion, between the bookshelves and a vase of flowers, sometimes put in the kitchen, near the refrigerator. It has become a household appliance, and we, in an armchair, clutching our remote, wield over these little images a total power, fighting against what is alien to us, and what bores us." Fellini in Grazzini, *Comments on Film* (Trans. Joseph Henry, Fresno: California State University, 1988), p. 207.

20) Here I am not considering the projections specific to all kinds of installations in art galleries and museum spaces. See on this point, apart from my two volumes *L'Entre-Images. Photo, Cinéma, Vidéo* (Paris: La Différence, 1990) and *L'Entre-Images 2. Mots, Images* (Paris: P.O.L., 1999), my essays "Le Cinéma seul/ Multiples 'cinémas'" in Jacques Aumont (ed.), *Le Septième Art. Le cinéma parmi les arts* (Paris: Léo Scheer, 2003), p. 257–280; and "Du photographique", in *Trafic*, no. 55 (Autumn 2005), p. 20–37.

21) Serge Daney, *Devant la recrudescence des vols de sacs à main* (Lyon: Aléas, 1991), p. 12.

22) Benjamin, "The Work of Art," p. 272.

film in various situations, but only if, first time around, it has been seen and received according to its own aura.

All that is left now is to swiftly indicate why this privilege of the *dispositif* is so absolute.

I have also read, for this contribution, five recent books, all fine and important, and (for a French reader) all foreign, whose combined titles are eloquent. Paolo Cherchi Usai's *The Death of Cinema: History, Cultural Memory and the Digital Dark Age* (2001), Victor Burgin's *The Remembered Film* (2004), Francesco Casetti's *Eye of the Century: Film, Experience, Modernity* (first Italian edition 2005), Laura Mulvey's *Death 24x a Second: Stillness and the Moving Image* (2006), and David N. Rodowick's *The Virtual Life of Film* (2007).

These five books—all very personal, and thereby as different as their authors—have in common their reckoning with the digital revolution and its symbolic dating made to more or less coincide with, on the one hand, the end of the century and, on the other, the centenary of cinema and the feeling it produced that something, thus, is ending. Casetti, for example, in order to categorically constitute cinema as the 'eye of the 20th century,' goes about distinguishing a 'Cinema 2.0' which, succeeding the first, would be something completely different, even including the very look-back it allows upon what thus now becomes 'Cinema 1.0.' Mulvey, for her part, revisits the idea of the *pensive spectator* with which I once described the psychic suspension introduced into the unfolding of a film by the immobility of still photography—making it, in fact, the hero of what she calls 'delayed cinema,' in which the film experience is transformed by every operation (freezing, suspending, metamorphosing) that the digital image—more broadly than even the electronic image—now provides.

It seems to me that these books, to which I feel so close, nonetheless misunderstand the way in which Cinema 2.0 (to adopt Casetti's term) simultaneously remains, in its very principle, identical to Cinema 1.0: in both cases, the spectator—no matter how transformed by the prostheses that offer him access to film in a new ways—finds himself in a cinema-*dispositif* and projection situation that has remained, in a sense, unchanged since the 1916 that Münsterberg described. For, apart from and beyond those new memory-prostheses, and in this sense independent of them—and even if a film takes these developments as its subject, as Chris Marker did in *Level Five* (1997)—something unique is testified to by a projected film: it is *the lived experience in real time of a cumulative process of remembering and forgetting, each of which nourishes the other, an experience according to which our attentiveness (more or less drifting or concentrated)—naturally varying according to the specific subject and the particular projection—becomes the testing ground for all the subtle shocks of which any film worthy of the name offers a more or less differentiated variety, according to its own style.* It seems especially the case that this relation between drifting attentiveness and concentrated or exacerbated attentiveness, and thus between passivity and activity—so essential to the free, cumulative working of oblivion and memory—can have no real equivalent in any of the concurrent *dispositifs*, which always lean too far, alternatively, and each according to its own format, in one direction or another. It is this *in vivo* work of active memory, becoming more or less self-conscious within the terms that each person chooses to cultivate (so as to better understand) its effects, that is specific to the projection experience, and it alone. There must be silence, darkness, a uniform time that allows us to gauge a temporality—to what extent, and how, it develops in continuity—a temporality that is at the same time striated with events, between the shots and within the shots of which every film is composed.

In *The Remembered Film*, Burgin borrows from Michel Foucault the concept of *heterotopia* (i.e., the reality of incompatible spaces) to then describe cinema. He thus invokes all the "variously virtual spaces in which we encounter displaced places of films: the Internet, the media and so on, but also the psychical spaces of a spectating subject that Baudelaire first identified as a 'kaleidoscope equipped with consciousness.'"[23] But it seems that we can invoke—along these lines but also in a contrary direction—via the mental heterotopia specific to each spectator and across a cinema shattered into different phases of technological and social reality, a return to a true *utopia*, a utopia at once real and current: the very experience of film, as such, the totality of suspended time that lasts for a projection and effects in the film an assembling of memory in a sole place, no matter how dispersive it may be or how diverse all the places it convokes.

The pensive spectator (an idea I have reformulated in my recent book *Le Corps du cinéma. Hypnoses, émotions, animalités*, P.O.L., 2009) thus has no meaning outside its coincidence with the strict temporality of film projection—regardless of his prior anticipation and the returns to it he can later stage by other means, in line with his curiosity and his eventual desire to work on the film.

I do not have the space here to give the slightest example of the way in which films invite us to reflect, always more or less consciously or unconsciously, but always according to this unshakeable principle: what can only have been more or less forgotten has been also necessarily inscribed, so that it can enter into a resonance with what has been recalled and—by that very process—refound.

This is what François Truffaut was talking about when he wrote in 1954, in relation to Hitchcock: "The homage that one can pay to an author or film-maker is to attempt to know and understand his book or his film as well as he does himself."[24] And, by laying out the systematic organization of the 'number two' and the rhymed construction of multiple figures in *Shadow of a Doubt* (1943), Truffaut himself thus gave us the example of what might be the first film analysis.

Such a vision presumes an attentiveness, a kind of seizure before the shocks and mini-shocks more or less immediately memorized,

23) Victor Burgin, *The Remembered Film* (London: Reaktion, 2004), p. 10.

24) François Truffaut, "Skeleton Keys," in *Film Culture*, no. 32 (Spring 1964), p. 66.

and amplified as the film unfolds, in order to comprise an uncertain block of memory—the guarantee of an experience that one can say must have been like that on a first viewing, in order to trigger the desire, afterwards, to go deeper. This always somewhat hallucinated 'first time' seizure seems the essential condition of what constitutes—despite all the other means of access to images which gather everywhere—the true nature of the film spectator, transformed, threatened and ironed out by history but also, in a sense, transhistorical.

I guess, retrospectively, that it was the series of extremely subtle shocks provoked at the outset by the second shot of Kenji Mizoguchi's *Miss Oyu* (1951)—when the hero strolls into the depth of frame followed by the camera which floats up and along while passing a cannily graduated succession of dark, knotted tree trunks and clear, straight bamboos—that aroused my attentiveness and the memory attached to these figures of trees and pillars that are deployed throughout the film, imprinting their mark upon the characters' bodies in so many frames. I also know that it was by making the mistake of wanting one night to watch an older Mizoguchi film, *The Story of the Last Chrysanthemums* (1939), on a bad TV set that I progressively lost my memory of it—to the point of experiencing, through this sensory loss of images, trouble in following the very plot they trace, and even in telling the characters apart.

I have deliberately left aside, until now, a problem without any clear answer: the modification occurring in the spectator, due not to any global change in the *dispositif* strictly speaking, but to one of its essential elements—the material base (for recording and/or distribution) which has today moved, to an extent that has become unstoppable, from analogue to digital. Rodowick's *The Virtual Life of Film* is essentially devoted to an evaluation of this shift: he does so with exemplary care in handling some difficult equilibriums and their related uncertainties—in a way that contrasts sharply (and all for the better) with the theoretical monologism of Lev Manovich's *The Language of New Media* (2001), a trait which Rodowick is compelled to limit. His clearest impression relates, ultimately, to time—the absence of a feeling of time transmitted by the digital image, for which it substitutes a material succession of frames regulated by the light generated from an informatic table formed by mathematical algorithms. Rodowick takes as an example Alexander Sokurov's *Russian Ark* (2002), with its sole ninety-minute shot, filmed in digital and largely recomposed in postproduction—a film which "does not involve me in time."[25] One cannot really object to this impression, which is at any rate unassailable insofar as such statements are always difficult to ground theoretically. On this level, it will always be a war of impression vs. impression, sensation vs. sensation, memory vs. memory, perhaps (or above all) work against work, and the adopting of formal positions. It is enough for me to have seen, several years ago, Ingmar Bergman's *Saraband* (2003), shot and (unusually) projected digitally in a Paris cinema, to grasp—in the face of this accomplished example of what Barthes called a "festival of affects"[26] based on the insistent relation between strata, returns of time and the intensive effects of shot changes—that the potential gap attached to the experience is not primarily due to its material base (i.e., digital) but, as ever, in the theater and the screening session.

But how can I suggest, in just a few words, the effect that grips a spectator in the singular situation of attentiveness which I believe is specific, above all, to theatrical projection, before a film that demands it? This effect is comprised, at the least obvious but most decisive level, of subtle commotions, suspensions, interruptions, associations, recalls and returns—all of which trace always infinitely variable circles of extension, as the film progresses and builds itself, and which the modes of attentiveness particular to each spectator elaborate in it. Virtualities never cease propagating themselves, faced with this trait, that element, this shot-event—between shots, and radiating out to the entire film, in its infinite opening, along every possible direction. It is thereby clear that a mental virtuality never ceases doubling the film, in the form of a returning back of associations as recurrences. It seems that intermittent fixities never stop being projected, reprojecting themselves, between the film and its spectator. In the same sense that the photographer Gisèle Freund stated her extremely strong intuition or assumption that it is through still images that one retains the most striking memory of things. This accounts for the outstanding feature we find in so many modern and experimental films, more and more resulting from technological mutation: the presence of the still photo in films, frozen images, every kind of interruption. As if the work of memory in action mimicked, in this fashion, the very same energy that bears along the thread of movement and time. But it is perhaps too simple to think of these interruptions, these permanent memory-in-action recalls—that also extend the film into the individual life of every spectator—as instants of actual fixity. No more than they exist in the film itself which, despite every possible fixity, moves ahead in time. Maybe it is a question, rather, of accumulated fixities, thus producing from among themselves something like a particular, aberrant movement, corresponding better to the psychic interruption whereby the spectator never ceases inscribing this dual movement that he both perceives and interiorizes. This could be exactly what Godard sought to specify, this singular animation, via the decompositions that have entered his films since *France/tour/détour/deux/enfants* (1979) and *Sauve qui peut (la vie)* (1979). This movement that is frozen, or stirred up in its movement. And that thereby ceaselessly returns time upon itself. The strongest point is surely that Godard has been driven to finally imagine himself as a meta-spectator, seated behind his typewriter, facing the entirety of cinema which then parades itself—fragmented, frozen, fixed, carried off, set in movement, mentally mixed—all throughout his *Histoire(s) du cinéma*. These *His-*

25) David N. Rodowick, *The Virtual Life of Film* (Cambridge: Harvard University Press, 2007), p. 164 and the entire analysis which follows.

26) Roland Barthes, "Upon Leaving the Movie Theater," in Theresa Hak Kyung Cha (ed.), *Apparatus* (New York: Tanam Press, 1980), p. 1.

*toire(s)* shot on video and produced for television, but that only (I believe) acquire their greatest effect in relation to the very thing they are aiming to invoke—a gigantic memory—when they receive a theatrical projection, the type of projection of which, all throughout his interminable monologue, Godard never ceases recalling the singular, unique power.

In order to know, somewhat more precisely, what this work of memory is all about—and how it can be just as easily brought about (or not), and above all with what meaning and in which proportion, by the mutation of the analogue into the digital image—it is solely neurobiology, I believe, to which we may perhaps one day turn to illuminate some aspect of how it all functions, at the basic level of likely variations in intensity between neuronal connections, and be able (by analogy if need be) to give names to such innumerable and obscure processes.

There remains one other, final hypothesis—or rather, the phantom hypothesis to my hypothesis, an idea to which I cannot really respond, since it is a delusion to think you can truly get outside of yourself enough to be constituted as a historical object. It is possible that such a view of cinema as I have presented here belongs to a generation for which "cinema, alone" actually existed, and for whom, as such, it is forever inscribed. Jean Louis Schefer called this, in a formula very swiftly appropriated by Daney, "the films that have looked at our childhood."[27] Perhaps, lacking a comparable predestination which will soon be without any witness, such a utopia of film as the special memory place will lose all reality.

But this would be to erase the *memory of memory* of which art and culture are made, to the extent that they manage to reinvent themselves. For such a loss would also assume a real death of cinema, and that still seems unlikely, seeing that today's world still produces true cinema films, and that the limited but immense community of their spectators reactivates this ritual, in ways both real and virtual, each time that the experience of a film is lived out according to its own specific reality, within that unchanging *dispositif.*

At the end of one of the most beautiful books ever written on the reality of literature, *The Book to Come* (originally published 1959), Maurice Blanchot arrives at a hypothesis concerning the "death of the last writer." What would happen if, suddenly, "the little mystery of writing [...] would disappear, without anyone noticing it?"[28] Not, contrary to what one might imagine, a great silence. But rather a murmuring, a new sound: "It speaks, it doesn't stop speaking, it is like the void that speaks, a light murmuring, insistent, indifferent, that is probably the same for everyone, that is without secret and yet isolates each person, separates him from the others, from the world and from himself. [...] A writer is one who imposes silence on this speech, and a literary work is, for one who knows how to penetrate it, a rich resting place of silence, a firm defense and a high wall against this eloquent immensity that addresses us by turning us away from ourselves. If, in this imaginary Tibet, where the sacred signs could no longer be discovered in anyone, all literature stopped speaking, what would be lacking is silence, and it is this lack of silence that would perhaps reveal the disappearance of literary language."

Blanchot adds to his hypothesis that, on the day that this murmuring imposes itself, on the death of the last writer, "the treasure of old works, the refuge of Museums and Libraries" would be, again contrary to what one would imagine, of little help, because "we have to imagine that, on the day this wandering language imposes itself, we will witness a distinctive disturbance of all the books."

You will have guessed, I think, that the murmur accompanying the death of the last film and of the utopia it once incarnated will be the sound of the universal reign of media, of which cinema will merely be just another element, just an image-skeleton floating among all the other images; and that the day on which no film is any longer made to be seen in a cinema theater, we cannot expect much help from the refuge of Museums and Cinémathèques.

*Translated by Adrian Martin*

27) Jean Louis Schefer, *L'homme ordinaire du cinéma* (Paris: Cahiers du cinéma/Gallimard, 1980).

28) Maurice Blanchot, *The Book to Come* (Trans. Charlotte Mandell, Stanford: Stanford University Press, 2003), pp. 218–220 (for this and the following quotations).

Miriam Hansen

# Max Ophuls and Instant Messaging

*Reframing Cinema and Publicness**

This paper is *not* about digital cinema, nor is it about the "death of cinema" debate. A number of film scholars assembled here have participated in and shaped this debate, and I don't presume to be making an original contribution to it. I'm going to be talking about something else. Still, allow me to briefly situate myself in relation to some of the key issues that have defined that debate. The arguments mobilized around the fate-of-cinema question largely revolve around two claims made by digital enthusiasts and cinephiles alike: (a) that the shift from photochemically-based indexicality to digital coding has substantially attenuated cinema's relation to reality, its supposedly medium-specific affinity with the material world; (b) that digital technologies of circulation and delivery have marginalized theatrical projection and dispersed the viewing of films to a variety of small screens and multiple media platforms. Let me say first off that I consider the debate on indexicality to some extent a red herring, useful only as part of a larger discussion on referentiality. As to the second proposition, I'm not quite sure where I stand, given the proliferation of hybrid forms involving film and video in the contemporary art world as well as the new life given to collective reception in the context of political movements and alternative venues (e.g. film clubs and movie bars in China and elsewhere).

Accounts of what has changed in and about cinema tend to be linked to the rhetoric of a break. Film theorists such as Phil Rosen have rightly pointed out that the rhetoric of a break itself is nothing new, considering that it has accompanied major junctures of technological innovation, from the invention of cinema itself, through the advent of sound and proliferation of television, video, and cable.

While I agree with this caveat, I do think we are dealing with something more fundamental today—not merely a matter of technological and institutional adjustment but a palpable, seismic shift in the cinema's relation to publicness or *Öffentlichkeit*, as the unstable matrix through which individual and social experience is articulated and organized.[1] This shift encompasses but goes way beyond changes in the production of moving images and the threat to the

*) Editors' note: This is the manuscript of a talk that Miriam Hansen (1949–2011) gave at the conference *Perspectives on the Public Sphere: Cinematic Configurations of "I" and "We"* (Berlin, April 23–25, 2009). The text was preceded by a short abstract: "Looking again at the opening sequence from Max Ophuls's *Liebelei*, this paper asks how earlier reconfigurations of publicness in and through the cinema appear from the perspective of the current threshold period. The ongoing major changes in the organization of human experience urge us to rethink the relationship between cinema and the

status of cinema as a public space of projection. Rather, it relates to the transformation of just about everything surrounding the cinema—the amazing reorganization of everyday experience in terms of spatiotemporal coordinates, modes of sensory perception and attention, cognition, affect, and memory, sociability and the circulation of knowledge. Obviously, I am referring to the rise of the Internet and the worldwide web, to phenomena such as *YouTube,* videogames, social networks, GPS, cell phones and instant messaging, and the seemingly inexorable tendency to combine all these media into single mobile pieces of hardware. Given that these developments are driven by a still booming market in consumer electronics and an explosion of electronic marketing and consumption, we are dealing with an unprecedented degree of acceleration in their adaptation, yet also the possibility that some products will go the way of all fashion.

These developments have been described in terms of a culture of "convergence" (Henry Jenkins), in which cinema disappears "into the larger stream of the audiovisual media, be they photographic, electronic, or cybernetic,"[2] in which content and communication have priority over the materiality of the medium. They have been celebrated—or, as the case may be, decried—for principles of instantaneity and simultaneity, mobility, ubiquity, and constant and potentially global access, and they have spawned a new participatory culture which lends itself both to unprecedented surveillance and to new forms of grassroots mobilization that have already demonstrated their political effectiveness worldwide, not just (but crucially) with the last Presidential election in the U.S.[3] While this is a vast and fast-changing, violently contested and contradictory field, my concern here is primarily with the implications of these changes from the vantage-point of the cinema—with their effect on the sensory-perceptual, aesthetic dimensions of experience and configurations of intimacy and publicness. Whether we like it or not, these changes constitute the horizon within and against which the cinema will not only survive, if it survives, but also remain a living cultural form.

As you may have guessed, I am arguing that we need to translate Benjamin's paradigmatic gesture of 1936—his claim that technological reproducibility, in particular the emergence of film, radio, and photography has fundamen-

public sphere. These changes encompass but go beyond the issue as to what effect and to what extent digital technologies have transformed the way films are produced, delivered, and consumed; as they reframe film history, they also resituate the cinema in relation to the traditional arts. The question posed by *Liebelei* is, among other things, about how to negotiate generational gaps in the field of cinema studies."

1) The manuscript adds in brackets: "Negt & Kluge, *Public Sphere and Experience* [1972] rather than Habermas." See Alexander Kluge and Oskar Negt, *Public Sphere and Experience. Toward an Analysis of the Bourgeois and Proletarian Public Sphere* (Trans. Peter Labanyi, Jamie Owen Daniel, and Assenka Oksiloff, Minneapolis: University of Minnesota Press, 1993).

2) Robert Stam, *Film Theory. An Introduction* (Malden: Blackwell, 2000), p. 314.

3) The manuscript adds in brackets: "sentence or two about difference from televisual publicness."

tally reframed the traditional arts—for the present and consider the cinema, whatever its internal changes, as thoroughly reframed by this new media environment. And this concerns not only what the cinema *is* but what it *was*. Which is the reason I'd like to take a detour through the cinema of Max Ophuls (prompted by my teaching once again a course on the director which presented a greater challenge this time around than only a few years ago). While Ophuls was clearly not as radical as Benjamin in defining the fault lines between cinema and the "classical" arts—and in terms of political temperament closer to Kracauer—I take his films to be concerned with remarkably similar issues, in particular the gap between human consciousness and modern systems of technology and exchange, as well as the relationship between cinema and the traditional arts, in Ophuls's case music and theater.

Re-watching Ophuls's films with a generation of students who do not know a world before computers, cell phones, and videogames highlights the distance between this kind of cinema—the cinephile's dream—and current configurations of publicness and experience.[4] That distance is palpable even if we argue, as I do, that Ophuls is a modernist (steeped in Weimar theater, radio practice, and debates on mass culture) who disguises his engagement with the contradictions and crisis of the present—his present—in turn-of-the-century costume dramas. However, looking at Ophuls's films again from the vantage point of our present makes us realize that they not only foreground the role of technology and exchange in the production of spectacle. They also engage with earlier moments of historic transition—the dynamics between old and new media, as between traditional and technologically mediated arts, and the conflicted cohabitation of different forms of publicness and spectatorship.[5]

For obvious reasons I let this clip run on into a new subsegment, even though the sequence arguably concludes with the Baron's departure from the theater, marked by the unpleasurably abrupt stop to the aria from the second act of *The Abduction from the Seraglio*.

Much could be said—and has been said—about this virtuoso opening to what I consider one of Ophuls's most heartbreaking films. It introduces all the protagonists in the same space (the Baroness by technological extension) and

4) Editors' note: In 2011, Miriam Hansen started to revise her talk. In its new, albeit unfinished version, the text starts by extending on this observation: "In 2009, I taught a seminar on the cinema of Max Ophuls, an upper-level undergraduate and first-year graduate course I had developed in 2002 and repeated in 2005. In the previous seminars we seemed embarked on a journey of collective discovery, with students turning out for second screenings of the same film (about half of them in 35mm) and joking among each other about their newfound infatuation. Only a few years later, I found it considerably more difficult to get the students to engage with these beautiful films; one of the few who did so early on enthusiastically reported that he had managed to download *Lola Montes* on his laptop. While the difference between these two teaching moments may have more to do with the glow of cinephile memory (and with the time warp afforded by a private university), it prompted me to revisit the debate on the changed status of cinema in contemporary moving image culture."

5) The manuscript adds in brackets: "Show the opening sequence of *Liebelei* (1933) in the Vienna opera theater up to the concierge's telephone conversation with the Baroness and, through a pneumatic communication device, with the stage manager."

*Liebelei*
(1933, Max Ophuls)

sets up the two fatally interlocking plot strands—the "old story" of Fritz's adulterous affair with the Baroness and his "new," deeply romantic love with Christine, triggered by the fall of the two girls' binoculars onto Theo's military cap, the first in a series of transfers of objects and a transgression in more than one sense. The sequence also introduces us to a pervasive motif in Ophuls's work—the displacement of the gaze from the anticipated spectacle to the diegetic spectators and the material preparations in the production of spectacle which itself is forever delayed. We hear parts of the music (which emotionally animates the action, just as the lyrics reflect and ironically refract it), but we never see the performance of the opera, and we never see the Kaiser whose entry further delays the beginning of the second act; in fact, a false match makes the offending girls in the gallery appear as the object of the collective gaze momentarily redirected—by means of electric lighting and Haydn's *Emperor Quartet*—from the stage to the empty space of power.

The sequence is structured by the dichotomy of competing public spheres and the media that subtend them. The setting places us in the distractive public sphere of the bourgeois and court theater, with its topography of class hierarchy and a regime of seeing and being seen that is at once sociable and panoptical. Yet the two girls pushing to the front of the gallery appear like visitors from a living future who happened into the wrong film, closer to the world of Ophuls's earlier "musical" *Die verliebte Firma (Company in Love*, 1931/32). Endowed with a conspicuously large instrument of vision, they are not only marked as transgressive of the old patriarchal taboo on the female gaze; they are also emissaries from a modern mass culture of female spectatorship that Kracauer in/famously pinpointed in his essay, "The Little Shopgirls Go to the Movies" (1927)—a trope for the public that Ophuls knew he had to contend with.[6] If the sequence inserts a splinter of a different, emergent public sphere into the diegesis, it also enacts that fracture at the level of cinematic discourse. In a more condensed form than any other Ophuls film I can think of, this sequence stages forms of vision not available to the theater: subjective shots and eye-line matching as in the stage manager's mobile look through the eye-socket of the grotesque mask painted on the curtain; Fritz's amused glance at the cap knocked out of his friend's hand; the Baron's registering of Fritz's empty seat; and, most conspicuously, Theo's narratively gratuitous, pronounced look through the girls' binoculars that brings his knocked-off cap into focus. Significantly, the subjects of all these acts of looking are male; the female transgressors of the taboo are not granted a comparable enunciatory power.

Whatever ambivalence Ophuls may have harbored toward the new public sphere of female spectatorial consumption, his characterization of the film's imaginary Viennese society as a deadly compact between the educated bourgeoisie and remilitarized, masculinist aristocracy leaves no illusions about turning back the historical clock. Irreversibility of time is thematized in *Liebelei* from the opening sequence's hyper-precise references to chronological time and its deceptive certainties to the deeper contradictions within the idea of romantic love as timeless and eternal, even as the film mobilizes the rebellious force of romantic love against rigid social conditions and values. Unlike Kracauer and Benjamin, Ophuls sought to salvage the utopian dimensions of classical art, and to do so within and against technological capitalist mass culture ("den schönen guten Waren")—an ambition to which we owe a film aesthetics that combines musical movement and mate-

6) I consider Kracauer's essay an important intertext for *Liebelei*, especially its dialectical take on romantic love (+ Mitzi as self-aware "little shopgirl"; Christine's glance at an illustrated magazine in a shopwindow during her silent walk with Fritz thoroughly nightly Vienna). While I cannot prove that Ophuls read this particular essay, it is obvious that he, like the left-liberal intelligentsia of the period, read Kracauer's writings in the *Frankfurter Zeitung*. Ophuls actually used Kracauer's pseudonymously published essay "Sie sporten" (FZ 13 January 1927), a deadpan satire on the Weimar sports and work-out cult, as the title piece of his radio program "Sie sporteln" [sic], (Westdeutscher Rundfunk, Cologne, 18 Nov. 1928). See Helmut G. Asper, *Max Ophüls. Eine Biographie* (Berlin: Bertz + Fischer, 1998), p. 686.

*Liebelei*
(1933, Max Ophuls)

rial, rhythm and temporality with theatrical choreographies of character and camera movement and other stylistic devices to produce complex artifices of sensory-affective intensity and reflection.

Perhaps, after all, the distance between this kind of cinema and contemporary configurations of experience and publicness is not such a bad thing. Perhaps we should think of cinema as an antidote to a quotidian culture of constant contact and instantaneity, offering an aesthetic experience that the small screen and iPod cannot. This would be the utopia of cinema as a *Zeit-Ort* or time-place in Alexander Kluge's sense, a heterotopia that is also a heterochronia—a place in which one can experience disparate and competing temporalities in the mode of play, transformed into the dynamic chunks of presentness that watching a film affords; a place that relies upon and enables memory and fantasy, that allows for encounters with otherness and mortality. In contrast with the alleged dematerialization of digital communication, cinema, with its second-order tactility and mixed materials of expression, offers a multi-sensorial, embodied experience. It allows us to abandon ourselves to the pleasure of passive receptivity, of having our perception manipulated by aesthetic illusion. It encourages a disposition that Adorno, quoting Hegel, referred to as "freedom to the object," liberating us from the obligation of instantaneous comprehension, appropriation, and interactivity, and instead giving license to delay, indeterminacy, and incommensurate feelings and thoughts. Such a cinema would allow us to experience films in their historical—and geopolitical—otherness, and give us glimpses of a history that does not include us; itself once a new medium that cannibalized older media and traditions, its very impurity and liminality would allow us to experience our own present as a historical threshold.

I assume that we all harbor such longings based on the cinema experience of our generation in the widest sense, to the extent that it was shaped in a pre-digital 20th century. But there are several problems with this vision of cinema as an antidote, refuge, or even counterpublic. For one, the industry has already thought of something like that in terms of the logic of product differentiation—think of the recent promotion of 3D as promising a unique experience not to be had in the home theater, a return to strategies familiar from the 1950s responses to the threat of television, that is, a nostalgic reflex reaction rather than a reinvention of cinema. For another, this utopian vision would situate cinema on the public map on the side of the institutions of traditional art—opera, symphony hall, museums—and thus accept that it is viable only as a subsidized or sponsored niche culture. This has of course been happening for quite a while and may not be the worst possibility, although the cinema might find a more energetic model in member-supported institutions such as National Public Radio (in the U.S.).

If cinema were indeed to join the ranks of the classical arts this would have implications for the discipline of cinema studies. The crisis of legitimation that is said to threaten the discipline—the danger of being swallowed up by media studies, new and old—could well cause a reaction formation in the other direction. Does this mean that cinema studies would simply be joining other disciplines in the humanities in their endeavor to bring into living thought and feeling what may no longer be a living art form? Will the study of what cinema has been for the 20th century cinema become analogous to that of 18th and 19th century opera? Pragmatically, this may be the preferable option. However, if we heed Benjamin's insight into how the emergence of cinema and other means of technological reproduction reframed the traditional arts, including his argument about the irrevocable decline of the aura, the reframing of cinema by the new media does not just replay that of the traditional arts by the cinema; rather, it makes for a constellation in which the cinema relates amphibiously to *both* old and new terms.

What distinguishes both cinema and the allegedly post-cinematic developments from the traditional arts is, now as before, their recursive relationship with technology, the possibility of engaging the impact of technology at large on the conditions of human living and experience on its own turf, as it were, in the mode of what Benjamin theorized as "second technology" or play (*Spiel*).[7] The political urgency of a mimetic, non-destructive innervation of technology made Benjamin invest, at least at the theoretical level, in children and childhood. "At first, granted, the technologically new gives the effect of being just that. But already in the next childhood memory it changes its characteristics. Every child accomplishes something great, something irreplaceable for humanity. Every childhood, through its interests in technological phenomena, its curiosity for all sorts of inventions and machinery, binds technological achievement [the newest things] onto the old world of symbols;"[8] that is, it incorporates it into the archive of images and experience. Perhaps we should defer cultural pessimism about the digital transformations of experience and publicness for a while and give the generations growing up with these technologies a chance to incorporate them into cultural memory and, along the way, to rediscover and reinvent cinema.

7) The idea of play or Spiel is a guiding trope in Ophuls' work and biography. (Editors' note: *Spiel im Dasein* is the title of his autobiography, published posthumously.)

8) Arcades Project, N2a,1. (Editors' note: See Walter Benjamin, *The Arcades Project* [Trans. Howard Eiland and Kevin McLaughlin, Cambridge: Harvard University Press, 1999], p. 462, where the translation slightly differs from the one Miriam Hansen uses.)

Jonathan Rosenbaum

# End or Beginning: The New Cinephilia*

It's a strange paradox, but about half of my friends and colleagues think that we're currently approaching the end of cinema as an art form and the end of film criticism as a serious activity, while the other half believe that we're enjoying some form of exciting resurgence and renaissance in both areas. How can one account for this discrepancy? One clue is that most of the naysayers tend to be people around my own age (68) or older whereas most of the optimistic ones are a good deal younger (most of them under 30).

I tend to feel much closer to the younger cinephiles on this issue than I do to the older ones. But I must admit that much of the confusion arises from the fact that the two groups typically don't mean the same things when they use terms like "cinema," "film," "movie," "film criticism," and even "available." The older group is usually referring to what they can see in movie theaters, on 35mm film, and what they read or write about in publications on paper that they either subscribe to by mail or purchase in book stores or newsstands. The younger group is mainly speaking about the DVDs or Blu-rays that they watch in their homes or at the homes of their friends and the blogs or sites that they access on the Internet, sometimes from their laptops or even from their mobile phones. Furthermore, when the older group speaks specifically about films that are "available," they mean films showing in theaters in their own towns or cities; what the younger group means by "available" is usually (a) available for rental at their local video store or by mail subscription (through American companies such as *Netflix*), or available via streaming, (b) available for purchase through the mail, either nationally or (at least if they have a multiregional DVD player) internationally, and/or (c) among the more hardcore and specialized cinephiles, available via swapping or copying among friends and acquaintances (either locally or internationally). In fact, after all the options get added up, even the potential meanings of nationality and territory get altered, along with those involving analog or digital means of communication and formats.

Both of these positions as well as my proximity to each can be neatly illustrated with a brilliant, hilarious three-and-a-half-minute short, *At the Suicide of the Last Jew in the World in the Last Cinema of the World* by David Cronenberg

*) Editors' note: This essay expands on material from the Introduction to Jonathan Rosenbaum's book *Goodbye Cinema, Hello Cinephilia* as well as from "Film Writing on the Web: Some personal Reflections," published in the same volume.

—who was born about two weeks after me, and who stars in the title role, in a grizzled one-take close-up, preparing to shoot himself inside a men's room in the world's last cinema while two airheaded TV newscasters, male and female, offer a continuous and inanely cheerful offscreen commentary about him. This film was made for the 60th edition of the Cannes film festival, in 2007, along with 32 other shorts of the same length by other famous directors—issued on a French DVD with English subtitles, *Chacun son cinéma*, that I was able to order fairly cheaply (it recently was still available from French Amazon for about ten Euros, plus postage) on the final day of the festival, so that I could watch it in Chicago on a multiregional player just a few days later. So in a way I qualify both as Cronenberg's Last Jew and as one of those dopey newscasters, equally untroubled by the loss of the last cinema because I could view this particular sketch feature at home.

Perhaps the strangest single aspect of this generational confusion about "cinema" that affects us all is that we're all still using the same terms for practices and objects that are radically different from one another. Our terminology is developing at a far slower rate than either our technology or what we call our film culture, producing a time lag that winds up confusing everyone.

~

It's hard for me to specify too precisely when my first encounter with cinema was, because from circa 1915 to 1960, film exhibition qualified as my family's business. My paternal grandfather, Louis Rosenbaum, opened his first movie theater, the Princess, in Douglas, Wyoming, around the same time that D.W. Griffith was shooting *The Birth of a Nation* (1915) three states west of there, in southern California. (The Princess's first program included *A Fool There Was*, with Theda Bara.) Later the same year, my grandfather built another movie theater called the Princess in North Little Rock, Arkansas, where he moved with his wife and four-year-old son, and four years after that he moved with them still again to Florence, Alabama, where he built his third, largest, and final movie theater to be called the Princess, this one also an opera house presenting an average of twenty-five stage shows a year as well as films. A few of the famous people who appeared at the Princess in Florence during its first two decades (1919-1939) were cowboy stars Gene Autry and Lash LaRue, violinist Mischa Elman, composer W.C. Handy (the composer of *St. Louis Blues*, who had been born in Florence), writer Carl Sandburg, former President William Howard Taft, and jazz musicians Gene Krupa and Fats Waller (who, during Prohibition, demanded and received a quart of vodka from the management before he would agree to appear).

I was born a little after this period, in 1943. By this time, my grandfather had opened at least half a dozen other movie houses in northwestern Alabama and hired his only child, Stanley, to help him manage them. Almost a year before I entered grammar school, the Rosenbaums opened their biggest establishment, the Shoals—the fourth largest in the state, with 1350 seats, named after nearby Muscle Shoals, with a sign whose flickering neon mimicked the tumbling spillways at Muscle Shoals' Wilson Dam on the Tennessee River, one of the largest such dams in the world. So already, by the time the Shoals opened, I had been attending movies at the Princess and perhaps other Rosenbaum theaters for at least a year and a half. I can still remember being frightened a little by the supernatural trappings of *That Lady in Ermine* (1948), the Shoals' opening attraction, starring Betty Grable as both Angelina, the ruling countess of an Italian principality in 1861, and her ancestor Francesca, three centuries earlier, who came to life from a painting to help Angelina out when the Hungarian army invaded.

Once I could enter theaters on my own, my consumption of movies went up considerably. In Florence, the Princess, the Shoals, and the Majestic, all three of which could be found within the same three-block radius, generally showed about a dozen films a week, and I usually got to see at least half of these. Then, after the Majestic closed its doors for good in mid-1951, I generally made it to almost everything that played at the two other theaters, some of them occasionally more than once, for the next eight years, until I left for boarding school in Vermont in the fall of 1959.

A little more than a year after that, while I was still off at school, the theaters that were still open were sold—Rosenbaum Theaters having shrunk by then from nine operating theaters to five. My grandfather retired, and my father began teaching American and English literature at Florence State University, known today as the University of North Alabama. And less than a decade after that, in New York, I became a professional film critic, a practice that I then continued for almost eight years in Europe (Paris and London) before I resumed it in the U.S., and which I sustained chiefly as a weekly reviewer for the *Chicago Reader* for about 20 years (1987–2007), after a previous decade (1977–1987) of working as a freelancer.

~

In March 2009, I returned to Florence to give the keynote address for a conference on world cinema held at the University of North Alabama. This lecture was given for about two dozen people in the balcony of the Shoals Theater which 29 years earlier had stopped showing movies for good, closed its doors, and then reopened them only sporadically for a few local stage productions, concerts, and similar events, meanwhile repainting the auditorium's walls and ceiling and rebuilding and expanding the stage. The conference—a private event, closed to the general public, which continued on the university campus the following day—was timed to overlap with the start of an annual film festival, then in its twelfth year. The latter event was named after and founded by George Lindsay, a TV actor and University of North Alabama alumnus, and was open to the general public; it showed films exclusively on projected DVDs, in various nearby shops and cafes. All the local commercial movie theaters in the area today are located in various shopping malls several miles away and have no connection of any kind with the film festival.

The night after I gave my keynote address, the Shoals launched the George Lindsay Film Festival with a tribute to two other journeyman actors who are mainly known for their TV work in the 60s and 70s, Rance Howard and Lee Majors, who had both recently been cast by a local woman filmmaker (who was interviewing them onstage at the Shoals) to play in a locally produced feature that's still in preparation. This time, none of the balcony seats but most of the thousand or so seats downstairs were filled, and the evening began with projected DVD clips from various TV shows and features that the two actors had appeared in, including a few films—such as *Cool Hand Luke* (1967, with Rance Howard) and *Will Penny* (1968, with Lee Majors)—that four decades earlier had been shown on the big screen at the Shoals, in 35mm. Only now the screen, a mere fraction in size, was planted directly behind the two actors and hostess, seated in swivel-chairs on the stage. Even though the brief excerpts from both of these Cinemascope films were letterboxed (that is, shown in the proper screen ratio), their impact was hardly the same. Perhaps no less depressingly (and significantly), the festival event that was clearly the hottest ticket and was handled the most professionally and conscientiously was the awards ceremony—clearly patterned after the Oscars, complete with full orchestra, standup routines, digital clips, and acceptance speeches—whereas a digital screening of the paltry prizewinners, held in a room with folding chairs at the festival hotel a couple of days later, was attended by practically no one.

I could mention many other changes that have taken place in Florence over the past half-century. Politically speaking, the area was both Democrat and relatively liberal while I was growing up; today it's so staunchly Republican that I'm told that only about 10 percent of the local white population voted for Barack Obama. While I was growing up, movies played a central role in the life of the entire community, including every age group—a role that was eventually superseded by television and then by the Internet, to the point where movies now cater mainly to teenagers and younger kids.

~

Even if the meaning and importance of filmgoing in Florence appear to have shrunk disastrously, I'm not persuaded that the overall changes in film culture everywhere are as bleak as I'm making them sound. Viewed from a different angle, film-viewing choices have expanded considerably, at least for those who care about having such choices, and it's been especially gratifying to me how many formerly unavailable films written about in my recent book *Goodbye Cinema, Hello Cinephilia* (2010) have become accessible at the same time I've been assembling it.[1] ("For a movie lover," says Tag Gallagher, a contemporary, in a recent interview on a German web site about his excellent film analyses on video, "there's been no

1) Jonathan Rosenbaum, *Goodbye Cinema, Hello Cinephilia: Film Culture in Transition* (Chicago: University of Chicago Press, 2010).

better time to be alive—with all due respect for those who claim that only nitrate is worth watching."[2])

Quite often, of course, a greater number of possibilities means greater chaos—one reason, I suspect, why my most popular efforts as a critic over the past several years have been lists of my 100 favorite American films and my 1000 favorite films, available, respectively, in my books *Movie Wars*[3] and *Essential Cinema*[4] (and on various online sites, easily found via search engines), which propose personal canons as a practical alternative to a surfeit of possible choices. And part of the potential chaos I'm speaking about, recalling in some ways the Patent Wars of a century ago, involves issues of copyright and territorial rights versus various forms of piracy (or anarchistic appropriation). For it surely matters that many films that were once literally or virtually impossible to see are now visible, sometimes by extralegal means (prompted in part by the ignorance or indifference of copyright holders, or in some cases by legal entanglements). One strong example is Jacques Rivette's 12-hour serial *Out 1* (1971), once regarded as the most invisible of all major contemporary films. In January 2011, when I checked most recently, it could still be downloaded for free with both English and Italian subtitles from a site called The Pirate Bay, even after this site was temporarily shut down on August 24, 2009 by order of a Swedish district court, and it can be obtained online from at least two other sources as well. As the critic Brad Stevens recently wrote in his first "AVI" column for *Video Watchdog*, striking a cinephilic chord that is characteristically both despairing and utopian (like *Out 1* itself), "It is surely evidence of how widely cinema is still considered a second-rate art that one of its supreme masterpieces has been denied to British and American audiences; if a similar situation existed where literature was concerned, we would only be able to read English translations of Proust's *À la recherche du temps perdu* in the form of clandestinely circulated photocopies. Yet one can hardly resist a wry smile upon discovering that *Out 1*, a work obsessively focused on conspiracies, has finally achieved widespread distribution thanks to what might described as an Internet 'conspiracy.'"[5]

And here is another cinephile/critic, Adrian Martin, writing in his column for *Filmkrant*, reflecting more on the dystopian side of the new film culture and even resorting to some horror-movie imagery: "Let us be honest. Despite the grumbles we all make or hear that IMDb [Internet Movie Database] is missing some important films, that it has a heavy bias towards the commercial mainstream, that it all looks so Hollywood and capitalistic—it is, by now, the Monster We All Have Sex With. And the scary children born of these couplings are beginning to appear, walking on the earth... Just as every living journalist now sneaks a peek at Wikipedia to verify (at their peril) facts and figures and names and places, everybody in the world of film, at whatever level, uses IMDb as the One Stop Shop for basic information. It has become as essential to us as email or Facebook or the mobile phone. I have even begun to spot serious university 'media sociology' studies which forego old-fashioned 'vox pop' sampling for a quick flick through the brain-dead 'user comments' on Amazon.com or IMDb..."[6]

~

This leads me to the subject of writing about film on the Internet. There's a part of me that understands perfectly why a minimalist like Jim Jarmusch and a 19th-century figure like Raul Ruiz won't have anything to do with email. "You can't *smell* email," Ruiz once said to me, to explain part of the reason for his distaste. But I find it tougher to feel nostalgic about film criticism before the Internet, because even though you *could* smell it, the choices of what you could lay your hands on outside a few well-stocked university libraries were fairly limited. Similarly, the choice of what films you could see outside a few cities like New York and Paris before DVD was pretty narrow, and possibly even more haphazard than what you could read about them.

2) Tag Gallagher, "Truly Doing Film Criticism. Ein Email-Interview mit Tag Gallagher," online at www.kunst-der-vermittlung.de/dossiers/filmgeschichte-gallagher/tag-gallagher-truly-doing-film-criticsm.

3) Jonathan Rosenbaum, *Movie Wars: How Hollywood and the Media Limit What Movies We Can See* (Chicago: Chicago Review Press, 2000).

4) Jonathan Rosenbaum, *Essential Cinema: On the Necessity of Film Canons* (Baltimore: John Hopkins University Press, 2004).

5) Brad Stevens, "AVI Watchdog," in *Video Watchdog*, no. 150 (summer 2009).

6) Adrian Martin, "World Wide Angle: Hierarchies of Value," in *Filmkrant*, no. 312 (July/August 2009). Online at www.filmkrant.nl/av/org/filmkran/archief/fk312/engls312.html.

These two developments shouldn't be considered in isolation from one another. The growth of film writing on the web—by which I mean stand-alone sites, print-magazine sites, chat groups, and blogs—has proceeded in tandem with other communal links involving film culture that to my mind are far more important than the decline in the theatrical distribution of art films and independent films, so I'll be periodically discussing those links here.

When I started out as a cinephile in New York in the early 60s, the English-language magazines that counted the most were the ones that went furthest in gathering together diverse constituencies: *Sight and Sound*, *Film Culture*, and *Film Quarterly*. Even the more local and partisan *New York Film Bulletin* was translating texts from *Cahiers du Cinéma*. Of course the film world was much smaller then, and some of the nostalgia for that era undoubtedly focuses on the coziness. By the time film writing on the web started, film culture had spread and splintered into academia and journalism, which often lamentably functioned as mutually indifferent or sometimes even mutually hostile institutions. So the theoretical golden age, I assume, took place before all the institutionalizing.

Significantly, the most enterprising early efforts to disseminate English-language film writing on the web were neither American nor English but Australian, most notably the academic and peer-reviewed *Screening the Past*, founded by classical and fine arts scholar Ina Bernard in Melbourne in 1997, and the more journalistic *Senses of Cinema*, founded by filmmaker Bill Mousoulis in the same city in 1999.

Both publications are still going strong, having published 29 and 58 issues respectively by spring 2011, meanwhile continuing to keep all their previous issues online, although *Senses* underwent several changes after the departure circa 2002 of Mousoulis and another editor, critic Adrian Martin, the latter of whom went on to cofound the no less ambitious *Rouge* in 2003. It's easy to hypothesize that this Australian concentration came from both a highly developed and interactive local film community and a desire both to be recognized by and to communicate with the wider world of cinephilia.

More generally, apart from these examples and the more recent www.movingimagesource.us, which appears much more frequently and regularly, there are the sites maintained by film magazines (e.g., *Sight and Sound, Film Comment, Cineaste, Cinema Scope*), which offer samples rather than exhaustive duplications of their latest issues, and those sites that have replaced former magazines on paper, such as *Bright Lights*. And finally, there are sites that are extremely useful as summaries of and indexes to the activity occurring on other sites, such as David Hudson's www.mubi.com/notebook/posts, Movie Review Query Engine (www.mrqe.com), and a portal mainly devoted to the film industry, www.moviecitynews.com.

My acquaintance with blogs and chat groups has started more recently, and has been more limited, but a few of each might be mentioned here. Among the more notable critics' blogs are one devoted to Serge Daney in English (www.sergedaney.blogspot.com) and others in English maintained by David Bordwell (an academic who largely uses his beautifully designed site to update and expand many of his writings on paper), Fred Camper, Steve Erickson, Chris Fujiwara, Glenn Kenny (who calls his own site *Some Came Running*, after the 1958 Vincente Minnelli feature), and myself. And the main chat groups I'm familiar with—which differ from the blogs by virtue of the fact that others can and often do contribute to the discussions on them—are an excellent one maintained by the *New York Times* critic Dave Kehr (who contributes a weekly DVD column), the auteurist "a film by" maintained by Yahoo, www.mubi.com and a few separate chat groups located on the elaborate site www.wellesnet.com ("the Orson Welles web resource"). (The latter calls to mind a slew of other director-based sites which are *not* chat groups, including especially impressive ones devoted to Robert Bresson, Carl Theodor Dreyer, Jonas Mekas, and Jacques Tati.)

How wide are the readerships of such resources? Klaus Eder, who for many years has been the general secretary of FIPRESCI, the international film critics organization, told me in 2006 that *Undercurrent*—an online, English-language magazine established that year on their website and edited by Chris Fujiwara, that had published only three issues (with four subsequent issues since then)—had about 100,000 readers per month. Considering how highly specialized this magazine's turf is—encompassing such arcane topics as the late film critic Barthélemy Amengual, Alexander Dovzhenko, the acting in Don Siegel's *Madigan*, Austrian cinema, sound designer Leslie Schatz, assorted short films, and recent features about Cameron Crowe, Philippe Garrel, Danièle Huillet, Terrence Malick, Park Chan-wook, and Tsai Ming-liang—and considering that 100,000 readers seems to comprise more than those of all film magazines on paper combined, this was a startling piece of information, and one that initially beggared belief. It was also hard to square this figure with one given to me the same year by Gary Tooze regarding a piece of mine called "Ten Overlooked Fantasy Films on DVD (and Two That Should Be!)" on his much more commercial and consumer-oriented web site, DVDBeaver.com. (In that case, he estimated about 10,000 hits during the first week the article was posted.)

But once Klaus added that the average length of time spent by each reader of *Undercurrent* was roughly two minutes, I started to realize that my shock was premature, and that my superimposition of two incompatible grids—one devoted to subscribers and readers of paper magazines such as *Cahiers du Cinéma, Film Quarterly*, and *Sight and Sound*, the other devoted to web surfers—could only lead to muddled conclusions. And I'm not sure that the comparison with DVDBeaver is very meaningful without the average length of time of each hit in that case, which I don't know.

Regarding my own web site, which I launched in May 2008, I can be somewhat more precise. According to Google Analytics' Dashboard, checked most recently on January 5, 2011, this site received 45,874 visits from 32,193 people (roughly four times as many people who visited the site in early 2009) and 72,888 "pageviews" over the previous month. These visitors used 103 languages and came from 147 countries or territories. 20,861 came from the U.S., 3,113 from the U.K., 2,850 from Canada, 1,608 from Germany, and 1,136 from Australia. Among the non-English-speaking countries apart from Germany, I'll cite only a few figures: 1,036 from Spain, 908 from France, 881 from India, 753 from Italy, 702 from Brazil, 576 from Sweden, 539 from Argentina, 467 from Japan, 427 from Russia, 332 from China, 285 from Iran, 207 from the Czech Republic, 174 from Austria, 98 from Taiwan, 31 each from Iceland and Latvia, 16 from Sri Lanka, and four each from Afghanistan, Bolivia, the Dominican Republic, and Uganda. In the top 15 cities represented, I should add, the only ones where English isn't the primary language are Buenos Aires (385), Madrid (323), Paris (292), and Berlin (291).

Extrapolating from all this, I think that current claims that film criticism is becoming extinct, and counter-claims that it's entering a new golden age, are equally misguided if they assume that film criticism as an institution functions the same way on paper and in cyberspace, as two versions of the same thing rather than as separate enterprises. Related debates about the distribution of foreign films in the English-speaking world (drastically shrinking in theaters, drastically expanding in the production and distribution of DVDs), or the sophistication of young filmgoers regarding film history (growing if you follow some chat groups, declining if you follow certain others), or the number of films that get made (even more difficult to determine if videos and films are treated interchangeably) seem equally incoherent due to the disparity of reference points, creating a Tower of Babel in a good many discussions. As suggested above, it's a central aspect of our alienated relation to language that when someone says, "I just saw a film," we don't know whether this person saw something on a large screen with hundreds of other people or alone on a laptop—or whether what he or she saw was on film, video, or DVD, regardless of where and how it was seen.

In short, we're living in a transitional period where enormous paradigmatic shifts should be engendering new concepts, new terms, and new kinds of analysis, evaluation, and measurement, not to mention new kinds of political and social formations, as well as new forms of etiquette. But in most cases they aren't doing any of those things. We're stuck with vocabularies and patterns of thinking that are still tied to the ways we were watching movies half a century ago. And the way critics as well as films become canonized continues to be a rather haphazard process. A major figure such as the late English film critic Raymond Durgnat is almost completely unknown today, even in the U.K., because most of his major books have long been out of print and very little of his work has ever become available online. And it's no less anomalous that there's a web site devoted to Serge Daney in English, but not one devoted to his writings in French.

Indeed, one could argue that film overall has fared better than film criticism. When I taught film history at the University of California, Santa Barbara in the mid-80s, I felt seriously hampered by the fact that I couldn't rent copies of anything by one of my favorite filmmakers, Louis Feuillade, apart from one section of his *Fantômas* (1913–1914), and his work was so poorly known by my colleagues that none of my predecessors who taught film history had ever included him in the syllabus. Today, all of *Fantômas* and two of Feuillade's subsequent serials, *Les Vampires* (1915) and *Judex* (1916), are available on DVD in excellent editions, complete with English subtitles. And practically all of the major works of another favorite filmmaker, Carl Theodor Dreyer, are currently available on DVDs with superb sound and image, something that was almost never the case when I was trying to discover his work during previous decades.

Yet if I wanted to support the argument that we're approaching the end of cinema as an art form, I could probably point towards certain depressing aspects of the George Lindsay Film Festival such as the total absence of any films shown there (as opposed to DVDs) and the terrible quality of much of what was shown (judging by the prizewinners that I saw on the festival's final day). I could also point towards the anti-art biases of academic film study in the U.S., not to mention the fragmented and alienated notion of film culture reflected and even encouraged by the fact that the conference I spoke at in Florence was closed to the general public.

In fact, there are times when I think pessimistically that we're kept further apart than we ever were before—subdivided into separate target audiences, markets, and DVD zones, territorialized into separate classes and cultures—in spite of our common experiences. This suggests that the technology that supposedly links us all together via phones and computers is actually keeping us all further apart, and not only from each other but also, in a sense, from ourselves. In other words, our sense of our own identities, including especially our social identities, becomes fragmented and compartmentalized, and even the operations of Internet chat groups might be said to provide a major illustration of this trend.

Perhaps this paradox about so-called "communications" impeding communication has always been the case. But I think the example of mobile phones illustrates such a cultural difference more vividly than many of the others. Personally, I despise mobile phones when I encounter other people using them on the buses and streets of Chicago, because I experience them as a rejection of myself as a fellow passenger or pedestrian. One used to assume, whenever one saw a person walking down the street speaking loudly to no one in particular, that this person was insane. Today one commonly assumes that this same person is a sane individual speaking to someone else on a phone, but it might also be possible to assume that the implied rejection of one's immediate surroundings suggests another kind of insanity, based on a no less antisocial form of behavior.

Yet I have to acknowledge that for a young person who lives with her or his family and feels in desperate need of some kind of privacy, a mobile phone may also represent a kind of liberation. Indeed, according to front-page story in the *New York Times* a few years ago, "About 27 percent of China's 1.3 billion people own a cell phone, a rate that is far higher in big cities, particularly among the young. Indeed, for upwardly mobile young urbanites, cell phones and the Internet are the primary means of communication."[7] And the fact that many films today can be watched on cell phones and discussed on the Internet only underlines the transformation that our film culture is currently undergoing.

~

It might help our discussion if we start redefining what we mean by community in relation to geography, which is central to all these paradigmatic shifts. It becomes relevant, for example, that Chris Fujiwara edits *Undercurrent* from Tokyo as well as from Boston, and that the editor of *Film Quarterly*, published by the University of California Press, works out of London—and perhaps even that this sentence was initially written while I was on a plane between Chicago and Vancouver—especially if we persist in regarding the discourse of both magazines as being aimed at a specific geographically-based constituency seen in relation to a particular nation-state, town or city, university or other institution. Speaking as someone who currently feels that he lives on the Internet more than he lives in Chicago or Richmond (where I have recently been teaching), I consider this distinction vital to the ways that I

7) Jim Yardley, "A Hundred Cellphones Bloom, and Chinese Take to the Street," in *New York Times* (April 25, 2005).

function as a writer. Maybe it's also relevant that *Rouge*, the most ambitious of the international online film magazines (translating some of its texts into English from Chinese, French, German, Italian, Japanese, Portuguese, and Spanish sources), originates from Australia—or at least from three Australian editors, who may at any given time be in France, Greece, or elsewhere while doing part of their editorial work. But if it *is* relevant, this is largely because Australia is itself multicultural, also yielding a multicultural, state-run TV channel, SBS, that similarly has few counterparts.

It's my own conviction that the nation-state itself is fast becoming an outdated and dysfunctional concept, apart from the special interests of politicians and corporations and their own highly functional designation of countries as markets. The choices of ordinary filmgoers are said to be steadily shrinking at the same time that most of the known riches of world cinema are becoming internationally available for the first time on DVD. So if I wanted to counter the argument that we're approaching the end of cinema as an art form, there's plenty of hopeful evidence that I could point towards as well.

Thanks to the site of the Canadian film magazine *Cinema Scope*, where I write a regular column called "Global Discoveries on DVD" that usually appears online (at www.cinema-scope.com), I received one of the most exciting glimpses of the utopian possibilities inherent in film writing on the web. For some time, I have been fantasizing that ciné-clubs, a major spur to French cinephilia over most of the past century, could be making a comeback, this time in global terms, thanks to DVDs. These ciné-clubs could be situated almost anywhere, in houses and apartments as well as in storefronts, and a model configuration might be touring "retrospectives" on DVD in which the DVDs could be sold at the screenings (perhaps along with relevant books and/or pamphlets), in much the same way that CDs are now often sold by music groups in clubs between their sets. And if enough circuits for these retrospectives could become established in this fashion, this could ultimately finance the production of these packages. In some ways this dream has already been realized in the U.S. by www.moveon.org and the way it has arranged private showings of such Robert Greenwald documentaries as *Uncovered* (2004), *Out-Foxed* (2004), *Wal-Mart* (2005), and *Iraq for Sale* (2006), but it doesn't appear to have caught on with other kinds of films. Yet if I started to dream about another direction that the George Lindsay Film Festival could take—one which concentrated on great films of the past or near-past rather than mediocre films of the present (even if they're all still screened on DVD), and one which bypassed the dubious standards of the multiplexes for more challenging and interesting fare—there are certainly some precedents I could cite.

I could start by mentioning some of my younger cinephile friends, including some who are still in their 20s and already know more about film history, thanks to multiregional DVD players, than I possibly could have known in my own early 30s, when I was educating myself about such matters in New York, Paris, and London. Some of these friends, moreover, live in relatively remote places, such as rural England (in two cases) or a small town in Spain, implying that the cultural dominance previously enjoyed by critics and viewers living in the major capitals of Europe and the U.S is no longer the same thing that it used to be. Today one can live just about anywhere—even Florence, Alabama—and still have access to a surprising number of the major works of film history, at least if one knows where and how to go looking for them.

While attending the Mar del Plata film festival in Argentina a few years ago, I met a schoolteacher based in Córdoba named Roger Alan Koza who had established a few ciné-clubs in separate small towns that he visited on a regular basis, and the films he showed included some of the more specialized and esoteric films I had written about, including Forough Farrokhzad's *Khaneh siah ast* (*The House is Black*, 1963), an Iranian short about a leper colony by one of that country's greatest poets, and Kira Muratova's *Chekhovskie motivy* (*Chekhov's Motifs*, 2002). He told me the combined audiences of such screenings for each film was somewhere between 700 and 800 people. Considering how unlikely it would be to fill single auditoriums of that size in most major cities of the world for such films, I realized that the shifting paradigms of today might also transform what we normally regard as a minority taste. Once the paradigm of a single geographical base changes, all sorts of things can be transformed. Maybe Muratova's craziest feature is too difficult for most New Yorkers and Parisians, but once it can be acquired globally on DVD with the right subtitles, anything becomes possible—including a sizable group of viewers in Córdoba.

And indeed, in late July 2010, in the city of Córdoba, I participated in a four-day event devoted to film criticism organized by Koza and held at the Cineclub Municipal Hugo del Carril that was not only well-attended but exceptionally well-focused and organized. Not only was every presentation translated into English for my benefit, but two of the principal talks, given respectively by Quintín (Eduardo Antin) and myself, lasted around seven hours each—approximately the same length as Béla Tarr's *Sátántangó* (1994)—and the sophistication of the questions posed by the audience was apparent throughout.

It might be argued, of course, that the knowledge about film history found in much of the general public may be decreasing at the same time that the film culture of Córdoba appears to be on the rise. It's much too soon to try to be conclusive in any way about an overall transition that is still in progress. But it's worth adding that a certain amount of the future—and perhaps a crucial amount—depends on our own initiatives.

Tom Gunning

# Moving Away from the Index

*Cinema and the Impression of Reality*

## INDEXICAL REALISM AND FILM THEORY

While cinema has often been described as the most realistic of the arts, cinematic realism has been understood in a variety of ways: from an aspect of a sinister ideological process of psychological regression to infantile states of primal delusion, to providing a basis for evidentiary status for films as historical and even legal documents. Cinematic realism has been praised as a cornerstone of film aesthetics, denounced as a major ploy in ideological indoctrination, and envied as a standard for new media. I believe the time has come to return to this issue without some of the polemics that have previously marked it but with a careful and historically informed discussion of cinema's uses and definitions of the impression of reality. In film theory over the last decades, realist claims for cinema have often depended on cinema's status as an index, one of the triad of signs in the semiotics of Charles Sanders Peirce. Film's indexical nature has almost always (and usually exclusively) been derived from its photographic aspects. In this essay I want to explore alternative approaches that might ultimately provide new ways of thinking about the realistic aspects of cinema.

Peirce defined the index as a sign that functions through an actual existential connection to its referent "by being really and in its individual existence connected with the individual object."[1] Thus, frequently cited examples of indices are the footprint, the bullet hole, the sundial, the weathervane, and photographs—all signs based on direct physical connection between the sign and its referent—the action of the foot, impact of the bullet, the movement of the sun, the direction of the wind, or the light bouncing from an object.[2] A number of these examples (such as the weathervane and the sundial) perform their references simultaneously to the action of their referents. This fact reveals that the identification of the photographic index with the pastness of the trace (made by several theorists) is not a characteristic of all indices (and one could point out that it only holds true for a fixed photograph, but not of the image that appears within a camera obscura).

For Peirce the index functions as part of a complex system of interlocking concepts that comprise not only a philosophy of signs but a theory of the mind and its relation to the world. Peirce's triad of signs (icon, index, and symbol), rather than being absolutely opposed to each other, are conceived to interact in the process of signification, with all three operating in varying degrees in specific signs. However, (with the exception of Gilles Deleuze, for whom Peirce's system, rather than the index, is primary) within theories of cinema, photography, and new media, the index has been largely abstracted from this system, given a rather simple definition as the existential trace or impression left by an object, and used to describe (and solve) a number of problems dealing with the way the light-based image media refer to the world. In fact, Peirce's discussion of the index includes a large range of signs and indications, including "anything which focuses attention"[3] and the general hailing and deictic functions of language and gesture. Peirce therefore by no means restricts the index to the impression or trace. I do not claim to have a command of the range of Peirce's complex semiotics, but it is perhaps important to point out that the use of the index in film theory has tended to rely on a small range of the possible meanings of the term.

I have no doubt that Peirce's concept has relevance for film and that (although more complex than generally described) the index also provides a useful way of thinking through some of these problems; indeed, even the restricted sense of the index as a trace has supplied insights into the nature of film and photography. However, I also think that what we might call a diminished concept of the index may have reached the limits of its usefulness in the theory of photography, film, and new media.[4] The nonsense that has been generated specifically about the indexicality of digital media (which, due to its digital nature, has been claimed to be nonindexical—as if the indexical and the analog were somehow identical) reveals something of the poverty of this approach. But I also feel the index may not be the best way, and certainly should not be the only way, to approach the issue of cinematic realism. Confronting questions of realism anew means that contemporary media theory must still wrestle with its fundamental nature and possibilities. I must confess that this essay attempts less to lay a logical foundation for these discussions than to launch a polemic calling for such a serious undertaking and to reconnoiter a few of its possibilities.

It is worth reviewing here the history of the theoretical discourse by which a relation was forged between cinematic realism and the index. Without undertaking a thorough historiographic review of the concept of the index in

1) Charles Sanders Peirce, "Prolegomena to an Apology for Pragmaticism," in James Hoopes (ed.), *Peirce on Signs* (Chapel Hill: University of North Carolina Press, 1991), p. 251.

2) See Charles Sanders Peirce in Justus Buchler (ed.), *Philosophical Writings of Peirce* (New York: Dover, 1955), pp. 106–111.

3) *Ibid.*, p. 108.

4) In a series of carefully argued and provocative articles, historian and theorist of photography Joel Snyder has questioned the usefulness of the index argument in describing photography. Compare Joel Snyder, "Res Ipsa Loquitur," in Lorraine Daston (ed. ), *Things That Talk: Object Lessons from Art and Science* (New York: Zone Books, 2004), pp. 195–222. See also Joel Snyder, "Visualization and Visibility," in Peter Galison and Caroline Jones (eds.), *Picturing Science, Producing Art* (London: Reaktion, 1998), pp. 379–400; *id.*, "Picturing Vision," in *Critical Inquiry*, Vol. 6, Issue 3 (Spring 1980), pp. 499–526; and *id.*, "Pointless," in James Elkins (ed.), *Photography Theory* (New York: Routledge, 2006), pp. 369–400.

film and media theory, the first influential introduction of the concept of the index into film theory came in Peter Wollen's groundbreaking comparison of Peirce to the film theory of André Bazin.[5] But to understand this identification, a review of certain aspects of Bazin's theory of film is needed. Bazin introduced in his essays and critical practice an argument for the realism of cinema that was, as he termed it in his most quoted theoretical essay, "ontological."[6] The complexity and indeed the dialectical nature of Bazin's critical description of a realist style have become increasingly recognized.[7] For Bazin, realism formed the aesthetic basis for the cinema, and most of his discussion of cinematic realism dealt with visual, aural, and narrative style. Although Bazin never argued the exact relation between his theories of ontology and of style systematically (and indeed, one could claim that Bazin's discussion of realism across his many essays contains both contradictions and also a possible pattern of evolution and change in his work taken as a whole—not to mention multiple interpretations), at least in the traditional reception of Bazin's theory, cinematic realism depended on the medium's photographic nature.

A number of frequently quoted statements containing the essence of Bazin's claim for the ontology of the photographic image and presumably for motion picture photography warrant consideration. Bazin's account of the realism of photography rests less on a correspondence theory (that the photograph resembles the world, a relation Peirce would describe as iconic), than on what he describes as "a transference of reality from the thing to its reproduction," referring to the photograph as "a decal or approximate tracing."[8] Bazin extends these comments saying: "The photographic image is the object itself, the object freed from temporal contingencies. No matter how fuzzy, distorted, or discolored, no matter how lacking in documentary value the image may be, it proceeds, by virtue of its genesis, from the ontology of the model; it is the model."[9] He adds shortly after this: "The photograph as such and the object in itself share a common being, after the fashion of a fingerprint. Wherefore, photography actually contributes something to the order of natural creation instead of providing a substitute for it."[10]

To cite one more famous description from another essay, Bazin also describes the photograph as "the taking of a veritable luminous impression in light—to a mold. As such it carries with it more than a mere resemblance, namely a kind of identity."[11]

5) Peter Wollen, "The Semiology of the Cinema," in *Signs and Meaning in the Cinema* (Bloomington: University of Indiana Press, 1969), pp. 116–54.

6) André Bazin, "Ontologie de l'image photographique," in *Qu'est-ce que le cinéma? Vol. 1. Ontologie et langage* (Paris: Cerf, 1958), pp. 11–19; published in English as "The Ontology of the Photographic Image," in Hugh Gray (ed. and trans.), *What Is Cinema? 2 vols.* (Berkeley: University of California Press, 1967), Vol. 1, pp. 9–16.

7) For a recent reevaluation of Bazin, once dismissed as a naive realist, one could cite Philip Rosen, *Change Mummified: Cinema, Historicity, Theory* (Minneapolis: University of Minnesota Press, 2001), esp. pp. 1–42.

8) I use here the translation proposed by Daniel Morgan in his essay "Rethinking Bazin: Ontology and Realist Aesthetics" in *Critical Inquiry*, Vol. 32, Issue 3 (Spring 2006), pp. 441–81, which revises the widely available

Bazin's descriptions are both evocative and elusive, and Wollen was, I think, the first to draw a relation between Bazin's ideas and Peirce's concept of the index. In his pioneering essay on "Semiology of the Cinema," Wollen said of Bazin: "His conclusions are remarkably close to those of Peirce. Time and again Bazin speaks of photography in terms of a mould, a death-mask, a Veronica, the Holy Shroud of Turin, a relic, an imprint. [. . .] Thus Bazin repeatedly stresses the existential bond between sign and object, which, for Peirce, was the determining characteristic of the indexical sign."[12]

The traditional reception of Bazin's film theory takes his account of the ontology of the photographic image as the foundation of his arguments about the relation between film and the world. Wollen's identification of Bazin's photographic ontology with Peirce's index has been widely accepted, (although critics have rarely noted Wollen's important caveat: "But whereas Peirce made his observation in order to found a logic, Bazin wished to found an aesthetic."[13])

I must state that I think one can make a coherent argument for reading Bazin's ontology in terms of the Peircean index, as Wollen did. However, I have also claimed elsewhere that this reading of Bazin in terms of Peirce does some disservice to the full complexity of Bazin's aesthetic theory of realism.[14] Likewise, in a recent essay Daniel Morgan makes a convincing and fully argued case (different from mine) that Bazin's theory of cinematic realism should not be approached through the theory of the index at all.[15] I would still maintain, however, that parallels between aspects of Bazin's theory of cinematic realism and the index do exist, even if they cannot explain the totality of his theory of cinematic realism (or, as Morgan would argue, its most important aspects).

I do not intend to rehearse here either my own or others' arguments about why the index might not supply a complete understanding of

translation by Hugh Gray. Gray translates this as "a decal or transfer" (see Bazin, 1967, "Ontology," p. 14). The original French is "transfert de réalité de la chose sur la reproduction" and "un décalique approximatif" (see Bazin, 1958, "Ontologie," p. 16). Unless otherwise noted, translations are Gray's.

9) Again, this is Morgan's revised translation (*op. cit.*, p. 450). Gray has: "The photographic image is the object itself, the object freed from the conditions of time and space that govern it. No matter how fuzzy, distorted, or discolored, no matter how lacking in documentary value the image may be, it shares, by virtue of the very process of its becoming, the being of the model of which it is the reproduction; it is the model" (in Bazin, 1967, "Ontology," p. 14). Morgan discusses the misinterpretation inherent in Gray's addition of the phrase "and space" (absent in Bazin) in "Rethinking Bazin." The original French reads "cet objet lui-même, mais libéré des contingences temporelles. L'image peut être floue, déformée, décolorée, sans valeur documentaire, elle procède par sa genèse de l'ontologie du modèle; elle est le modèle" (see Bazin, 1958, "Ontologie," p. 16).

10) Bazin, 1967, "Ontology," p. 18.

11) André Bazin, "Theater and Cinema," in *What Is Cinema? op. cit.* pp. 76–124.

12) Wollen, *op. cit.*, pp. 125–126.

13) *Ibid.*, p. 126.

14) Tom Gunning, "What's the Point of an Index? Or Faking Photographs," in Karen Beckman and Jean Ma (eds.), *Still Moving* (Durham: Duke UP 2008), pp. 23–40.

15) Morgan, *op. cit.*

Bazin's theory of cinematic realism, but some summary remarks are in order. The chief limitation to the indexical approach to Bazin comes from the difference between a semiotics that approaches the photograph (and therefore film) as a sign and a theory like Bazin's that deals instead with the way a film creates an aesthetic world. When Bazin claims that "photography actually contributes something to the order of natural creation instead of providing a substitute for it," he denies the photograph the chief characteristic of a sign, that of supplying a substitute for a referent. While it would be foolish to claim that a photograph cannot be a sign of something (it frequently does perform this function), I would claim that signification does not form the basis of Bazin's understanding of the ontology of the photographic image and that his theory of cinematic realism depends on a more complex (and less logical) process of spectator involvement. Bazin describes the realism of the photograph as an "irrational power to bear away our faith."[16] This "magical" understanding of photographic ontology is clearly very different from a logic of signs. In Peirce's semiotics, the indexical relation falls entirely into the rational realm.

## BEYOND THE INDEX: CINEMATIC REALISM AND MEDIUM PROMISCUITY

The indexical argument no longer supplies the only way to approach Bazin's theory. Rather than assuming that the invocation of Peirce's concept of the index solves the question of film's relation to reality, I think we must now raise again the question that Bazin asked so passionately and subtly (even if he never answered it definitively): What is cinema? What are cinema's effects and what range of aspects relates to its oft-cited (and just as variously defined) realistic nature? Given the historically specific nature of Bazin's arguments for cinematic realism as an aesthetic value (responding as he did to technical innovations such as deep focus cinematography and to new visual and narrative styles such as Italian Neorealism), it makes sense for a contemporary theory of cinematic realism to push beyond those aspects of cinematic realism highlighted by Bazin. Specifically, we need to ask in a contemporary technical and stylistic context: What are the bounds that cinema forges with the world it portrays? Are these limited to film's relation to photography? Is the photographic process the only aspect of cinema that can be thought of as indexical, especially if we think about the term more broadly than as just a trace or impression? If the claim that digital processing by its nature eliminates the indexical seems rather simplistic, one must nonetheless admit that computer-generated images (CGI) do not correspond directly to Bazin's description of the "luminous mold" that the still photograph supposedly depends on. But can these CGI images still be thought of as in some way indexical? In what way has the impression of reality been attenuated by new technology, and in what ways is it actually still functioning (or even intensified)? But setting aside the somewhat complex case of computer-generated special effects, is it not strange that photographic theories of the cinema have had such a hold on film theory that much of film theory must immediately add the caveat that they do not apply to animated film? Given that as a technical innovation cinema was first understood as "animated pictures" and that computer-generated animation techniques are now omnipresent in most feature films, shouldn't this lacuna disturb us? Rather than being absorbed in the larger categories of cultural studies or cognitive theory, shouldn't the classical issues of film theory be reopened? I will not attempt to answer all these questions in this essay, but I think they are relevant to the issues I will raise.

Within the academy, the study of film theory has often been bifurcated between "classical film theory" and "contemporary film theory." Insofar as this division refers to something more than an arbitrary sense of the past and present, "classical" film theories have been usefully defined as theories that seek to isolate and define the "essence" of cinema, while "contemporary" theories rely on discourses of semiotics and psychoanalysis to describe the relation between film and spectator.[17] While the classical approach has been widely critiqued as essentialist, it seems to me that a pragmatic investigation of the characteristics of film as developed and commented on through time hardly needs to involve a proscriptive quest for the one pure cinema. Therefore, if I call for new descriptions of the nature(s) of the film medium, I am not at all calling for a return to classical film theory (and even less to a neo-classicism!). But I do think the time has come to take stock of the historical and transforming nature of cinema as a medium and of its dependence and differentiation from other media.

Considering historically the definitions of film as a medium helps us avoid the dilemma of either proscriptively (and timelessly) defining film's essence or the alternative of avoiding any investigation into the diverse nature of media for fear of being accused of promoting an idealist project. As a new technology at the end of the nineteenth century, cinema did not immediately appear with a defined essence as a medium, but rather displayed an amazing promiscuity (if not polymorphic perversity) in both its models and uses. Cinema emerged within a welter of new inventions for the recording or conveying of aspects of human life previously felt to be ephemeral, inaudible, or invisible: the telephone, the phonograph, or the X-ray are only a few examples. Before these devices found widespread acceptance as practical instruments, they existed as theatrical attractions, demonstrated on stage before paying audiences. Indeed, the X-ray, which appeared almost simultaneously with the projection of films on the screen, seemed at one point to be displacing moving pictures as a popular attraction, and a number of showmen exchanged their motion picture projectors for the new apparatus that showed audiences the insides of their bodies (and unknowingly gave themselves and their collaborators dangerous doses of radiation). It is in this competitive context of novel devices that Antoine Lumière, the father of Louis and Auguste Lumière, who managed the theatrical ex-

16) All quotes Bazin, 1967, "Ontology," p. 14.

17) Noël Carroll, *Philosophical Problems of Classical Film Theory* (Princeton: Princeton University Press, 1988), pp. 10–15.

hibition of his sons' invention, warned a patron desirous of purchasing a Cinématographe that it was an "invention without a future."[18]

Rather than myths of essential origins, historical research uncovers a genealogy of cinema, a process of emergence and competition yielding the complex formation of an identity. But cinema has always (and not only at its origin) taken place within a competitive media environment, in which the survival of the fittest was in contention and the outcome not always clear. As a historian I frequently feel that one of my roles must be to combat the pervasive amnesia that a culture based in novelty encourages, even within the academy. History always responds to the present, and changes in our present environment allow us to recognize aspects of our history that have been previously obscured or even repressed. At the present moment, cinema finds itself immersed in another voraciously competitive media environment. Is cinema about to disappear into the maw of undefined and undifferentiated image media, dissolved into a pervasive visual culture? To be useful in such an investigation where theory and history intertwine, the discussion of cinematic realism cannot be allowed to ossify into a dogmatic assertion about the photographic nature of cinema or an assumption about the indexical nature of all photography.

My history lesson resists either celebration or paranoia at the prospect of a new media environment, seeing in our current situation not only a return to aspects of cinema's origins but a dynamic process that has persisted in varying degrees throughout the extent of film's history—an interaction with other competing media, with mutual borrowings, absorptions, and transformations among them. Cinema has never been one thing. It has always been a point of intersection, a braiding together of diverse strands: Aspects of the telephone and the phonograph circulated around the cinema for almost three decades before being absorbed by sound cinema around 1928, while simultaneously spawning a new sister medium, radio; a variety of approaches to color, ranging from tinting to stencil coloring, existed in cinema as either common or minority practices until color photography became pervasive in the 1970s; the film frame has changed its proportions since 1950 and is now available in small, medium, and super-sized rectangles (television, cinemascope, IMAX, for example); cinema's symbiotic relation to television, video, and digital practices has been ongoing for nearly half a century without any of these interactions and transformations—in spite of numerous predictions—yet spelling the end of the movies. Thus anyone who sees the demise of the cinema as inevitable must be aware they are speaking only of one form of cinema (or more likely several successive forms whose differences they choose to overlook).

Film history provides a challenge to rethinking film theory, arguing for the importance of using the recent visibility of film's multiple media environment as a moment for reflection and perhaps redefinition. In contemporary film theory, a priori proscriptions as well as a posteriori definitions that privilege only certain aspects of film have given way to approaches (like semiotics, psychoanalysis, or cognitivism) that seem to ignore or minimize differences between media in favor of broader cultural or biological conditions. My view of cinema as a braid made of various aspects rather than a unified essence with firm boundaries would seem to offer a further argument against the essentialist approach of classical film theory. But we also increasingly need to offer thick descriptions of how media work, that is, phenomenological approaches that avoid defining media logically before examining the experience of their power. And while I maintain the various media work in concert and in contest rather than isolation, I also maintain that the formal properties of a specific medium convey vital aesthetic values and do not function as neutral channels for functional equivalents. An attempt to isolate a single essence of cinema remains not only an elusive task but possibly a reactionary project, yet most earlier attempts by theorists to define the essence of cinema can also be seen as attempts to elucidate the specific possibilities of cinema within a media environment that threatens to obscure or dismiss the particular powers that film holds. In other words, while the naming of a specific aspect of cinema as its essence must always risk being partial, it once had the polemical value of drawing attention to those aspects, allowing theorists to describe their power. This was true of the emphasis given to editing by the Soviet theorists in the 1920s, who established that film could function not simply as a mode of mechanical reproduction but that it could create a poetics and a rhetoric that resembled a language. Partly as a corrective to this earlier claim that editing formed the essence of film as a creative form, the emphasis on film's relation to photography found after World War II in the work of Bazin, Siegfried Kracauer, and Stanley Cavell also performed this sort of vital function of attracting attention to a neglected aspect of cinema. In the current environment, probing the power of cinema, its affinities with and differentiations from other media, must again take a place on our agenda.

### WHAT REALLY MOVES ME...

Photography's relation to cinema comprises one of the central concepts in classical film theory's attempt to characterize the nature of cinema, and it remains a rich area for investigation. However, to offer alternative paradigms, I want to return to the generation of film theorists of the 1920s, primarily the work of filmmaker theorists such as Sergei Eisenstein, Jean Epstein, and Germaine Dulac,[19] who wrote before the dominance of photography that marks the work of Bazin and Kracauer (and arguably Walter Benjamin). Although photography played a key role in film theories of the 20s as well, (especially in the concept of Photogénie—the claim that film produced a unique image of the world more revelatory than other forms of imagery—championed by Epstein, Dulac, and Louis Delluc), I want to focus on the centrality

18) Quoted in Bernard Chardère, *Le roman des Lumière* (Paris: Gallimard, 1995), p. 313.

19) Key essays by Dulac and Epstein can be found in Richard Abel, *French Film Theory and Criticism: 1907–1939, A History/Anthology. 2 vols.* (Princeton: Princeton University Press, 1988). An excellent selection of Eisenstein's essays is in Jay Leyda (ed. and trans.), *Film Form: Essays in Film Theory* (New York: Harcourt, 1949).

of cinematic motion in the discussions of cinema's nature that marked this foundational period of classical film theory. Dulac declared in 1925, "Le cinéma est l'art du mouvement et de la lumière" [Cinema is the art of movement and light]. In her writings and her innovative abstract films, she envisioned a pure cinema uncontaminated by the other arts (although aspiring to the condition of music), which she described as "a visual symphony, a rhythm of arranged movements in which the shifting of a line or of a volume in a changing cadence creates emotion without any crystallization of ideas."[20] The concerns that preoccupied both the French Impressionist filmmakers and the Soviet montage theorists of the 1920s—cinematic rhythm as a product of editing, camera movement, and composition; the physical and emotional reactions of film spectators as shaped by visual rhythms; even the visual portrayal of mental states and emotions—were all linked to cinema's ability both to record and create motion.[21]

The role of motion in motion pictures initially appears to be something of a tautology. Rather than simply recycling this seemingly obvious assumption—that the movies move—theories of cinematic motion can help us reformulate a number of theoretical and aesthetic issues, including film spectatorship, film style, and the confluence of a variety of new media. Further, a renewed focus on cinematic motion directly addresses what I feel is one of the great scandals of film theory, which I previously mentioned as an aporia resulting from the dominance of a photographic understanding of cinema: the marginalization of animation.[22] Again and again, film theorists have made broad proclamations about the nature of cinema, and then quickly added, "excluding, of course, animation." Perhaps the boldest of new media theorists, Lev Manovich, has recently inverted this cinematic prejudice, claiming that the arrival of new digital media reveals cinema as simply an event within the history of animation. While I appreciate the polemic value of this proclamation, I would point out (as Manovich's archeology of the cinema also indicates) that far from being a product of new media, animation has always been part of cinema and that only the over-emphasis given to the photographic basis of cinema in recent decades can explain the neglect this historical and technological fact has encountered.

Stressing, as Manovich does, the nonreferential nature of animation implies that only photography can be referential—a major error that comes from a diminished view of the index. But if cinema should be approached as a form of animation, then cinematic motion rather than photographic imagery becomes primary. Spectatorship of cinematic motion raises new

20) Germaine Dulac, "Aesthetics, Obstacles, Integral Cinegraphie," (Trans. Stuart Liebman) in Abel, *op. cit.*, p. 394. The French original appears in Germaine Dulac, *Écrits sur le cinema*, 1919–1937 (ed. Prosper Hillairet, Paris: Paris Expérimental, 1994), pp. 98–105.

21) The recuperation of motion in contemporary film theory will immediately evoke Deleuze's two-volume philosophical work *Cinema: The Movement Image* and *Cinema: The Time Image*; see Gilles Deleuze, *Cinema 1: The Movement-Image* (Trans. Hugh Tomlinson and Barbara Habberjam, Minneapolis: University of Minnesota Press, 1986) and *id.*, *Cinema 2: The Time-Image* (Trans. Hugh Tomlinson and Barbara Habberjam, Minneapolis: University of Minnesota Press, 1989). There is much to learn from

issues, such as the physical reactions that accompany the watching of motion. Considering this sensation of kinesthesia avoids the exclusive visual and ideological emphasis of most theories of spectatorship and acknowledges instead that film spectators are embodied beings rather than simply eyes and minds somehow suspended before the screen. The physiological basis of kinesthesia exceeds (or supplements) recent attempts to reintroduce emotional affect into spectator studies. We do not just see motion and we are not simply affected emotionally by its role within a plot; we feel it in our guts or throughout our bodies.

Theories of cinema's difference from the other arts that appeared in the 20s derived from the excitement that filmmakers of the 10s and 20s experienced in their new-found ability to affect viewers physiologically as well as emotionally through such motion-based sequences as chase scenes involving galloping horses or racing locomotives, rapid camera movement, or accelerated rhythmic editing. While kinesthetic effects still play a vital role in contemporary action cinema, nowadays these devices of motion rarely generate theoretical speculation or close analysis. Nonetheless, critical attention to cinematic motion need not be limited to action films, however rich this mainstay of film practice may be. Motion, as Eisenstein's analysis of the methods of montage makes clear, can shape and trigger the process of both emotional involvement and intellectual engagement.[23] Analysis of motion in cinema should address a complete gamut of cinema, from the popular action film to the avant-garde work of filmmakers such as Stan Brakhage, Maya Deren, or Abigail Child.

In many ways these avant-garde filmmakers took up the legacy of Dulac's pure cinema and explored the possibilities of filmic motion outside of narrative development. Although Deren in particular stressed the importance of the photographic basis of film in her theoretical writings, she made the analysis and transformation of motion essential to all her films, especially her later films inspired by dance and ritualized bodily movement such as *Ritual in Transfigured Time* (1946), *A Study in Choreography for Camera* (1945), *Meditation on Violence* (1948), and *The Very*

this work, although its background in and understanding of itself as an essay in philosophy, rather than film theory or history, should be taken seriously. I do not want to undertake a full-scale discussion of Deleuze's work here, since I feel that will pull us away from the issue of movement to a consideration of Deleuze's methods, terms, and assumptions. As Deleuze announces about his work in his preface, "This is not a history of the cinema. It is a taxonomy, an attempt at the classification of images and signs" (*Cinema 1*, p. xiv). Although a number of Deleuze's taxonomic distinctions provide insights into cinematic motion, an in-depth discussion of them would lead us astray from this issue. I want instead to consider the discussion of cinematic motion that preceded Deleuze, emerging primarily from film practice and theory. Most of the issues I want to raise here, while having a relation to Deleuze, remain marginal to his discussions, but they are central to the earlier theorists I will refer to. The best treatment of Deleuze's book, fully informed of the history and theory of film, is by Rodowick. See David Norman Rodowick, *Gilles Deleuze's Time Machine* (Durham: Duke University Press, 1997).

22) Notably, Deleuze devotes no real discussion to animation.

23) A key essay in this regard by Eisenstein would be "Methods of Montage" in *Film Form: Essays in Film Theory*, *op. cit.*, pp. 72–83.

*Eye of Night* (1958).[24] Brakhage's use of hand-held camera movement and complex editing patterns, as well as frenetic kinetic patterns created by painting directly on celluloid, produced types of motion that evoked a crisis of perception and lyrical absorption in the processes of vision.[25] Filmmaker Abigail Child's recent volume of writings on film and poetry is actually titled *This Is Called Moving*, testifying to her commitment to cinema as a means of deconstructing the dominant cultural forms of media through an intensification of cinematic perception that relies in part on new patterns of motion, often created through editing.[26] As cinematic experience, motion can play a strong role both in sensations of intense diegetic absorption fostering involvement with dramatic, suspenseful plots à la Hitchcock and in kinetic abstraction, thrusting viewers into unfamiliar explorations of flexible coordinates of space and time.

Theoretical exploration of cinematic motion need not contradict, but can actually supplement photographic theories of cinema such as those of Kracauer and Bazin. Kracauer in particular deals extensively with cinema's affinities with motion (discussing especially the cinematic possibilities of the chase, dancing, and the transformation from stillness to motion) as a part of cinema's mission to capture and redeem physical reality.[27] Even if movement never receives a detailed discussion as a theoretical issue within Bazin's work, he clearly sees camera movement as an essential tool within a realist style, as in his analysis of the extended track and pan in Jean Renoir's *The Crime of M. Lange* (1936),[28] or his description of the shot in Friedrich Wilhelm Murnau's *Tabu* (1931) in which "the entrance of a ship from left screen gives an immediate sense of destiny at work, so that Murnau has no need to cheat in any way on the uncompromising realism of a film whose settings are completely natural."[29]

## METZ AND CINEMATIC MOVEMENT

While Bazin and Kracauer saw motion as contributing to (or at least not contradicting) the inherent realism of the film medium, another film theorist went farther and made movement the cornerstone of cinema's impression of reality. I want to turn now to a neglected essay by a theorist usually associated with postclassical film theory, Christian Metz. "On the Impression of Reality in the Cinema," a short essay that directly superimposes the issues of motion and cinematic realism, opens the first volume of Metz's writings and is among Metz's presemiotic essays that the section heading characterizes as "phenomenological" (and that most theorists have zoomed past, treating them as juvenilia).[30]

Metz attempts in this essay to account for the "impression of reality" that the movies offer

24) See also Maya Deren in Bruce R. McPherson (ed.), *Essential Deren: Collected Writings on Film* (Kingston, New York: Documentext, 2005).

25) A fine collection of Brakhage's writing is in Bruce R. McPherson (ed.), *Essential Brakhage* (Kingston, New York: Documentext, 2001). See also the discussion of Brakhage in P. Adams Sitney, *Visionary Film: The American Avant-Garde, 1943–2000* (New York: Oxford University Press, 2001), and his recent work *Eyes Upside Down: Visionary Filmmakers and the Heritage of Emerson* (New York: Oxford University Press, 2008).

26) See Abigail Child, *This Is Called Moving: A Critical Poetics of Film* (Tuscaloosa: University of Alabama Press, 2005).

("Films release a mechanism of affective and perceptual *participation* in the spectator [...] films have the *appeal* of a presence and of a proximity"[31]). While later apparatus theorists (including Metz himself in later writings) would see realism as a dangerous ideological illusion (while Bazin, on the contrary, would deepen cinematic realism into the possibility of grasping the mysteries of Being), in this early essay Metz simply attempts to give this psychological effect a phenomenological basis. Metz begins by contrasting media, claiming this degree of spectator participation and investment does not occur in still photography. Following Roland Barthes, Metz claims that still photography is condemned to a perceptual past tense ("This has been there"), while the movie spectator becomes absorbed by "a sense of 'There it is'."[32]

Metz locates the realistic effect of cinematic motion in its "participatory" effect. "Participation" seems to be a magic word in theories of realism that seek to overcome the dead ends encountered by correspondence theories of cinema. For Bazin, participation describes the relation between the photographic image and its object. Likewise, his description of the spectator's active role in the cinematic style that makes use of depth-of-field composition ("it is from [the spectator's] attention and his will that the meaning of the image in part derives"[33]) indicates an active participation by the viewer. For Metz, similarly, participation in the cinematic image is both "affective and perceptual," engendering "a very direct hold on perception," "an appeal of a presence and proximity."[34]

Metz points out that "participation, however, must be engendered."[35] What subtends this sense of immediacy and presence in the cinema? "An answer immediately suggests itself: It is *movement* [. . .] that produces the strong impression of reality."[36] While Metz admits other factors in film's effect on spectators, he ascribes a particular affect to the perception of motion, "a general law of psychology that movement is always perceived as real—unlike many other visual structures, such as volume, which is often very readily perceived as unreal."[37] In terms that seem to recall Bazin's claim that a photograph "is the object," Metz adds, "The strict distinction between object and copy, however, dis-

27) Siegfried Kracauer, *Theory of Film: The Redemption of Physical Reality* (Princeton: Princeton University Press, 1960), esp. pp. 41–45.

28) See André Bazin, *Jean Renoir* (New York: Da Capo, 1992), pp. 43–46.

29) André Bazin, "Evolution," in *What Is Cinema? op. cit., Vol. 1*, p. 27. Morgan's detailed discussion of the camera movement in Rossellini's *Voyage to Italy* in "Rethinking Bazin" shows one way camera movement can function within Bazin's realist aesthetic. See Morgan, *op. cit.*, pp. 465–468.

30) Christian Metz, "On the Impression of Reality in the Cinema," in *Film Language: A Semiotics of the Cinema* (Trans. Michael Taylor, New York: Oxford University Press, 1974), pp. 3–15.

31) *Ibid.*, pp. 4–5.

32) Both quotes *ibid.*, p. 6.

33) Bazin, 1967, "Evolution," p. 36.

34) All quotes Metz, *op. cit.*, p. 4.

35) *Ibid.*, p. 5.

36) *Ibid.*, p. 7.

37) *Ibid.*, p. 8.

solves on the threshold of motion. Because movement is never material but is always visual, to reproduce its appearance is to duplicate its reality. In truth, one cannot even 'reproduce' a movement; one can only re-produce it in a second production belonging to the same order of reality, for the spectator, as the first. [...] In the cinema the impression of reality is also the reality of the impression, the real presence of motion."[38] Metz gives here a very compressed account of a complex issue, and his assumptions would take some time to isolate and explicate (such as exactly what the "reality of an impression" might be and the begging of the question through the assertion that cinema delivers "the real presence of motion"). But the relation he draws between motion and the impression of reality provides us with a radical course of thought. We experience motion on the screen in a different way than we look at still images, and this difference explains our participation in the film image, a sense of perceptual richness or immediate involvement in the image. Spectator participation in the moving image depends, Metz claims, on perceiving motion and the perceptual, cognitive, and physiological effects this triggers. The nature of cinematic motion, its continuous progress, its unfolding nature, would seem to demand the participation of a perceiver.

Although Metz does not refer directly to Henri Bergson's famous discussion of motion, I believe Bergson developed the most detailed description of the need to participate in motion in order to grasp it. Bergson claims, "In order to advance with the moving reality, you must replace yourself within it."[39] For Bergson, discontinuous signs, such as language or ideas, cannot grasp the continuous flow of movement, but must conceive of it as a series of successive static instants, or positions. Only motion, one can assume, is able to convey motion. Therefore, to perceive motion, rather than represent it statically in a manner that destroys its essence, one must participate in the motion itself. Of course, analysis provides a means of conceptual understanding, and Bergson actually refers to our tendency to conceive of motion through a series of static images—a distortion he claims our habits of mind and language demand of us—as "cinematographic." Great confusion (which I feel Deleuze increases rather than dispels) comes if we do not realize that the analytical aspect of the cinematograph that Bergson took as his model for this tendency to conceive of motion in terms of static instants derives from the *film strip* in which motion is analyzed into a succession of frames, not the *projected image* on the screen in which synthetic motion is recreated.

Cinema, the projected moving image, demands that we participate in the movement we perceive. Analysis of perceiving motion can only offer some insights into the way the moving image exceeds our contemplation of a static image. Motion always has a projective aspect, a progressive movement in a direction, and therefore invokes possibility and a future. Of course, we can project these states into a static image, but with an actually moving image we are swept along with the motion itself. Rather than imagining previous or anterior states, we could say that through a moving image, the progress of motion is projected onto us. Undergirded by the kinesthetic effects of cinematic motion, I believe "participation" properly describes the increased sense of involvement with the cinematic image, a sense of presence that could be described as an impression of reality.

Metz claims that the motion we see in a film is real, not a representation, a claim I take to be close to Bergson's discussion of the way movement cannot be derived simply from a static presentation of successive points. According to Metz, what we see when we see a moving image on the screen should not be described as a "picture" of motion, but instead as an experience of seeing something truly moving. In terms of a visual experience of motion, therefore, no difference exists between watching a film of a ball rolling down a hill, say, and seeing an actual ball rolling down a hill. One might object to this identification of motion and its visual sensation by pointing out that our sensation of motion (kinesthesia) does not depend entirely on vision but on a range of bodily sensations. But I believe Metz could respond to this in two ways. First, the most extreme sort of kinesthesia primarily refers to the sensation of ourselves moving bodily, traversing space, not simply watching a moving object. Insofar as we do experience kinesthesia when we observe a moving object other than ourselves, the same sensations seem to occur when we watch a moving object in a film. Thus, perceiving motion in the cinema, while triggered by visual perception, need not be restricted to visual effects. Clearly, cinema cannot move us, as viewers, physically (we don't, for instance, leave our seats or get transported to another place, even if we have a sensation of ourselves moving as we watch films in which the camera moves through space). However, while acknowledging that Metz can only claim that cinema possesses visual motion, not literal movement through space—a change of place—the fact remains that even visual motion, such as camera movement, doesn't only affect us visually but does produce the physiological effect of kinesthesia.

Metz questions whether there could be a "portrayal of motion" that did not actually involve motion, a representation parallel, say, to the use of perspective drawing to render volumes. In a way, it is not hard to conceive of such a portrayal. A diagram conveying the trajectory of a moving object, such as a graph of the parabola described by a baseball hit by David Ortiz, could be said to portray motion. The speed lines used by comic book artists to indicate a running figure also portray the idea of motion visually but in static form. Indeed, the chronophotographs of Étienne-Jules Marey, with their composite and successive figures tracing the path of human movement, or the blurred image of simple actions like turning a head found in the photo-dynamist photographs of Futurist Anton Giulio Bragaglia, all portray motion without actually moving. But that is the point, precisely. These diagrammatic por-

38) *Ibid*., p. 9.

39) Henri Bergson, *Creative Evolution* (Trans. Arthur Mitchell, Lanham: University Press of America, 1983), p. 308. The discussion of motion extends over pages 297–314.

trayals of motion strike us very differently from actual motion pictures. Such portrayals of motion recall Bergson's descriptions of attempts to generate a sense of motion from tracing a pattern of static points or positions, which miss the continuous sweep of motion. In contrast to these diagrams of the successive phases of motion or indications of its pathways, we could say, perhaps now with even more clarity, that cinema shows us motion, not its portrayal.

Ultimately, I think there is little question that phenomenologically we see movement on the screen, not a "portrayal" of movement. But what does it mean to say the movement is "real"? As I understand Metz's claim, it does not at all commit us to the nonsensical position that we take the cinema image for reality, that we are involved in a hallucination or "illusion" of reality that could cause us to contemplate walking into the screen, or interacting physically with the fictional events we see portrayed. In the cinema, we are dealing with realism, not "reality." As Metz makes clear, "on the one hand, there is the impression of reality; on the other, the perception of reality."[40] Theater, for instance, makes use of real materials, actual people and things, to create a fiction world. Cinema works with images that possess an impression of reality, not its materiality. This distinction is crucial.

#### THE REALISTIC MOTION OF FANTASY

Metz's description of cinematic motion supplies at least part of (and probably a central part of) an alternative theory of the realistic effect of the cinema (one I find much more compelling and flexible than the ideological explanation of psychological regression offered by Jean-Louis Baudry and, in a sense, the later Metz of *The Imaginary Signifier*). But we should keep in mind that this is a theory of the impression of reality (based, as he says, on the reality of the impression), rather than an argument for a realist aesthetic such as that offered by Bazin or Kracauer. Part of the flexibility of Metz's theory of the reality of cinematic motion lies in its adaptability to a range of cinematic styles. As Metz indicates, the "feeling of credibility" film offers "operates on us in films of the unusual and of the marvelous, as well as in those that are 'realistic.'"[41] But his description also shows that movement can be an important factor in describing a realist style (one need only think of the role of camera movement in Welles and Rossellini, undertheorized by Bazin, or in Renoir, which Bazin describes beautifully). But the fantastic possibilities of motion, or rather its role in rendering the fantastic believable, and I would say visceral, shows the mercurial role motion can play in film spectatorship and film style.

It is this mercurial, protean, indeed *mobile* nature of cinematic motion that endows it with power as a concept for film theory and analysis. Not only does the concept of cinematic movement unite photographic-based films and traditional animated films (not to mention the hybrid synthesis of photographic and animation techniques that Computer Generated Images represent), movement also displays a flexibility that avoids the proscriptive nature of much of classical film theory.[42] While the formal aspects of cinematic movement (and the range of ways it can be used, or even the number of aspects of cinematic motion possible) make it an important tool for aesthetic analysis (and even useful in a polemical argument like Dulac's or Bazin's for a particular style of film), nothing restricts movement to a single style.

The impression of reality that cinematic movement carries can underwrite a realist film style (think of the use of hand-held camera movement in the films of the Dogma 95 movement), a highly artificial fantasy dependent on special effects (the importance of kinesis in the *Star Wars* films), or an abstract visual symphony (animator Oskar Fischinger). Metz describes the role of the impression of reality enabled by cinematic motion as "to inject the reality of motion into the unreality of the image and thus to render the world of imagination more real than it had ever been."[43] Like Mercury, winged messenger of the Gods, cinematic motion crosses the boundaries between heaven and earth, between the embodied senses and flights of fancy, not simply playing the whole gamut of film style but contaminating one with the other, endowing the fantastic with the realistic impression of visual motion.

The extraordinary writings Sergei Eisenstein produced in the 1930s on the animated films of Walt Disney accent this double valence of movement, tending not only toward realism but also, as the animated film and new digital processes demonstrate, toward fantasy.[44] Movement in the cinema not only generates the visual sense of realism that Metz describes, but bodily sensations of movement can engage spectator fantasy through perceptual and physical participation. Thus, movement created by animation, freed from photographic reference, can endow otherwise "impossible" motion and transformations with the immediacy of perception that Metz claims movement entails. In some ways this returns us to Dulac's concept of a pure cinema based entirely on the motion of forms (and the forms of motion). In his writings on Disney, Eisenstein focuses on the possibility of the animated line to invoke precisely this aspect of motion, which he calls "plasmaticness" and defines as "a rejection of once-and-forever allotted form, freedom from ossification, the ability to dynamically assume any form."[45] Rather than simply endowing familiar forms with the solidity and credibility that Metz de-

40) Metz, *op. cit.*, p. 13.

41) *Ibid.*, p. 8.

42) Would a focus on movement entail a proscriptive definition that all films must include motion? Insofar as we are referring to the movement of the apparatus, the film traveling through the projector gate, this might be tautological. Duration as a measure of this motion of the film certainly provides the sine qua non for cinematic motion and all cinema, technically defined. However, I think we can certainly conceive of films that exclude motion, made entirely of still images. Interestingly, many films that use still images seem to do so to comment on movement. Clearly, the dialectical relation between stillness and movement provides one of the richest uses of motion in film. But I think it would be an essentialist mistake to assume a film could not avoid cinematic motion, even if the examples of such are very rare and possibly debatable.

43) Metz, *op. cit.*, p. 15.

44) See Sergei Eisenstein in Jay Leyda (ed. and Trans.), *Eisenstein on Disney* (London: Methuen, 1988).

45) *Ibid.*, p. 27.

scribes, movement can extend beyond familiarity to fantasy and imagination, creating the impossible bodies that throng the works of animation, from the early cartoons of Emile Cohl to the digital manipulation of Gollum in *The Lord of the Rings* (Peter Jackson, 2001).[46] While flaunting the rules of physical resemblance, such animation need not remain totally divorced from any reference to our lived world. As I once heard philosopher Arthur Danto explain, the cartoon body can reveal primal phenomenological relations we have to our physical existence, our sense of grasping, stretching, exulting.[47] For Eisenstein, this plasmatic quality invokes "[a] lost changeability, fluidity, suddenness of formations—that's the 'subtext' brought to the viewer who lacks all this by these seemingly strange traits which permeate folktales, cartoons, the spineless circus performer and the seemingly groundless scattering of extremities in Disney's drawings."[48]

Motion therefore need not be realistic to have a "realistic" effect, that is, to invite the empathic participation, both imaginative and physiological, of viewers. Eisenstein's discussion of motion as a force that does not simply propel forms but actually creates them not only refers back to the theories of Bergson but makes clear the multiple nature of the participation that motion invokes, from the perceptual identity described by Metz to the realm of anticipation, speculation, and imagination of the possibly transforming aspects of line described by Eisenstein. Unlike the literalness of pointing to an actual individual that a narrow adherence to the diminished indexical theory of film and photography forces on us, as Metz emphasizes, the cinematic impression of reality affects the diegesis, the fictional world created by the film, and thus escapes the straitjacket of exclusive correspondence or reference to any preexisting reality. Metz's concept of cinematic movement's "novel power to convince [...] was all to the advantage of the imagination."[49] The realist claim offered for cinema's indexical quality, based in still photography, actually operates in a diametrically different direction than the role Metz outlines for cinematic movement in the medium's impression of reality. An indexical argument, as it has been developed, based in the photographic trace, points the image back into the past, to a preexisting object or event whose traces could only testify to its having already been. Metz's concept of the impression of reality moves in the opposite direction, toward a sensation of the present and of presence. The indexical argument can be invoked most clearly (and usefully) for films used as historical evidence. It remains unclear, however, how the index functions within a fiction film, where we are dealing with a diegesis, a fictional world, rather than a reference to a reality. Laura Mulvey, in her extremely important discussion of indexicality in film, has pointed out how it relates to the phenomenon of the Star, clearly an existing person beyond the fictional character he or she plays and therefore a reference outside the film's diegesis.[50] The effect of an index in guaranteeing the actual existence of its reference depends on the one who makes this connection invoking a technical knowledge of photography, understanding the effect of light on the sensitive film. Metz's cinematic impression of reality depends on "forgetting" (that is, on distracting the viewer's attention away from—not literally repressing the knowledge of) the technical process of filming in favor of an experience of the fictional world as present. As he claims, "The movie spectator is absorbed, not by a 'has been there' but by a sense of 'There it is'".[51]

Even if the indexical claim for cinema is granted, I am not sure it really supplies the basis for a realist aesthetic. Although Bazin invokes something that sounds like an index in his description of the ontology of the photographic image, maintaining the exact congruence of his claims with a strictly indexical claim seems fraught with difficulty. Rather than an argument about signs, Bazin's ontology of the photographic and filmic image seems to assert a nearly magical sense of the presence delivered by the photographic image. In any case, at best, the index would only function as one aspect of Bazin's realist aesthetic.[52] Once again, I am not claiming no use exists for the index in theories of film and photography, but simply that it has been entrusted with tasks it cannot fulfill and that reading it back into classical realist theories of the cinema probably obscures as much as it explains.

But I would also have to admit that "motion," even when specified as "cinematic motion," probably includes multiple aspects, not just one perceptible factor. The extreme spectator involvement that movement can generate needs further study, both in terms of perceptual and cognitive processes (which I think call for both experimental and phenomenological analysis) and in relation to broader aesthetic styles. Metz's description is based on the classical fiction film: what role does motion play in non-classical films? (I have, of course, argued for its vital role in avant-garde film.) I am offering only a prolegomena to a larger investigation; my comments here aspire to be provocative rather than definitive. Motion, I am arguing, needs to be taken more seriously in our exploration of the nature of film and our account of how film style functions. At the same time, giving new importance to movement (or restoring it) builds a strong bridge between cinema and

46) See my discussion of Gollum and CGI-generated characters in Tom Gunning, "Gollum and Golem: Special Effects and the Technology of Artificial Bodies," in Ernest Mathijs and Murray Pomerance (eds.), *From Hobbits to Hollywood: Essays on Peter Jackson's Lord of the Rings* (Amsterdam: Rodopi, 2006), pp. 319–350.

47) Danto discussed this more than a decade ago at the Columbia Film Seminar in New York City. He specifically referred, as I recall, to the way Mickey Mouse and other cartoon characters often have fewer than five fingers but cogently convey the role of the hand in grasping. If my memory is faulty, I apologize to Mr. Danto (with humble admiration).

48) Eisenstein, 1988, "Disney", p. 21.

49) Metz, *op. cit.*, p. 14.

50) Laura Mulvey, *Death 24x a Second: Stillness and the Moving Image* (London: Reaktion, 2006). See esp. pp. 54–66.

51) Metz, *op. cit.*, p. 6.

52) Kracauer's arguments for the realist mission of cinema, although also based in its photographic legacy, most certainly exceeds, if it implies at all, the index.

the new media that some view as cinema's successors. Like the animated line Germaine Dulac described, whose movement directly creates an emotion, motion involves both transformation and continuity (film history involves both the transformation of its central medium and a recognition of an ever-shifting continuity, a trajectory, to this transformation). As an art of motion, cinema has affinities to other media: dance, action painting, instantaneous photography, kinetic sculpture. But it also possesses its own trajectory, one in which I suspect the new media of motion arts will also find a place, or at least an affinity.

Vinzenz Hediger

# Lost in Space and Found in a Fold

*Cinema and the Irony of Media*

According to a number of theorists, in the age of mobile media, ubiquitous screens and moving images on the move, an age where only 25 percent of the box office returns of an average film come from the sale of cinema tickets,[1] ontology and the question "What is cinema?" have been replaced by topology and the question "Where is cinema?" as the key concern of film theory. In a recent essay for *Cinema & Cie*, Malte Hagener proposes a suggestive chronology of film studies: From the 1950s onward and in the vein of André Bazin, film scholars asked what cinema was. Beginning in the 1970s with the study of early cinema and new methodologies of film historiography, the focus shifted to questions about the historical emergence of cinema, of when cinema was. And now, in the light of the new ubiquity of moving images, film theorists ask where cinema is, and what it means to be surrounded by moving images or to be and move with and within them, instead of looking at them.[2]

In the same issue of *Cinema & Cie*, Alexandra Schneider approaches the topology of the moving image from a historical point of view. Pointing to the long history of the circulation of moving images outside the theater, Schneider challenges the canonical status of the cinematic screening and the classical cinema space as the frame of reference for film theory's thinking about cinema. While the cinematic screening may be the norm, Schneider argues, it is also just *a* norm, and film theory, in order to continue its work, must come to terms with what lies beyond this norm.[3]

Combining the insights of Hagener and Schneider, contemporary film theory could indeed move in the direction of a topology of the moving image, thinking from within the image, and thinking both inside and outside the cinema.

In this essay, I would like to take up this challenge, but in a somewhat oblique manner. I would like to address the complexities and perplexities of film theory in an age of ubiquitous moving images through what might be called a concrete geography of film: a geography of the boundaries and walls at stake in terms like "Entgrenzungen des Kinos" and "Cinema with-

1) See Harold L. Vogel, *Entertainment Industry Economics. A Guide for Financial Analysis* (Cambridge, UK: Cambridge University Press, Eighth Ed. 2011), pp. 71ff.

2) Malte Hagener, "Where is Cinema (Today)? The Cinema in the Age of Media Immanence," in *Cinema & Cie*, no. 11 (Fall 2008), p. 15–22.

3) Alexandra Schneider, "'The Cinema is the Theater, the School and the Newspaper of Tomorrow': Writing the History of Cinema's Mobility," in *Cinema & Cie*, no. 11 (Fall 2008), p. 57–64.

out walls."[4] I propose to take these metaphors quite literally as markers of an inherent spatiality of film theory. I contend that the question of what is, and what is not cinema has always been a question of concrete spatial boundaries. The ontology of film, I would argue, has always had a topological undertow. This becomes evident—and has its consequences—in a moment when film seems to be leaving its assigned territory, the spatial framework of the cinema, which happens to be the territory within which it first became an object of theoretical reflection. In what follows, I will first provide some evidence for the spatial element sustaining some of the established answers to the question "What is cinema?" I will then turn to the history of film theory in order to address what I just proposed to call its inherent spatiality, but also to such recent concepts in media theory as "convergence," and explore the dynamics of that spatiality. In particular, I will argue that the spatial metaphors and modes of argument in film and media theory point to what I propose to call the "irony of media," i.e. the fact that from a theoretical point of view film and media, in a way, are bound to remain indeterminate, or limitless.

## I.

The topology of film is concerned with questions of space, place, territories, boundaries and delimitations. But the ontology of film has also been sustained by questions of boundaries and limitations. In fact, the question "What is cinema?" has long been a question of space, place and territory as much as it has been a question of essence or media specificity. While early film theorists engaged in what we might call, with Étienne Souriau, a "comparative aesthetics" of cinema as a *language* or an art form, teasing out the specifics of cinematic language as opposed to the languages, or forms, of other arts, film culture from the 1920s onwards evolved around a comparative aesthetics of cinema as a cultural practice, based on a "confrontation of tastes, styles, artistic functions with different peoples, historical periods or distinct social groups."[5] Consider the classical definition of cinema in film culture, shared—implicitly or explicitly—by critics, cinephiles, film clubs, festivals, film archives, and also by academic film scholars working on canonical films and national cinematographies. According to this definition, cinema is a corpus of films created by directors who deserve to be called "auteurs," and who hail from a specific place of origin, usually defined as a modern nation state with a cultural output that can be classified as nationally specific.

Beginning in the 1920s, and certainly since the 1950s, the cinema of film culture and most of film scholarship, as defined mostly by French theorists and authors, whose writings developed a worldwide reach, has been routinely been defined as both an auteur cinema and a national cinema.[6] Thus, in film culture, the ontological question "What is cinema?" has mostly been answered by using a list and a map: A list of directors' names and a map that indicates their place of origin. While the question "What is cinema?" may point to an atemporal, universal essence of cinema that is the same everywhere and at all times, in the terms of film culture it is quite possible for some people or ethnic groups not to share in this seemingly universal essence of cinema and *not* to have a cinema. If in the inventory of cinema, the list and the map of cinema, a certain place comes up short in the column of directors that can make the list of auteurs, it is possible for this place to be considered more or less devoid of "cinema."

A case in point would be Spain which has a very limited number of directors in the canon of auteurs and hence, to some observers who closely adhere to the "list and map approach" to cinema, does not have much of a cinema to speak of. Even more dramatic is the case of Switzerland, a country that produces dozens of films annually but currently has no director of international standing, while the country's most notable director, Alain Tanner, had his most productive phase in the 1970s and is routinely co-opted by the French as a French director anyway, a neo-colonial gesture of appropriation to which Tanner himself happily agrees. In epistemological terms, the list-and-map concept of cinema is a hybrid, confounding aesthetic with political and geographical categories and mingling the descriptive with the normative, thereby generating a discursive and regulative onto-topology of film. As such it has been, and continues to be, a powerful conceptual operator, combining and conjugating a diverse set of actors and institutions in a discourse about film that provides a framework for the policies of a number of institutions, from festivals and archives to universities and the academic study of film.

With regard to individual films, the list-and-map approach is a powerful operator in that it not only helps to classify films in a broader sense but can, and will, if the conditions are met, turn films into cinema. Once the auteur/artist credentials of a director are established by the relevant institutional players—which in the world of film include critics, festival selection committees and directors, film scholars, archivists and curators—a film of a given auteur, as in fact any film of any accredited auteur, will be considered as part of "cinema" (quite analogous to the world of art, where the list of players who turn artists into eminent artists includes critics, art historians

4) Editors' note: The conference where an earlier version of this essay was presented was entitled *Entgrenzung des Kinos—Grenzen des Films / Cinema without Walls—Borderlands of Film*.

5) Étienne Souriau, *La correspondance des arts* (Paris: Flammarion, 1969), p. 27 ["confrontation des goûts, des styles, des fonctions artistiques chez différents peuples, ou à diverses époques historiques ou dans des groupes sociaux distincts"].

6) For a history of the nationalization of film culture and film historiography in the wake of the First World War see Christophe Gautier, "Le cinéma des nations: Invention des écoles nationales et patriotisme cinématographiques (années 1910–années 1930)," in *Révue d'histoire moderne et contemporaine*, Vol. 51, Issue 4 (October 2004), pp. 58–77. For a history of the film club movement and its contribution to this process see Malte Hagener, *Moving Forward, Looking Back. The European Avantgarde and the Invention of Film Culture, 1919–1939* (Amsterdam: Amsterdam University Press, 2007). Open access online version: http://dare.uva.nl/document/171983.

and museum curators, among others).[7] In that sense, the list and the map constitute a Deleuzian discursive machine that ceaselessly turns the raw material of individual films into the product known as "cinema." And for all the talk about the imminent death of cinema, there is no reason to assume that that machine will grind to a halt anytime soon. As it is, no edition of the Cannes film festival has as yet been announced as the last of its kind.[8]

But even beyond the realm of the discursive onto-topology of the list and the map, in the realm of film theory and film aesthetics, the ontological question "What is cinema?" has often been answered, and continues to be answered, in topological rather than purely ontological terms. In a recent essay, Annette Kuhn highlights a notable division in the study of film since the 1990s. In the wake of cultural studies and in the light of Janet Staiger's radical methodological claim that the meaning of a film can only be grasped through the ways in which an audience makes sense of it,[9] reception studies have delved into the many historical layers of film culture, focusing on the cultural practice of moviegoing and on individual memories of the cinema experience rather than on individual films or the aesthetics of the medium.[10] On the other hand, film theory and film philosophy have focused on the aesthetic rather than the pragmatic side of cinema and developed ever more sophisticated theories of the cinematic body, the cinematic illusion or cinema as a haptic medium.[11] Far from attempting to bridge this impasse I want to highlight the spatial framework that marks much of the philosophical and aesthetic reflection on cinema's specificity to this day. "Le cinema est un corps de mémoire," is the wonderful and powerful first sentence of Raymond Bellour's recent book on *Menschen am Sonntag* (1929).[12] As Bellour argues in this and other books, most notably in his latest work *Le corps du cinéma*, the cinema's body of memory can come to life only within the confines of the *dispositif* of cinema, i.e. the standard situation of the theatrical screening.[13] A film watched on a television set is at risk of dispelling the body of memory, and one can assume that the *corps de mémoire* will fare even worse if the film is viewed on a mobile phone device. As Bellour puts it in his contribution to the present volume, when it comes to the cinema there is a "privilège absolu du dispositif," an absolute privilege of the *dispositif*. In that sense, the *definition* of cinema is really a *de-*

7) The classic study of this dynamic in the art world is Howard S. Becker, *Art Worlds* (Berkeley: University of California Press, 1982). On the role of film festivals in shaping national cinema canons see Liz Czach, "Film Festivals, Programming, and the Building of a National Cinema," in *The Moving Image*, Vol. 4, Issue 1 (Spring 2004), pp. 76–88. A comprehensive study of the role of critics in creating the lasting reputation of individual films and directors, based on a sample of 1,277 films from 1929 to 1991, is: Michael Patrick Allen and Anne E. Lincoln, "Critical Discourse and the Cultural Consecration of American Films," in *Social Forces*, Vol. 82, Issue 3 (March 2004), pp. 871–894. Despite a recent surge in studies of film festivals, the most thorough and detailed studies of the institutional interactions of festivals, critics, academics and cinema programmers have so far been devoted to smaller fields such as the American experimental film of the 1960s and 1970s. See Todd Bayma, "Art World Culture and Institutional Choices: The Case of Experimental Film," in *The Sociological Quarterly*, Vol. 36, Issue 1 (Winter 1995), pp. 79–95; Kathryn Ramey, "Between Art, Industry and Academy: The Fragile Balancing Act of the Avant-Garde Film

*limitation* of cinema: A defintion of cinema in terms of the space where the screening and the experience of the film take place. In such a delimitative theory of film real estate literally matters: If contemporary cinema is indeed a cinema without walls, the question arises whether it still is cinema at all. But while Raymond Bellour affirms—plausibly to me, I might add—that the tone of his analysis is neither elegiac nor melancholic, for other theorists the essence of cinema is not only at stake beyond the walls of cinema, but condemned to be lost if and when these walls come down. For Heide Schlüpmann, for instance, cinema is the inheritor of the enlightenment, a continuation of the enlightenment by other means. But for Schlüpmann cinema can only provide the experience of sensory enlightenment under the conditions of the public screening and the shared space of cinema. In that sense the dispersion of the film image in our current culture of ubiquitous moving images is a threat to the very essence of cinema and undermines the cinema's potential mission to continue and complete the enlightenment.[14] But if such theories of film, or rather of cinema, depend on spatial delimitations, they are quite specific in a temporal sense as well. Stanley Cavell, a close reader of Heidegger's *Sein und Zeit* and as such not a stranger to the existential stakes and situated nature of philosophy, is straightforward in acknowledging that his philosophy of film is grounded in a specific biographical experience, namely his experience of the classical Hollywood cinema of his youth and early adulthood. Similarly, theories such as those of Bellour and Schlüpmann reveal themselves—or are revealed by their authors to be—rooted in a specific time of cinema,

Community," in *Visual Anthropology Review*, Vol. 18, Issue 1 (March 2002), pp. 22–36. The network aspects of the international film festival circuit have been studied by Marijke de Valck in her recent book on festivals. Marijke De Valck, *Film Festivals: From European Geopolitics to Global Cinephilia* (Amsterdam: Amsterdam University Press, 2007). Open access online version: http://dare.uva.nl/document/165315.

8) For the cultural politics of the Cannes film festival and the discursive practices of reframing Hollywood films as "cinema" see Christian Jungen, *Hollywood in Cannes. Die Geschichte einer Hassliebe, 1939–2008* (Marburg: Schüren, 2009).

9) Janet Staiger, *Interpreting Films. Studies in the Historical Reception of American Cinema* (Princeton: Princeton University Press, 1992); Janet Staiger, *Perverse Spectators. The Practices of Film Reception* (New York: New York University Press, 2000).

10) Annette Kuhn, "Was tun mit der Kinoerinnerung?" in *Montage AV*, Vol. 19, Issue 1 (2010), pp. 117–134. For one of the most thorough applications of this approach to the study of cinema culture see the work of Daniel Biltereyst and Philippe Meers and his research group on the cinema culture of Antwerp, Belgium, which has been replicated for similar studies in Guadalajara, Mexico, and Brno, Czech Republic. See for instance Philippe Meers, Daniel Biltereyst and Lies Van de Vijver, "Metropolitan vs. Rural movie-going in Flanders, 1925–75," in *Screen*, Vol. 51, Issue 3 (Autumn 2010), pp. 272–280.

11) Of particular note here is the work of Gertrud Koch, Vivian Sobchak and Christiane Voss, all of whom propose theories of film, film spectatorship and film aesthetics grounded in philosophy, but without a particular regard to the pragmatics of the medium.

12) Raymond Bellour, *Les hommes, le dimanche, de Robert Siodmak et Edgar G. Ulmer* (Paris: Yellow Now, 2009).

13) Raymond Bellour, *Le corps du cinéma. Hypnose, emotions, animalités* (Paris: POL, 2009).

14) Heide Schlüpmann, "Das Aufklärungsversprechen des Kinos, oder die Ablösung der Metaphysik durch die Medien," in *Montage AV*, Vol. 19, Issue 1 (2010), pp. 164–171; Heide Schlüpmann, *Die Abendröthe der Subjektphilosophie. Eine Ästhetik des Kinos* (Frankfurt am Main: Stroemfeld, 1998).

namely the cinephile film culture of the 1950s through the 1970s. While it is perhaps ironic that the florescence of film culture in the mid-twentieth century coincides with the early stages of the massive circulation of theatrical films through television, "cinema" in that period most emphatically means both a body of films compiled according to the list-and-map criterion and the visual and corporeal experience of such films within the confines of the theatrical *dispositif*. And so it does to theorists like Bellour and Schlüpmann (but not quite to Cavell, whose point of reference is Hollywood cinema before it became an art and acquired a history—that is before American films became integrated into the global order of the list-and-map definition of cinema, which implies, among other things, that cinema has a history of authors, masterpieces and formal innovations, all of which Hollywood cinema could splendidly do without until the late 1950s).

As the "cinema" of the mid-20th century fades into memory it would be easy to argue that the force of the claims made by Bellour, Schlüpmann and others who lived that moment of cinema, must wane. In fact, since the cinema that made Cavell think disappeared even before (and partly because) the "cinema" of the 1960s and 1970s emerged, one should expect his theoretical claims to be of even less relevance to us now. Yet those claims are important to an understanding of the current situation of cinema, or "cinema," precisely because they are "unzeitgemäß," unfashionable. Rather than merely becoming dated by recent advances in filmmaking and screening technologies, they are a challenge to theorists who have come to film later, in some cases very recently.

So what are we to make of such paradigmatic claims made by film theory as cinema theory? Should we just adopt the opposite position and claim that, yes, films are cinema even outside the cinema? Or should we just shrug off the problem of cinema space as part of cinema's essence and treat it as a generational thing, an idiosyncratic material fetish developed by a generation of theorists raised on a diet of classical cinephilia and without the blessings of portable screen devices, DVD collections and online streaming platforms for films? As I've outlined in my introductory remarks, a number of authors have addressed the question of cinema's spatiality, which the current debate reveals to be one of the core elements of the medium's specificity, head on. Where Alexandra Schneider proposes to historicize the norm of "cinema" and focus on the circulation of moving images in a broader sense, and where Malte Hagener proposes to approach cinema from a Deleuzian perspective, i.e. from within the moving image itself, Francesco Casetti uses another spatial metaphor of sorts when he talks about the current "explosion of cinema" and describes the shift from "cinema" to contemporary moving image culture as a shift from a film culture of *attendance*, where audiences share the public space of cinema, to a culture of *performance* where viewers create their own spaces of viewing and patterns of programming.[15]

Rather than contributing yet another approach to the new spatial aesthetics of cinema I would like to take a different approach. I would like to take seriously the possibility of what might be called an inherent spatiality of film theory, and with it media theory. In fact, with the benefit of hindsight, that is from the vantage point of contemporary film theory's interest in the overtly topological aspects of cinema, it is quite possible to argue that even beyond the question of the *dispositif*—and before that question was ever raised—the ontological question "What is cinema?" has carried with it a topological undertow. In that spirit, I would now like to turn to the history of film theory and, in a way, use it as a resource for addressing the current perplexities in film theory.

## II.

In any discussion of the ontology of film, André Bazin would probably have to be the first name to be mentioned. Instead, I would like to start with another classical theorist, Siegfried Kracauer (before returning, albeit briefly, to Bazin, at the end of this article). In their writings, both Bazin and Kracauer offer definitions of the medium specificity of photography, which in turn prepare the way for definitions of the medium specificity of film. Kracauer's first major statement on photography came in an article originally published in the *Frankfurter Zeitung* in the 1920s.[16] In this essay Kracauer first articulates an interest in a perceived analogy between photography and historiography, which he explores again in his last, unfinished book about historiography, in the second chapter of *The Last Things Before Last*, which was first published in 1969.[17] In the essay on photography Kracauer argues that photography is analogous to, and in line with, historicist approaches to historiography. As such, photography is at odds with any attempt at writing a more penetrating and potentially more just form of history. Even though the essay is rather muted on the issue, Kracauer has a dialectial approach to history and historiography in mind as he writes his critique of photography and historicism. Roughly forty years later, in the history book, he develops a more relaxed and nuanced version of the analogy between historiography and photography. He maintains the anology, but he no longer sees it as inherently pernicious. While I do not want to elaborate on the relative merits of Kracauer's arguments from the 1920s and the 1960s at this point, I want to focus on the common thread that binds the two texts together. In both cases, the argument is based on what might be called a classical definition of the essence of photography, i.e. of what photography is. The definition is classical in that it follows a pattern that was probably first fully developed by Lessing in his Laokoon essay and has been followed by subsequent philosophers of art, including Georg Lukács in his early essay on the cinema from 1911 and Étienne Souriau and his comparative aesthetics, which included

15) Francesco Casetti, "Die Explosion des Kinos. Filmische Erfahrung in der post-kinematographischen Epoche," in *Montage AV*, Vol. 19, Issue 1 (2010), pp. 11–35.

16) Siegfried Kracauer, "Photography," in *The Mass Ornament. Weimar Essays* (Cambridge: Harvard University Press, 1995 [1927]), pp. 47–64.

17) Siegfried Kracauer, *History. The Last Things Before Last* (New York: Oxford University Press, 1969).

film in particular:[18] the pattern of defining the essence of an art through its comparison with another art. It is a comparison in terms of an art's medium specificity, that is in terms of what specifically an art or a medium can do, and which features a given work has to display in order for it to be considered to be a successful example of the art to which it belongs. According to this definition, every successful work of art is an exemplification of the specifics of a given art as compared to other, similar arts.

The question of the essence of a given art form has been around at least since Aristotle's poetics and Horace's identification of painting with poetry, which Lessing addresses and criticizes in the Laokoon essay. The comparative aesthetics inaugurated by Lessing, however, may be characterized as a specifically modern phenomenon. Comparative aesthetics of this type first appear and unfold their appeal at the threshold of the 19th century. Variously characterized as a shift from the classical *episteme* to a modern regime of knowledge by Foucault or as a "Sattelzeit," a saddle epoch, by Reinhart Koselleck, this threshold marks a historical passage from the established order and hierarchy of the arts to what Jacques Rancière calls the "aesthetic regime of art," when all art forms become essentially equivalent and anything can become the subject of an artwork. In this dynamic new regime, in which all arts are equivalent, comparative aesthetics of the kind proposed by Lessing provide a procedure and a tool by which to assess if no longer the value, then at least the specific potential and merits of a given art form.

As W.J.T. Mitchell has pointed out, Laokoon-essay type of arguments operate with a series of dichotomies, of fundamental distinctions. In terms of the thought process involved, it is interesting to note that such dichotomies create a spatial layout of defining opposites.[19] In a replay of the standard set-up of scientific observation and working towards what Lorraine Daston proposes to call "a-perspectival objectivity,"[20] it is as if the two art forms or media were laid out before the eyes of the theorist, and his eyes wander from one to the other and back, defining and delineating their differences, eventually putting one term of the dichotomy on one side and one on the other.

Returning to Kracauer, the photography essay attempts to define the specificity, or essence, of photography, through a comparison with painting. Kracauer's key point is this: "For in the artwork the meaning of the object takes on spatial appearance, whereas in photography the spatial appearance of an object is its meaning."[21]

As Kracauer argues, painting, and art in general, expresses the meaning of an object in the form of a spatial appearance, whereas photography conversely reduces the meaning of any object to that spatial appearance. Kracauer's Lessingian definition of photography's medium specificity contains an obvious residue of Platonism: Photography is suspect because it is mere appearance, because it does not allow for the transcendence of meaning and provides no room for the intention of the artist. In a way, this amounts to a quasi-Platonic rephrasing of a well-established trope in the theory of photography. In his "Salon of 1859" Baudelaire deplores the fact, which he considers to be indisputable, that photography, as an automatic procedure of generating images, leaves no room for the artist and eliminates the artist's subjectivity.[22] Thus, to the Kracauer of the 1920s, as to Baudelaire in 1859, photography is all appearance and no ideas. The Kracauer of the 1960s, the Kracauer after the *Theory of Film*, has a slightly different view of photography. In the second chapter of the history book, Kracauer writes about a photograph by Alfred Stieglitz: "Alfred Stieglitz' print of a group of huddled trees is a photograph of really existing trees and at the same time a memorable image—or should I say allgeory?—of autumnal sadness."[23]

All of a sudden, one is tempted to say, photography can do both. It can do what photography always could, namely record the physcial or spatial appearance of things. But photography can also do what painting can, namely express ideas: "Der Bedeutung des Gegenstandes räumliche Erscheinung verleihen." It is as if things had taken a McLuhanian turn where the content of the new medium is, among other things, the old medium. Photography has its limits and limitations—it is and remains the medium that reduces the meaning of an object to its physical appearance. But now photography encompasses and contains within itself the limits and limitations of the medium from which it was previously delimited: It can do both.

But if photography has now acquired what used to be the key defining feature of painting, then what happens to painting? What, if any, are the defining features of painting now? I want to try and answer this question with an example, a painting that was created just ten years after Kracauer wrote his second chapter of the book on history, the painting *Central Savings* by Richard Estes from 1975. Estes is one of the key figures of the photorealist movement in

18) In Lukács' text the comparison is between cinema and the theater, with the latter posited as the "tragic" art, whereas cinema, the art in which every object can be juxtaposed with every other through montage, is the "romantic" art par excellence. See Georg Lukács, "Gedanken zu einer Ästhetik des ‚Kino'," in Jörg Schweinitz (ed.), *Prolog vor dem Film: Nachdenken über ein neues Medium 1909–1914* (Leipzig: Reclam, 1992 [1911]). See also Tom Levin, "From Dialectical to Normative Specificity: Reading Lukács on Film," in *New German Critique*, no. 40 (Winter 1987), pp. 35–61.

19) W. J. T. Mitchell, "The Politics of Genre: Space and Time in Lessing's Laocoon," in *Representations*, no. 6 (Spring 1984), pp. 98–115.

20) Lorraine Daston, "Objectivity and the Escape from Perspective," in *Social Studies of Science*, Vol. 22, Issue 4 (November 1992), pp. 597–618.

21) Kracauer, "Photography," p. 52. "Denn in dem Kunstwerk wird die Bedeutung des Gegenstandes zur Raumerscheinung, während in der Photographie die Raumerscheinung eines Gegenstandes seine Bedeutung ist." Siegfried Kracauer, "Die Photographie," in Siegfried Kracauer, *Das Ornament der Masse. Essays* (Frankfurt am Main: Suhrkamp, 1977 [1927]), p. 27.

22) Charles Baudelaire, "The Salon of 1859: The Modern Public and Photography," in Francis Frascina, Charles Harrison and Deirde Paul (eds.), *Modern Art and Modernism: A Critical Anthology* (London, New Delhi: Sage 1982 [1859]), pp. 19–21.

23) Siegfried Kracauer, 1969, *History*. p. 57.

American painting of the 1960s and 1970s, alongside such figures as Don Eddy and Chuck Close. The painting, which looks very much like a large photograph of a New York street scene, shows the empty interior of a cafeteria with long, U-shaped red counters. Superimposed on this interior are the reflections of facades, shop signs and street signs. Their source is supposedly the other side of the street, behind the onlooker or painter. It is a confusing image in that the spectator has to sort out the various layers of objects and reflections, as well as the implied point of view of both the artist/camera and the spectator, and the perspectives of her view on the scene.

Inasmuch as *Central Savings* confounds the physical appearance of a photograph with that of a painting, it also belongs to the baroque tradition of the trompe l'oeil. What interests me here, however, is that one can argue that Estes' painting exemplifies the theory of photography of both the early Kracauer and Baudelaire. Clearly, this painting reduces the meaning of the object to spatial appearance: There is nothing that meets the eye but spatial appearance. In fact, because of the reflection in the window, there is a virtual overkill of spatial appearance. There is no obvious transcendence of meaning. Even the writing on the street signs and the business signs means, literally, what it says on the plates and marquees. "Die räumliche Erscheinung ist die Bedetung des Gegenstandes," the spatial appearance is the meaning of the object. At the same time, this painting does what photography does according to Baudelaire and Kracauer: It eliminates the artist, both figuratively and allegorically. Looking at the painting, somewhere in the middle of that window there should be a reflection of the person taking the photograph, if it is a photograph indeed. But there is no such reflection. One might argue that the photographer is standing in the shadow. Hence there is no reflection of his physical presence in the window. But regardless of the explanation one proposes: There is no source of the image present in the image itself, not a painter, not a photographer, not an onlooker. Exactly like the implied onlooker, the artist is absent and eliminated from the picture—suffering the same fate as that of Baudelaire's generic artist who falls prey to the automatism of photomechanical image production.

My point here is this: If we frame Richard Estes' painting in terms of media theory rather than art history, what we are looking at when we look at *Central Savings* is an ironic figure of media history—and I take the term "irony" here in its Socratic sense, as "not knowing." Estes' painting marks the *Vollendung*, the perfection and completion of photography as understood by theorists like Baudelaire and the early Kracauer. With this painting, photography comes to its end in the sense that it fully explores the medium's possibilities, that it goes to its limits, the boundaries that delimit photography from other arts and media and thus define the specificity of photography. Here photography is what it is meant to be: mere physical appearance, with no transcendence of meaning and no space for an artist and her intentions. Estes' painting exemplifies the essence of photography as defined by Baudelaire and Kracauer.

Richard Estes, *Central Savings*, 1975
Oil on canvas, 36 × 48 inches

The irony lies in the fact that Estes' *Central Savings* exemplifies the essence of photography in another, older medium, the medium of painting. For the later Kracauer, the Kracauer of *The Last Things Before Last,* photography can do what painting can do, if only you put the camera in the hands of an artist like Stieglitz. In Estes' *Central Savings* painting does what photography can do, and to perfection.

According to Arthur Danto, modern art comes into its own at the point where we can no longer tell whether something is an object of everyday life or an object of art, that is with Andy Warhol's *Brillo boxes* and Marcel Duchamp's ready mades.[24] The key question of a thoroughly modernist aesthetics, then, is not what art is, but when something is art. Such an aesthetics is primarily concerned with the fundamental undecidability of the status of the art object. At any given moment in time the status can shift from non-art to art object. Similarly, but addressing a problem of spatial rather than one of temporal indecidability, Estes' painting exemplifies what may be called the *ironic condition of modern media*: The undecidability of the question, "Which medium, or which of n+1 media, is it?" However much we try to establish an art's or a medium's specificity through a comparative aesthetics in the line of Lessing-Baudelaire-early Kracauer, the ironic condition of modern media sooner or later catches up with us. What both Kracauer's 1969 analysis of Stieglitz' photograph and Estes' painting from 1975 show is that the dichotomies that delimit one art form or medium from another in an argument about media specificity in the vein of Lessing, are never stable: As W.J.T. Mitchell observed in his Derridean reading of Lessing in 1984, the terms of the dichotomy begin to shift as soon as you fix them. Taking the argument one step further, I would like to suggest that the boundary that delimits the specificity of the medium is, in fact, a *fold*: The delimitation demarcates a line around which the space in which the terms of dichotomy are laid out begins to fold as soon as those terms are defined and fixed. The boundary-as-fold separates an inside from an outside, only to see the inside flip to the outside, and vice-versa. The ontology of cinema which, as in Kracauer, usually starts out with a definition of the medium specificity of photography, has long been a topology not so much of blurred boundaries as a topology of folding spaces, a geography of boundaries as folds that separate insides from outsides and turn outsides into insides, and back again.[25]

One could argue that for some time now media theory has had an intuition that the question of media specificity and the practice of drawing boundaries, of setting distinctions in the space of media—while necessary in order to provide a sense of order in a modern, post-hiearchical regime of the arts and of media—is a futile operation in the sense that the space of delimitation starts to fold at the moment the markers are set. In German media theory, for instance, at a certain moment about twenty years ago, the computer was widely celebrated as the end, the *Vollendung,* of media history. Rephrasing Hegel's phenomenology of the spirit in terms of hardware, German media theorists argued that the computer was media history's equivalent to the *Weltgeist*. If the *Weltgeist* was an expression of all philosophy up to Hegel in the terms of Hegelian philosophy, the computer was the one medium that, *Weltgeist*-like, could encompass and express all media that came before it in digital code. Such Techno-Hegelianism, if we are to call it that, is a far-reaching attempt to reduce, and resolve, the folding spaces of aesthetic theory into a new metaphysics of the digital code. Thus the answer to the question "What is cinema?" comes down to "At the level of hardware and the code, which is the one that counts, for everything else is mere appearance, cinema is the same as every other 'medium,' namely code." More recently, and in a somewhat more communitarian spirit, new media theorists have started to talk about the "convergence" of media, a term which implies that media as pre-existing entities are moving toward each other, in a supposedly harmonious process of slowly, but steadily becoming each other in the realm of the digital. No material object exemplifies the idea of convergence, but in substance and tone, better than the iPhone, the Apple gadget that can do everything in the field of media, communication and entertainment, everything except popcorn. If the Techno-Hegelianism of German media theory presents a materialist, bellicose hard-core version of the metaphysics of the code, convergence theory provides a somewhat more cuddly, communitarian replay of what is basically still a metaphysics of the code, and the iPhone is the spatial appearance of that particular advance in contemporary metaphysical ideas. For the film theorist who tries to come to terms with what for most film theorists is their point of departure, namely some form of experiential reality of cinema, both Techno-Hegelianism and convergence theory turn film into a lost object: Neither has space for a consideration of the essence of cinema as distinct from that of other arts or media. It remains to be seen, however, if these post-specific theories of media escape the fundamental ironies of modern media theory, of which the folding dichotomies of comparative media aesthetics are perhaps merely the most salient expression.

III.

It would seem, then, that the current ubiquity of digitized moving images puts film theory at a loss as to what its object really is: Cinema disappears into the unfolding of the folds of comparative aesthetics at the hands of post-specific media and post-aesthetic media theory. Yet at the same time the post-specific condition of

24) Arthur Danto, "The Artworld," in *The Journal of Philosophy*, Vol. 61, Issue 19 (October 1964), pp. 571–584.

25) Perhaps significantly, in his writings on cinematic emotions Raymond Bellour proposes to replace the established model of film spectatorship of 1970s film theory, which was grounded in an Althusser-Lacanian conception of interpellation, with a Deleuzian model of the spectator subject as fold. It is also important to note that one of the main points of Deleuze's cinema books was to, literally, fold the spectator into the image and work with a concept of the image as a self-contained entity.

media reveals retrospectively, through a focus on the topological aspects of classical film theory, that film theory has always dealt with boundaries that were really folds, folds around which the space of delimitation instantly folded as soon as the boundary was drawn. In such a moment of crisis, when we do not seem to know any longer what cinema is and when the grounds are moving and shifting, we, as theorists, can always turn to cinema itself to try and find some answers. After all, cinema, whatever it may be exactly and specifically, is still there, more or less in its classical *Gestalt* of films available on screens and ready, like the sphinx, to answer our questions.

Let us see, then, how cinema itself, that elusive object, draws the boundaries and how it delineates, and folds, the spaces of medium specificity.

One obvious reason why it seems like a good idea to ask cinema itself about its medium specificity is that cinema, and particularly Hollywood cinema, has a long history of applied comparative aesthetics. Hollywood has, in fact, long extolled the relative merits and potentials of cinema and staked out its claims in the territories of adjacent arts and media, and it continues to do so today.

For a look at the map drawn by cinema itself let me turn to a recent example. It is a scene from *Frost/Nixon* (2008), a film directed by Ron Howard, a former child actor. Thus far, Howard has not made any of the lists in the list-and-map definitions of cinema, but there may still be hope, so I won't let that get in the way of my argument. *Frost/Nixon* is based on a stage play which in turn is based on the events surrounding a somewhat legendary television interview that the British game and talk show host David Frost conducted with disgraced U.S. president Richard Nixon in 1977. Where Frost, played in the film by British actor Michael Sheen, saw the interview as his ticket to journalistic respectability, Nixon, played by veteran Broadway actor and film star Frank Langella, chose Frost as the journalist for his first television interview after his resignation because he considered him a lightweight. Frost, Nixon believed, would not stand in the way of his ambition to redefine the public perception of his legacy. It was a long interview, and throughout most of it, Nixon actually dominated the proceedings and set the pace and terms of the discussion. But in the final segment, Frost finally got to Nixon with a surprise question about Watergate. The question derailed Nixon and led him to confess to his misdemeanors and apologize to the "American people" on camera. This moment is the key scene in the film, its final turning point. The film tells the story of this moment in a montage that combines scenes from the interview, both framed as film footage and as television footage, with shots of the reactions of Nixon's support team of loyal advisers and Frost's team of producers, as well as excerpts from an on-camera interview with the historian and journalist James Reston (played by Sam Rockwell), the scientific consultant for Frost's preparation team. The film assigns the role of the interpreter of Nixon's on-camera breakdown to Reston, who has the following to say about the

Frank Langella in *Frost/Nixon* (2008, Ron Howard)

power of the close-up of Nixon's face in the moment of his confession: "The first and great sin or deception of television is that it simplifies. It diminishes great complex ideas, trenches of time. Whole careers become reduced to a single snap shot. At first I couldn't understand why Bob Zelnick was quite as euphoric as he was. Or why John Purr felt the urge to strip naked and rush into the ocean to celebrate. But that was before I really understood the reductive power of the close-up. Because David had succeeded on that final day in getting for a fleeting moment what no investigative journalist, no state prosecutor, no judiciary committee or political enemy had managed to get. Richard Nixon's face, swollen and ravaged by loneliness, self-loathing and defeat. The rest of the project and its failings would not only be forgotten, they would totally cease to exist."

If for the young Kracauer photography reduced history to a fragment and a shred of memory, television—according to the film's resident historian—reduces history to a close-up. Or, more specifically: Television vanquishes the disgraced president's attempt to rewrite history by substituting a close-up of his shrunken face for his version of that history. For the television crew in the film, this is a cause for celebration. But the celebration is also a celebration of cinema, or rather a case of cinema celebrating itself and its power relative to other media. In fact, in this scene, cinema defines television. Cinema writes the history of television and explains a historical event of and on television based on a theory of what the defining property of television is: Its capacity to reduce history to a close-up. In this scene, cinema shows that it can do what television does, by reconstructing the television close-up and framing, or rather re-framing it as a film image. At the same time the film claims, and demonstrates, through its framing and interpretation of the television closeup, that it can write history, too—the "factual history," or *Realgeschichte*, as some historians would call it, and the media history of the event. So while in Howard's film, cinema shows how television vanquishes the enemy, the triumph of television is, after all, a triumph of cinema: There is no territory claimed by other media that cinema cannot cover. Cinema here adresses what I propose to call the ironic condition of modern media. Cinema folds, if you will, the folding spaces of media ontology into the limitless space of the moving image and, in doing so, provides an answer to the question "Which art, and which of n+1 media, is it?" The answer of cinema, it would seem, is that in the end, it is always cinema.

~

In the end, I would like to argue, we are where Malte Hagener sees us: Inside the moving image, no matter where that moving image is, and no matter where we are in relation to that moving image. But what about the outside, you might ask? What about "reality," the *dispositif* and all that? In his "Ontology of the photographic image" André Bazin argues that the photographic image does not represent its objects. It is not a sign that stands for the object in its absence, but a "natural sign" that partakes in the being of the object. The photographic image transforms, or better still, transubstantiates the object: it renders the object itself present in the image. Rather than an ontology of the photographic image, then, Bazin proposes a cosmology of the photographic media: A theory of photography's and film's limitless potential to transform, or transubstantiate, the world into the world-as-image.[26] Transubstantiation is a miracle, of course, and contemporary theory, secular and critical as it is, has little patience for miracles. Still: What if Bazin were onto something? What if the real question were not how cinema represents the world, but how it transubstantiates and transforms the world, and what if the real question were not where or what cinema is, but how cinema folds the space in which it appears into itself as image? After all, as Hollywood films such as *Frost/Nixon* demonstrate, there is no frame outside the frame of cinema's moving image, and there is nothing that cannot be contained within that frame.

Kant defines the sublime as a mental operation: a framing of the infinite in terms of the finite. In a recent essay entitled "On magnification," based on Kant as well as on an analysis of scientific films and discussions of magnification techniques in manuals from the early years of cinema, Scott Curtis argues that the cinematic frame combined with magnification constitutes an objective correlate of the sublime.[27] Expanding on Curtis' point, one could ask whether the onto-topology of cinema in an age of ubiquitous moving images, rather than focusing on the various transformations of the *dispositif* or the essential properties of the medium, should start with a discussion of the technological sublime of the cinematic frame:[28] cinema's performative capacity of drawing a line in the infinite folding space of modern media. Or, to put it differently, the answer to the question "What is cinema?" and "Where is cinema?" is best understood as a continuous process of framing, and reframing.

26) Vinzenz Hediger, "Das Wunder des Realismus. Transsubstantiation als medientheoretische Kategorie bei André Bazin," in *Montage AV*, Vol. 18, Issue 1 (2009), pp. 75–104.

27) Scott Curtis, "On magnification," paper delivered on the occasion of the "Science/Film" Workshop, Weimar, Graduiertenkolleg "Mediale Historiographien," May 6, 2011.

28) I am borrowing the term „technological sublime" from David Nye, *American Technological Sublime* (Cambridge: MIT Press, 1994).

Volker Pantenburg

# 1970 and Beyond

*Experimental Cinema and Installation Art*

When it comes to historicizing the gallery and the museum as alternative venues to the movie theater, critics tend to highlight two periods of time. To describe the earlier one, roughly the 1960s and 70s, the term Expanded Cinema is often invoked, whereas the later period, roughly the last two decades, invites a number of competing terms: "cinematographic installation," "artists' cinema," "cinéma d'exposition," to name just a few.[1] More often than not, both phenomena are thought of in terms of continuity and succession: Expanded Cinema is interpreted as a potential precursor of installation art, and the film and video installations developed since the early 1990s—for instance, Doug Aitken's large and spacious multi-screen works—are understood as a continuation of aspects featured in the earlier movements.

It seems to me that this now canonical account risks neglecting the historical differences and specificities that are at work. Hence, I would like to compare both historical phenomena in a less smooth and unproblematic way. Two of the guiding questions will be: Is there a potential misunderstanding that has led to the established genealogy of installation art and experimental cinema? At which points do we have to deal with differences and incongruities rather than with continuities and succession?

## THE SPATIAL MISUNDERSTANDING

Gene Youngblood's *Expanded Cinema*[2] is a good starting point for this kind of inquiry. Under the umbrella term Expanded Cinema, Youngblood ties together an extremely heterogeneous multitude of practices: Between his reading of the "stargate corridor" sequence of Stanley Kubrick's *2001* and technical utopias like "holographic cinema," a vast and rather entropic field emerges. To construct a continuous line between Expanded Cinema and installation art, it was therefore necessary to isolate one element of the term "expanded," namely its spatial aspect, at the expense of the other attributes that it also encompassed. As an example of this tendency, let me quote gallerist Tanya Leighton and her introduction to the valuable

1) The term "cinematographic installation" comes from Juliane Rebentisch's book *Ästhetik der Installation* (Frankfurt am Main: Suhrkamp, 2003). "Cinéma d'exposition" was an early suggestion by Jean-Christophe Royoux in "Pour un cinéma d'exposition, retour sur quelques jalons historiques," in *Omnibus*, no. 20 (April 1997), pp. 11–15. "Artists' cinema" was propagated by Maeve Connolly in her book *The Place of Artists' Cinema. Space, Site, and Screen* (Bristol: Intellect, 2009).

2) Gene Youngblood, *Expanded Cinema* (New York: Dutton, 1970)

3) "Introduction," in Tanya Leighton (ed.), *Art and the Moving Image: A Critical Reader* (London: Tate/Afterall, 2008), pp. 13/14.

source book, *Art and the Moving Image*: "The decade of the 1960s," she writes, "saw the contemporary exodus of film from the theater towards the site of the gallery (and an emphasis on screening situations); the beginning of an 'intermedia'-condition; the permeation of boundaries between art and film; and the creation of hybrid filmic objects, installations, performances and events."[3] However, what Leighton describes as an "exodus" and therefore as a form of relocation, characterizes only a small part of what was aimed at in those days. The term "expanded" suggests enlargement or amplification, rather than negation and renunciation, and it had at least two different implications: The British and Austrian varieties of Expanded Cinema would have to be described separately,[4] but the American movement was primarily aiming at the expansion of consciousness, toward which the migration to other venues would be merely one step. Youngblood leaves no doubt about this when, right at the beginning of his psychedelically saturated account, he claims, "When we say expanded cinema we actually mean expanded consciousness. Expanded cinema does not mean computer films, video phosphors, atomic light, or spherical projections. Expanded cinema isn't a movie at all: like life it's a process of becoming, man's ongoing historical drive to manifest his consciousness outside of his mind, in front of his eyes."[5] It is true that Youngblood's target remains abstract and universal, often veering toward the "expansion of consciousness." Still, he points the finger at the exact two ways of "dissolving boundaries" that have confronted cinema at an ever more rapid pace over the following four decades. One is the replacement of film stock by electronic or digital media, while the second is the migration to other venues and forms of presentation. Or, to put it differently, it is the problem of "remediation," as well as the diverse "relocations" of cinema.[6]

Stan Vanderbeek's films and texts[7] are good illustrations of yet another way to "dissolve boundaries." Already in the mid-1960s, he dreamed of image-based forms of knowledge that would be free from the restraints of verbal

4) For an analysis of British Expanded Cinema as an explicit engagement with TV and questions of live coverage, see Duncan White, "British Expanded Cinema and the 'Live Culture' 1969–79," in *Visual Culture in Britain*, Vol. 11, Issue 1 (March 2010), pp. 93–108. A number of valuable essays on Expanded Cinema have recently been published in A.L. Rees, Duncan White, Steven Ball, David Curtis (eds.), *Expanded Cinema. Art, Performance, Film* (London: Tate, 2011).

5) Youngblood, *op. cit.*, p. 43.

6) The classic account of remediation is, of course, Jay David Bolter, Richard Grusin, *Remediation: Understanding New Media* (Cambridge: MIT Press, 1999). Francesco Casetti has recently unfolded the question of "relocation" in various essays: "Elsewhere. The Relocation of Art," in *Valencia09/Confines* (Valencia: INVAM, 2009), pp. 348–351; "Back to the Motherland: The Film Theater in the Post-media Age," in *Screen*, Vol. 52, Issue 1 (Spring 2011), pp. 1–12. Both essays are accessible on Casetti's comprehensive website, http://francescocasetti.wordpress.com.

7) In spring 2011, the Contemporary Arts Museum in Houston presented a first museum survey of Stan Vanderbeek's work. See the catalogue: Bill Arning (ed.), *Stan VanDerBeek: The Culture Intercom* (Houston: Contemporary Arts Museum, 2011). The website www.stanvanderbeek.com is another excellent resource and makes a lot of historical material available in PDF format.

or written language. In Vanderbeek's case, "expansion" primarily aims at translating the question of art into a question of communication. It thus comes as no surprise that Vanderbeek did not focus his hopes on the museum or the gallery, but on the new media of television and the computer. Vanderbeek and many others built their utopias on these potentially less hierarchical media and their capacity to form networked, global communities. Thinking about migration in image practices only within the institutional contexts of cinema and the museum, while at the same time mythologizing Expanded Cinema as one of the origins of installation art, runs the danger of neglecting this media-technological framework. To exclude television and the computer from such considerations vastly underestimates their power and influence on the concept of Expanded Cinema.

#### QUESTIONS OF MOBILITY

Ever since narrative forms of cinema made a resurgence in the art context during the 1990s, the crucial difference between the two forms of presentation has regularly been described as the opposition between the "immobile" and "passive" spectator on the one hand, and the "mobile" and "active" visitor of museums and galleries on the other. This concept takes up or, to put it in more polemical terms, exhumes one of the central ideas developed in apparatus theory: As a bourgeois mode of representation, cinema deprives the spectator of his or her autonomous position and perpetuates classical forms of the gaze that have been present ever since Plato and the camera obscura. With Althusser and Lacan, the structural arrangement of the *dispositif* is interpreted and severely criticized as a mode of "interpellation" and "subjectivisation." What is overlooked in this adaptation of apparatus theory is that the concept of a transcendental spectator, which clearly had its political merits at the time, has been criticized and complemented at great length by numerous phenomenological, feminist, and historically oriented film theories ever since. There is no such thing as "the" spectator, just as there is no such thing as "the" cinema. The historical moment of 1970 (connected to a strong emancipatory project at the time) has therefore only been able to serve as a model since 1990 by stripping it of all its historical specificity. In a dubious theoretical move, concepts of mobility, participation, activity or critique are often placed on one and the same level and are mutually identified with one another. What remains vague in this argumentation is why a strolling visitor in a gallery or museum should automatically be more reflective, critical, or alert than someone sitting in a cinema seat. As Erika Balsom puts it, "The comparisons between the cinema hall and the gallery rest on a spurious mapping of passive/active binaries onto this architectural difference, as if to conflate physical stasis with regressive mystification and physical ambulation with clear-sighted, intellectual engagement."[8]

8) Erika Balsom, "Screening Rooms: The Movie Theater in/and the Gallery," in *Public*, no. 40 (Fall 2009), p. 31.

*Movie-Drome* interior, Stony Point, New York, ca. 1963–1965

### TIMES OF EXPERIENCE

I would argue that this tendency to privilege mobility is yet another effect of the spatial focus that I mentioned earlier. A different assessment of the moving picture presentation and the *dispositif* emerges as soon as the question is reformulated in terms of *time* instead of *place*. It then becomes clear that the spatial mobility proper to exhibition contexts like galleries and museums, usually implies a temporal dissociation of the film experience or, described in terms of perception, a permanent distraction that confronts the visitor. Immobility, on the other hand, might be reconsidered as one of the preconditions of temporal compactness and concentration. Around 1968, this question of concentrated perception appears as the second crucial issue—beside the issue of "expansion"—of experimental cinema. Two examples can illustrate this. The first one is a famous Hollis Frampton piece aptly entitled "A Lecture." At its initial performance at Hunter College on October 30, 1968, Michael Snow's taped voice read the text, while Frampton operated the projector in the back of the hall. The text begins as follows: "Please turn out the lights. / As long as we're going to talk about films, we might as well do it in the dark. / We have all been here before. By the time we are eighteen years old, say the statisticians, we have been here five hundred times. / No, not in this room, but in this generic darkness." Right after this atmospheric start, Frampton's text arrives at a surprising characterization of the institution of cinema, which he described as "the only place left in our culture intended entirely for concentrated exercise of one, or at most two, of our senses."[9]

The second, better-known example is Peter Kubelka's and Jonas Mekas' "Invisible Cinema," first realized in May 1970.[10] The goal of this unique architectural project was to create a movie theater that would not only guarantee, but also amplify the viewing conditions laid out by Hollis Frampton. "The construction of Anthology's cinema is premised upon the idea that the cinematic experience should be at once communal and extremely concentrated on the filmic image and sound, without distractions. The viewer should not get any sense of the presence of walls or the size of the auditorium. He should have only the white screen isolated in darkness as his guide to scale and distance. [...] In order to minimize the possibility of distraction during our performances, no one will be admitted to the theater after the program has begun."[11] The rift between this concept and the mobile and flexible museum experience could not be deeper. For Kubelka, Mekas, and P. Adams Sitney, modernist axioms such as autonomy and specificity are obviously paramount. Whereas Expanded Cinema, much in line with postmodern claims, asks for the abolition of the cinema experience in favor of a communal gathering and a blending with other media, techniques, and art forms, the Invisible Cinema and large parts of structural filmmaking propagate both the medium- and site-specificity of film and cinema.

It is thus necessary to emphasize that 1970 is a period involving two sharply contrasting utopias. The first one, Expanded Cinema, is a utopia of distraction and expansion. Its premise is that cinema is not—or is no longer—able to provide adequate forms of perception and communication for the contemporary, networked, and mixed-media world. Globally interlinked "movie-dromes" with thousands of synchronous images, immersive architectures of communication, TV, or the computer appear as tempting alternatives to the mono-directional model called "cinema." Yet, at the same time, there is also the utopia of concentrated perception (Frampton, Kubelka, Mekas, Sitney), which is dialectically connected to the former. It is based on the assumption that cinema has not yet existed in an adequate form, but has to be invented first. If we consider two of the most influential avant-garde films made around 1970, Michael Snow's *Wavelength* (1967) and Hollis Frampton's *(nostalgia)* (1971), we see that some of the most prominent filmmakers found themselves promoting the second utopia. What's more, their films are entirely based on the existence of the movie theater. For neither Snow's 40-minute zoom through a room, towards a photograph, nor Frampton's deferred, asynchronous reflections about photography, memory, text, and image would make any sense as installations. They would simply fail to work in black boxes and as loops. As they unfold either in a linear mode or along a pre-meditated structure, they both rely on being watched from start to finish. In an ironic mode, Snow himself has stressed the character of duration and linearity when, after being approached by galleries and museums numerous times to exhibit the film, he produced an instal-

Andy Warhol at the Invisible Cinema

9) Hollis Frampton, "A Lecture," in Bruce Jenkins (ed.), *On the Camera Arts and Consecutive Matters: The Writings of Hollis Frampton* (Cambridge: MIT Press, 2009), p. 125.

10) For an oral history of the Invisible Cinema, see Sky Sitney, "In Search of the Invisible Cinema," in *Grey Room,* no. 19 (Spring 2005), pp. 102–113.

11) Anthology Film Archives, "The Invisible Cinema," in *Filmmakers Newsletter,* Vol. 4, Issue 4 (February 1971), pp. 14 and 16.

lation version called *WVLNT—Wavelength for Those Who Don't Have the Time,* dissecting the film into three even segments and then copying them one on top of each other.

Time-based, durational works from the history of structural film were not easy to appropriate for art contexts. Artists like Sharon Lockhart, who specifically address either the cinema or the gallery and are as familiar with the history of experimental cinema as with that of conceptual art, remain exceptions.[12] It has only been a few years since attempts were made to pave a way for this line of experimental work to move into the museum. However, the side effects of this operation are sometimes severe, as when 16mm work is shown in the form of DVD loops, or when curators decide to show paratexts, books, and memorabilia, rather than the films themselves (because they need "objects" to display).

Why is the gallery visitor's flexible mode of perception so often deemed superior to the situation inside the cinema? One possible reason is that, in the wake of a radical critique of categories such as "author" and "work," it was important to shift authority to all kinds of recipients, no matter if they are readers, spectators, or visitors. In a temporal respect, this meant delegating the responsibility for time management to the visitor—and neglecting two other levels of time. In the aesthetic experience at least three different temporalities meet or collide: First, there is the time of the work and its duration; second, there is the temporal economy that the visitor brings with him or her; and third, there is a form of temporality that is "built into" the institution and its temporal conventions. "Going to the movies" and "visiting a museum" are subject to very different temporal agendas. In the cinema, temporality is prescribed by the duration of the film, whereas the temporal calculations of a visit to an exhibition are mostly made independently of the time required to actually see the works. The inevitable collision between different time regimes is most obvious at large group shows or biennials. The time demand simply adds up, whereas the visitor usually budgets time by rather schematically distinguishing between standard practices: thirty minutes for a simple gallery visit, two or three hours for a regular museum visit, one or two days for a biennial.

#### CONCENTRATION/DISTRACTION

Against this backdrop, I would suggest to reevaluate the constellation of cinema vs. museum by introducing "attention" as a conceptual framework, instead of reiterating once more the "mobility" of the museum visitor. Such an approach seems to be productive even if it produces contrasts and differences, rather than similarities. Jonathan Crary's extensive study on the dialectics of attention and distraction in the second half of the nineteenth century provides a good model for the examination of the cinema and museum situations.[13] His interpretations of paintings by Seurat, Monet, or Cézanne could be complemented by readings of Paul Sharits, Hollis Frampton, Sharon Lockhart, or Tacita Dean. Peter Osborne, in a short essay on "distracted reception," has already taken one step in this direction. Osborne characterizes the museum visit as a series of choices, where the visitor is constantly confronted with other works that could just as well take the place of the one he or she is contemplating at the moment. I might be watching James Coleman's 40-minute installation, *Retake with Evidence,* at *documenta 12*, but I cannot ignore the fact that, at the same time, hundreds of other works are competing for my attention. Osborne, therefore, proposes to analyze the museum's dialectical way of processing distraction. On the one hand, the institution has to provide an alternative to the distractions of everyday life, yet on the other hand, it has to do this precisely by implementing and modulating attention and distraction itself. Osborne goes so far as to identify this—at least hypothetically—as one important function of the typical museum show: minimizing the amount of attention required of the visitor. "Perhaps this is the function of grouping works together in the same visual space: they provide a psychic space of distraction which eases the anxiety involved in giving oneself up to a particular work."[14] The term "attention" can, I would argue, become a key concept for the analysis of the cinema / museum constellation, because it is positioned at the threshold between two economic fields: the economics of attention and the "real" economics of money, real estate and financial resources.

12) See Volker Pantenburg, "Sharon Lockhart. Raum, Medium, Dispositiv," in Ursula Frohne, Lilian Haberer (eds.), *Kinematographische Räume. Installationsästhetik in Film und Kunst* (Munich: Fink, 2012).

13) Jonathan Crary, *Suspensions of Perception: Attention, Spectacle, and Modern Culture* (Cambridge: MIT Press, 1999).

14) Peter Osborne, "Distracted Reception: Time, Art and Technology," in Jessica Morgan (ed.), *Time Zones: Recent Film and Video* (London: Tate, 2004), pp. 68 and 69.

### THE INSTITUTIONAL MISUNDERSTANDING

As I have tried to show, Expanded Cinema and structural film differ widely in the character of their critical interventions. I have distinguished a centrifugal impulse (expansion, alternative spaces, television, computers, postmodernism, dissolution of boundaries) from a centripetal one (concentration, examination of the medium, the single frame, modernism, delimitation). However, what unites both currents, as well as their impulses, is their anti-institutional impact. Given the politically charged background of the 1960s, it comes as no surprise that both initiatives were striving for self-administration and alternative forms of production, distribution, and presentation, which did not depend on capital or market criteria. Film cooperatives in the USA (Canyon Cinema, the Film-Makers' Cooperative) and Europe (London Film-Makers' Coop, Austria Filmmakers Cooperative, Hamburger Film-Cooperative, and others) envisioned independent networks that would gain maximum accessibility and circulation, instead of maximum profit. The whole economic idea of the "coop" was meant to create an alternative to the modes of commodification which the "dominant" cinema made in Hollywood or Moscow relied upon.

The rediscovery of narrative cinema in art contexts during the 1990s took place under very different circumstances. It emanated from museums, curators, and art galleries, whose relation to notions of value and profit is quite different. At the same time that DVDs and the Internet have rendered an ever-growing amount of historical and experimental films more visible, installation work remains scarce and hard to see. This, of course, is partly due to its site-specificity. Yet it also generates a feeling of exclusiveness that has economic implications. Experimental cinema of the 1960s and 70s was looking for alternatives to profit and commodification. Installation art, on the contrary, is deeply involved in the speculative economies of the art market, which functions like a mirror—some say, like an amplifier—of speculations on the stock market and in the financial realm. At the 2010 Berlin Film Festival, James Benning expressed his opinion that the success of film and video installation art in the 1990s only became possible with a new type of commodification; a commodification that, to him, is incompatible with the pragmatics of "showing movies" that characterized the experimental film tradition. "The return of the time-based images in installations and galleries comes out of the 80s art movement that created art stars and millionaires. And to have millionaires, you have to have an object. The past films weren't objects. They were something to put on the projector and the audience would watch them."[15]

#### INSTALLATION ART AND THE AURA

Let me expand on this thought for a moment. In 2001, Harun Farocki made a two channel installation piece called *I Thought I was Seeing Convicts*, co-produced by the Generali Foundation in Vienna. In a retrospective text he recalls, "Later, people were interested in this piece, but I couldn't sell it, because the contract with the Generali Foundation had declared it a 'unique copy.' Sabine Breitwieser, the artistic director of the Generali [at the time; VP], holds the opinion that a 'unique copy' cannot be shown or displayed at two different spots in the world at the same time." A little later in the same text, he adds a historical thought to this observation: "It is totally unfamiliar to me to limit my goods. For decades, I have been trying to disseminate my work, and now I am told to hold it back!"[16] In Farocki's account, the two kinds of logic collide: independent cinema's desire to spread the work as widely as possible, and the museum curator's desire to create impact, draw attention, and add value.[17] To understand the difference, it is important to take into consideration the changes that the art market underwent in the 1990s and 2000s. Lots of publicly funded institutions, such as museums, have been privatized, and private collectors and galleries have gained

15) James Benning, in a panel discussion called *Time after Time: The Return of the Time-Image in Contemporary Art and Cinema*; panelists: James Benning, Sharon Lockhart, Mark Lewis, Karl Kels, and Sandra Peters, February 16, 2010, Berlin, Arsenal Cinema. David E. James also stresses the incompatibility between paradigms of structural filmmaking and the art market: "Though structural film was an avant-garde art practice taking place within the parameters of the art world, it was unable to achieve the centrally important function of art in capitalist society: the capacity for capital investment. Massive public indifference to it, its inaccessibility to all but those of the keenest sensibility, and finally, its actual, rather than merely ostensible, inability to be incorporated excluded it from the blue-chip functions, the mix of real estate and glamour, that floated the art world [...] Film's inability to produce a readily marketable object, together with the mechanical repro-

increasing influence over the ways exhibitions and group shows are conceived. In this climate, the iconic qualities of stars and "Hollywood" are much more attractive than large portions of experimental cinema. This is at least one reason why, during the 1990s, many attempts in the contemporary art system to appropriate cinema relied heavily on cinema's narrative genres and tended to neglect experimental cinema. This has changed recently, even if this change may seem suspicious. Lars Henrik Gass, director of the Oberhausen film festival, expressed his doubts recently by stating, "In the last ten years, the art business has done at least two things: (1) It has brought new attention and sources of revenue to artists' films and videos; (2) It has cancelled out the historical and critical discussions about experimental filmmaking and about the standards of its presentation. I would go so far as to state that the price to pay for recognition in art circles was the exorcism of film and cinema history."[18]

**ASYMMETRY OF DISCURSIVE CAPACITIES**

At this point, it is important to mention—albeit in passing—the discursive conditions under which speaking and writing about cinema and the museum take place. Books on cinema, at least in Germany, are published in film critical or academic contexts. The number of film-oriented publishing houses is frustratingly small. Whereas in the 1970s, large publishing houses like Fischer or Hanser edited impressive series of film books, the intellectual debates about film have now retreated to (a) universities and academic institutions or (b) new forms of cinephilia, often articulated via festivals and the Internet.[19] Hardly any cinema has the financial resources to publish anything beyond program notes. This general difficulty concerning film publications gets even more problematic when it comes to experimental cinema. The times when the prestigious Suhrkamp published two volumes of *A Sub-History of Film* or Ullstein put out Birgit Hein's *Film im Underground* are long gone.[20]

ducibility of its texts, set very narrow limits to the possibility of structural film's being turned into a commodity." David E. James, *Allegories of Cinema: American Film in the Sixties* (Princeton: Princeton University Press, 1989), pp. 273–274. See also Jonathan Walley, "The Material of Film and the Idea of Cinema: Contrasting Practices in Sixties and Seventies Avant-Garde Film," in *October*, no. 103 (Winter 2003), pp. 15–30.

16) Harun Farocki, "Auf zwölf flachen Schirmen. Kaum noch ein Handwerk," *new filmkritik*, December 16, 2007, http://newfilmkritik.de/archiv/2007-12/auf-zwolf-flachen-schirmen (transl. VP).

17) For a sociological account of the economic and cultural background of experimental cinema, see Todd Bayma, "Art World Culture and Institutional Choices: The Case of Experimental Film," in *The Sociological Quarterly*, Vol. 36, Issue 1 (Winter 1995), pp. 79–95.

18) Lars Henrik Gass, "Experimentalfilm oder Film-Avantgarde? Ein Plädoyer für den Diskurs – und eine andere Aufführungspraxis," in *kolik.film*, no. 13 (March 2010), p. 66 (transl. VP). In 2007, the Oberhausen Festival hosted a series of film programs and talks devoted to the question of "Artists' Cinema." Some of the contributions and talks were published in Mike Sperlinger, Ian White (eds.), *Kinomuseum. Towards an Artists' Cinema* (Cologne: König, 2008).

19) See Jonathan Rosenbaum's contribution to this volume.

20) Hans Scheugl, Ernst Schmidt Jr., *Eine Subgeschichte des Films. Lexikon des Avantgarde-, Experimental- und Undergroundfilms*, 2 volumes (Frankfurt am Main: Suhrkamp, 1974) and Birgit Hein, *Film im Underground. Von seinen Anfängen bis zum Unabhängigen Kino* (Frankfurt am Main, Berlin, Vienna: Ullstein, 1971).

Compared to this, the situation of contemporary art is completely different. Large-format, lavishly designed publications, also known as catalogues, are the norm and not the exception to the rule. Whenever a major museum shows Farocki, Fassbinder, Warhol, Kenneth Anger, or Bruce Conner, a book automatically sees the light of day. It is therefore no surprise that most of the discussions about art and film or the museum and the cinema have taken place on the discursive turf of contemporary art. Only recently have interventions from film theory and film history started to complement this one-sided discussion.

It is easy to forget that the catalogue essay is a strange form of biased criticism, which oscillates uncannily between analysis, description, and promotion. I do not know if there has ever been an analysis of the catalogue essay along the lines of Brian O'Doherty's famous critique of the White Cube in the 1970s.[21] Which dynamics are at work, when the laudatory tone of a text is certain before it is even written? When the commissioning institution is the museum where the artist's work is being presented, or the gallery that has him or her under contract? No doubt, none of these precarious conditions are exclusive to contemporary art or the genre of the catalogue essay. Networks, friendships, and dishonest motivations exist everywhere in the cultural field (and elsewhere). Yet the difference, I would argue, is that, in the case of the catalogue essay, these things are a constitutive feature and not just a contingent background.

## FOUND FOOTAGE

In conclusion, and in order to go beyond the contexts that frame Installation art, I would like to briefly discuss some classical and contemporary works dealing with found footage. Ken Jacobs' *Tom Tom the Piper's Son* (1969) and Ernie Gehr's *Eureka* (1974) are, without a doubt, two incunabula of experimental cinema around 1970. Douglas Gordon's *24 Hour Psycho* (1993) is one of the most paradigmatic installations of the early 1990s. All three works turn to (and consist of) images from film history, yet the concept of cinema at work in these pieces is quite different. In *Tom Tom*, Ken Jacobs appropriates Billy Bitzer's 1905 film of the same title. Bitzer transformed a popular nursery rhyme into a turbulent, burlesque scene. On what seems to be a stage with different set pieces, we see boys escaping with the pig, people leaving a building through the chimney, lots of jumping around and hullabaloo. Jacobs starts by re-filming the original footage in its entirety. After this, he subjects the material to various kinds of analytical operations. He slows down certain sequences, emphasizes details in the overcrowded and confusing composition by zooming in or out, illuminates Bitzer's mise-en-scène and narration. The tools for all this are the camera and an optical printer. Bart Testa, to whose

21) See Brian O'Doherty, *Inside the White Cube: The Ideology of the Gallery Space* (Berkeley: University of California Press, 2000). Some skepticism toward the catalogue essay is expressed in James Elkins' essay, *What Happened to Art Criticism* (Chicago: Prickly Paradigm, 2003, pp. 18–23). However, his argument seems to be largely driven by the fear that sloppy art criticism might render serious art history obsolete.

*24 Hour Psycho*
(1993, Douglas Gordon)

*Eureka*
(1974, Ernie Gehr)

work on the relation between the avant-garde and Early Cinema I refer here, calls Jacobs' method a "shot analysis" and explains his method as a three-step procedure: "Although constantly varied, a similar three-step procedure shapes the structure of Jacobs' film: a clarification of the original tableau, the isolation of details and the decomposition of the illusion to its material infrastructure."[22]

Ernie Gehr's *Eureka* seems quite different from Jacobs' aggressive analytical interventions. The film basically restricts itself to slowing down the original material—a tram ride through San Francisco in 1903—to one-eighth of its speed by multiplying each frame eight times. The source is a so-called Phantom Ride: The camera is attached to the driver's cab of the train and is directed towards the depth of space. Gehr describes his method as follows: "This is a refilming of a remarkable movie depicting Market Street, San Francisco, around the turn of the century. The original film consisted of one long continuous take recorded from the front of a moving trolley from approximately Seventh Street all the way to the Embarcadero. I extended each frame six to eight times, full-frame, and increased the contrast and the light fluctuations. To some degree, the original film has obviously been transformed, but I hope that this simple muted process allowed enough room for me to make the original work 'available' without getting too much in the way. This was very important to me as I tend to see what I did, in part, as the work of an archeologist, resurrecting an old film as well as the shadows and forces of another era." In Gehr's work, two gestures overlap: (1) there is the attempt to give access to an otherwise nameless and invisible film from the early period of cinema, and (2) there is the attempt to emulate and etch out the hypnotic effect that the initial camera movement might have had at the time the movie was shot.

At first glance, Douglas Gordon's installation does quite the same thing, at least on a purely formal level. Like Gehr, Gordon also slows down the material, taken from Hitchcock's *Psycho*—even if, in his case, the result lasts twenty-four hours instead of Gehr's thirty minutes. Still, I would argue that Gordon's work presents an antithesis rather than a complement to *Eureka*. Considering the iconic images from Hitchcock's film, *24 Hour Psycho* undoubtedly is a work about cinema. Yet Gordon's approach to cinema is much more indirect than the one witnessed in Jacobs' and Gehr's films, for it clearly owes itself to re-mediated presentations of film history, namely the ones broadcast by British cable television. Gordon would be the first to acknowledge this. Asked when and under which circumstances he discovered the films which he refers to in his installation work, he answers: "I stumbled upon them by accident when I was maybe fifteen or sixteen years old. I used to work on a late shift in a supermarket and when I came back home the clock was already at midnight or 1 a.m., and everyone in the house was already asleep, but I needed to rest and calm down before going to bed. This was around the time in Britain when Channel 4 had just started. It was a very important thing: Channel 4 was the only thing on TV at that time of night. They ran a pretty esoteric film series, from what I can remember. And that's how I got to see Godard, that's how I got to see Truffaut, Rohmer, and everyone else. As well as the vague boys, I also got an introduction to B movies, and noirs—Nicholas Ray or Rudolph Maté or Otto Preminger, for example."[23] It seems to me that this difference has to be taken into account in any analysis of film and video installations since the 1990s: wherever questions of "cinema" seem to be addressed, "film" can just as well mean TV, DVD, or the Internet.

In contrast, for artists like Gehr and Jacobs around 1970, it was still comparatively clear that the appropriative gesture focused on the film archive and operated with tools such as the optical printer. While Jacobs and Gehr are interested in the materiality and peculiarities of an alternative, pre-narrative form of cinema, Gordon is less concerned about cinema and film than about the mythologies and the iconic value of Hitchcock's images. To put it somewhat polemically: whereas Gehr and Jacobs make an archaeological investment in one specific medium, Gordon skims off the glamorous surplus that film history and found footage filmmakers in particular have generated since the 1950s, and which has been disseminated across all kinds of media ever since.[24]

However, this does not necessarily have to be an argument against Gordon's installation, even if it may sound like one. Don DeLillo's novel *Point Omega* starts with an extensive scene in Gordon's installation, on display at New York's Museum of Modern Art in 2006, and shows that Gordon's deceleration of *Psycho* renders possible two contrasting spectatorial "uses." The attraction that the installation has for the protagonist is described as an immersive experience: "It was only the closest watching that yielded his perception. He found himself undistracted for some minutes by the coming and going of others and he was able to look at the film with the degree of intensity that was required. The nature of the film permitted total concentration and also depended on it."[25] This behavior, however, is exceptional, because the other visitors follow a completely opposite model: "They stayed a moment longer and then they left. [...] There were other gal-

22) Bart Testa, *Back and Forth: Early Cinema and the Avant-Garde* (Toronto: Art Gallery of Ontario, 1993), pp. 12 and 13.

23) David Sylvester, "Interview with Douglas Gordon," in *Douglas Gordon* (Cambridge: MIT Press, 2002), p. 157.

24) Alexander Horwath makes a similar case when he points to the distance between Peter Tscherkassky's work and Douglas Gordon's installation: "In this sense, Tscherkassky's practical film criticism on the basis of found footage differs radically from seemingly similar and very popular strategies in visual art, for example most installations by Scottish artist Douglas Gordon. Using the video medium, Gordon transfers well known Hollywood classics into the White Cube and leaves his signature by manipulating one single formal element. Polemically stated, films like *Psycho, The Searchers* or *Taxi Driver* are thus blown-up or, rather, artificially shrunk into one-joke-movies. As viewers, we watch the flaccid gaze of a media junkie who is mainly out to refine rather than fathom his/our drug and his/our addiction." Alexander Horwath, "Singing in the Rain. Supercinematography by Peter Tscherkassky," in Alexander Horwath, Michael Loebenstein (eds.), *Peter Tscherkassky* (Vienna: FilmmuseumSynemaPublikationen, 2005 [2000]), p. 10–48: 44.

25) Don DeLillo, *Point Omega* (New York: Scribner, 2010), p. 5.

leries, entire floors, no point lingering in a secluded room in which whatever was happening took forever to happen."[26] In my reading, these two possible reactions correspond precisely to the two different traditions of experimental film that I highlighted before. Whereas the nameless protagonist watches Gordon's installation as a structural film lasting twenty-four hours, the other viewers understand it as Expanded Cinema and use it accordingly.

~

The common link between contemporary art spaces and the history of experimental cinema can only be established by neglecting or excluding large parts of media history. The simple dichotomy of "cinema" and "museum," therefore, leaves too little room for considering other media and their impact since the 1970s.[27] Another problem with the genealogical short circuit between installation art and Expanded Cinema is that the latter is almost always reduced to critiquing the movie theater as space. In such a discourse, individual films or works hardly play any role; the dominant issues are usually the argument concerning the migration to other spaces and the alternatives to celluloid.

Against this backdrop, my proposition is to expand the debates about arrangements of spaces and screens by raising the issue of the cinema's peculiar temporality and duration. The concept of attention in its theoretical tradition, from Kracauer and Benjamin via Jonathan Crary to Bernard Stiegler's contemporary model of psycho-powers, offers a promising framework, since it helps interpret questions of perception in their interdependence with economic issues.[28] To a certain extent, this necessitates a theoretical refocusing on questions that were posed most explicitly around 1970, in the context of modernist projects connected to issues of medium- and site-specificity. The proliferation of films via a myriad of channels has tended to multiply these questions, rather than answer them.

26) *Ibid.*, pp. 3–4.

27) This dichotomy also ignores a third type of institution which is neither an art museum nor a cinema in the usual sense of the word (or both): A film museum like the one in Vienna collects, preserves, and exhibits films under adequate conditions and hence treats them with the same care that other museums treat their artifacts. In a conversation about his film program for *documenta 12*, Alexander Horwath, the director of the Austrian Film Museum, discusses similar issues as the ones taken up in this text: "Both in cinema theory and in everyday movie-going experience, the view of the cinema spectator as a 'prisoner' (of the fixed time and place, and of the illusions hurled at him or her) doesn't hold a lot of currency anymore. I would even suggest, a bit crudely maybe and still recognizing the barely diminished power of blockbuster cinema, that in today's socio-economic and cultural climate the spatially and durationally *unflexible* space of cinema is potentially more inviting to a reflective or critical experience of the world via images than most museum spaces are. The cinema is certainly not the hegemonic 'ideal space' anymore. Considering what the dominant 'flexibility machines' of commerce and culture demand today, the cinema is–thankfully–just not fluid and 'expanded' enough." Alexander Horwath, Michael Loebenstein, "Case Study #1: Curating the Documenta 12 Film Programme," in Paolo Cherchi Usai, David Francis, Alexander Horwath, Michael Loebenstein, *Film Curatorship. Archives, Museums, and the Digital Marketplace* (Vienna: FilmmuseumSynemaPublikationen, 2008), p. 132.

28) See Bernard Stiegler, *Logik der Sorge* (Frankfurt am Main: Suhrkamp, 2010). See also Ute Holl's contribution to this volume.

Victor Burgin

# Interactive Cinema and the Uncinematic*

André Bazin famously asked "*What is cinema?*" We may also ask: "*Where* is cinema?" In addition to being seen in a movie theater, or at home on DVD, a film may be encountered through posters, "blurbs," and other advertisements, such as trailers and clips seen on television or the Internet; it may be encountered through newspaper reviews, reference work synopses and theoretical articles (with their "film-strip" assemblages of still images); through production photographs, frame enlargements, memorabilia, and so on. In my book of 2004 *The Remembered Film*[1] I call this expanded space beyond the confines of the movie theater the *cinematic heterotopia*. For most of the history of cinema it was only within this space that the cinemagoer could physically intervene: for example, by compiling scrapbooks of clippings from fan magazines, or by assembling collections of such items as lobby cards, and so on. Towards the end of the 20th century, however, the arrival of the domestic video cassette recorder, and the distribution of industrially produced films on videotape, put the material substrate of the narrative into the hands of the audience. The *order* of narrative could now be countermanded—the VCR allowing such freedoms as the repetition of a favourite sequence, or the freezing of an obsessional frame. The subsequent arrival of digital video editing on "entry level" personal computers exponentially expanded the range of possibilities for dismantling and reconfiguring the once inviolable objects offered by narrative cinema. Most recently, such practices have been extended to the World Wide Web, where anyone with broadband access may use online video editors to mix their own "video mashups" from inexhaustible streams of online images and sounds. Since the Frankfurt School, cinema has been charged with producing a passively conformist subject for the social and political status quo; "interactivity" has consequently been seen as not only technologically progressive but as politically desirable. It is therefore worth considering the claims made for a putative "interactive cinema." The *New Oxford American Dictionary* which installs along with the Apple Macintosh operating system offers two definitions of "interactive:" one pertaining to social interactions between people, the other to the flow of information between a computer and a user. I shall begin with the computer-related sense of the word, in its

*) This essay combines material from talks given at the *Jeu de Paume*, Paris, on the 13th February and the 22nd May, 2010.

1) Victor Burgin, *The Remembered Film* (London: Reaktion, 2004).

relation to cinema, before considering the social implications of "interactivity."

Users of the Web may not only intervene in the narrative forms of commercial films, they may also put their own life stories on the screen, faintly replicating the "celebrity" of professional actors, in ways that owe little to traditional narrative practices. In 1996, an American college student, Jennifer Ringley, attached a video camera to her computer and set up an AppleScript to automatically and continuously upload images of her college dormitory room to the Internet. Ringley's "real time" presentation of her own life was transmitted as a series of still images taken at the rate of one every three minutes. There are a number of websites where these images are archived, tagged with date and time—the dormant components of a potential filmic narration of a life passed in time-lapse. Jennifer Ringley was the first to cross to the other side of the screen and put her life online. Today, albeit in less remarkable ways, social networking sites such as *MySpace* and *Facebook,* and image sharing sites such as *Flickr* and *Photobucket*, have made the practice normal. Writing in 1971 the photographer and filmmaker Hollis Frampton envisaged an "infinite film" that would consist of a spectrum of possibilities extending from the stasis of an image resulting from a succession of completely identical frames, to the chaos of an image produced by a succession of totally different frames.[2] A recently developed technology in effect turns every photograph on the Web into a frame in a boundless interactive movie.[3] The technology—*Photo Tourism*—was first presented at SIGGRAPH (an annual conference on interactive computer graphics) in 2006, since then Microsoft have made a client-server version of the software available on their website under the name *Photosynth*.[4] Suppose I have a photograph of myself taken on the south side of the Place des Vosges, and another taken on the north side. Once I have uploaded these to the Web *Photosynth* will take me from one photograph to the other in a smoothly morphed path passing through all the other photographs taken in the square that are available on the Internet. At the inaugural presentation of *Photosynth* at SIGGRAPH 2007, the presenter demonstrated how the software can automatically assemble a navigable 'three dimensional' space from a random collection of photographs found on the Internet by typing the expression "Notre Dame Cathedral" into the online photo sharing application *Flickr*. Following his demonstration, the presenter says: "What the point here really is ... is that we can do things with the social environment, [...] taking data from everybody, from the entire collective memory of what the earth looks like ... and link all of that together, all of those photos

2) See Hollis Frampton, "For a Metahistory of Film: Commonplace Notes and Hypotheses," in *Artforum*, Vol. 10, Issue 1 (September 1971), pp 32–35.

3) In a collaboration between Microsoft and the University of Washington: Noah Snavely and Steven M. Seitz (University of Washington) and Richard Szeliski (Microsoft Interactive Visual Media Group).

4) The organisation of the technology on this "public" site is focused entirely on the "synthing" of individual collections of photographs, foreclosing entirely the opening of the "synth" onto communal virtual space.

become linked together and they make something emergent that is greater than the sum of the parts."[5]

Another Microsoft spokesperson describes *Photosynth* as "still photography in motion."[6] With such technologies the cinematic heterotopia has merged with the endless process of becoming of a perpetual infinite film, the frames of which are the totality of all recorded images, reduplicating the real world in the virtual.

By my own defintion, these and other forms of interaction within the cinematic heterotopia take place alongside cinema rather than supersede cinema. From my initial topological question "Where is cinema?", therefore, I am returned to Bazin's ontological question: "What is cinema?" Ludwig Wittgenstein advised that we look not for the meaning of a word, but rather for its use. In the dominant understanding of the word "cinema" the history of cinema begins in 1895 with the Lumière brothers' first screening of a film to a paying audience—which is to say that cinema begins not with a technology but with a commercial exploitation of a technology. Its subsequent history unfolds as the story of a mass entertainment form inseparable from the setting of the movie theater[7]—a darkened space in which the spectator, as part of a collectivity, looks up to the proscenium-arched screen. The spectator in darkness is emotionally immersed in the film but immobile. Concurrently with the history of this space, and occasionally interweaving with it, is the history of other forms of immersive public spectacle in which the spectator is free to move. These other immersive technologies predate cinema and have their most obvious antecedents in the panorama. In the present century the panoramic principle continues to occupy real space mainly in the form of 'theme park' attractions and IMAX film technology, while in televisual space the panorama has been projected into a technologically perfected future in the form of the 'holodeck' of Federation starships. The fantasy of lucid dreaming that the holodeck represents (and which was dramatised in the 1935 film *Peter Ibbetson* that so fascinated the surrealists[8]) still haunts the technologically intensive immersive environments under development today in art and technology centres worldwide.[9] Again, such projects

5) Compare "Blaise Aguera y Arcas demos Photosynth," www.ted.com/index.php/talks/blaise_aguera_y_arcas_demos_photosynth.html

6) Rob Knies, "Photo Tourism: Still Photography in Motion," http://research.microsoft.com/en-us/news/features/phototourism.aspx

7) Roland Barthes remarked: "I can never, speaking of cinema, prevent myself thinking 'movie theater,' rather than 'film'." Roland Barthes, "En sortant du cinéma," in *Communications*, no. 23 (Paris: Seuil, 1975), p. 104: "... je ne puis jamais, parlant cinéma, m'empêcher de penser 'salle', plus que 'film'." Barthes' essay is published in English as "Leaving the Movie Theater," in *The Rustle of Language*, trans. Richard Howard (Berkeley: University of California Press, 1989), pp. 345–349.

8) *Peter Ibbetson* (USA 1935) directed by Henry Hathaway, starring Gary Cooper and Ann Harding, based on an 1891 novel by Georges du Maurier.

9) For example: *iCinema Centre for Interactive Cinema Research* in Sydney, the *Centre for Art and Media Technology* (ZKM) in Karlsruhe, the *MIT Interactive Cinema: Media Fabrics program* in Cambridge (Mass) and the *Applied Laboratory for Interactive Visualization and Embodiment (ALiVE)*, City University, Hong Kong.

evolve in parallel with cinema and do not supplant it.

If we accept the basic sense of the word "cinema" in common usage for about a century, then to speak of "interactive cinema" implies the familiar situation of people assembled in a movie theater but who may now exercise some influence over the course of events on screen. What is reputed to be the first example of interactive cinema in a modified theater setting was the "Kino-Automat" in the Czech Pavilion at the *Expo 67* World Fair in Montreal.[10] At a number of points in the Czech film *One Man and His World* the audience were asked to vote on how the film's hero should act, with the narrative then branching according to the consensus. Intervention by consensus was again tested in 1992 when the interactive film *I'm Your Man* was shown in specially equipped theaters; *I'm Your Man* was rereleased on DVD six years later, about the same time that a number of other interactive movies appeared on DVD. The most recent of these I have seen is the Canadian film *Late Fragment* (2007) in which the viewer may move between the interwoven story lines of the three main protagonists by operating the DVD player's remote control. The producers of the film describe *Late Fragment* as a "multi-plot, non-linear and interactive narrative." Although "non-linearity" is a claim frequently made for interactive films it is rarely justified. The viewer may choose, at select moments in the film, which way the narrative branches, but the ensuing narrative is no less linear for that. Moreover, the range of choices is predetermined, as are the places where choice may be exercised. Of course the same technology on which the interactive DVD depends may also be used to override its structuring determinations. Finding myself bored watching the interactive film *Tender Loving Care*[11] I interacted with it by ripping the DVD into its constituent files and laying them out in a grid on my 30 inch "Cinema" computer display. Having thus—in the words of the linguist Roman Jakobson—"projected the paradigm plane onto the plane of the syntagm," I could then assess the narrative world of the film in a spatial as well as a linear way.

Implicit in the popular understanding of the word "cinema" is the assumption that the cinema is an apparatus for telling a story, usually a fiction. A story usually implies an author, or at least a storyteller. No less prevalent than the claim to non-linearity is the claim that in interactive cinema such traditional roles are ceded to the spectator/user. For example, the author of a recent article on interactive cinema writes: "The unique participatory experience that interactive cinema can offer [...] lets anyone take a seat in the much-coveted director's chair and create the film that they want to see."[12]

This is somewhat equivalent to saying that if you give someone a dictionary and a manual of grammar they can write their own novel—certainly they can, but the literary quality of the outcome will be uncertain. Perhaps in recognition of this, some interactive films—*Tender Loving Care* is an example—are positioned somewhere between a conventional film and a video game. The claim is no longer that the user will become an author, but rather that through their exercise of choice they will have a uniquely individual ludic experience. For example, the video game designer Steve Gaynor writes: "Unlike a great film or piece of literature, [video games] don't give the audience an admiration for the genius in someone else's work; they instead supply the potential for genuine personal experience."[13]

These kinds of claims are very often made by interactive media artists who redefine the author's role as that of providing only the general preconditions for the user's own uniquely individual experience. Such claims invite the response first made by the Russian born artist Alexei Shulgin in a short essay posted on the Internet in 1996: "Media artists! Stop manipulat[ing] people with your fake 'interactive media installations' [...] don't regard people as idiots [...] [the] emergence of media art is characterised by [the] transition from representation to manipulation."[14] Shulgin's criticism was endorsed by Lev Manovich in his own net article in response, "On Totalitarian Interactivity," which he later adapted for his book *The Language of New Media*, where it appears under the sub-heading *The Myth of Interactivity*. Manovich finds it "meaningless" to apply the concept of "interactivity" to computer-based art as "it simply means stating the most basic fact about computers."[15] He further notes that the entire history of the arts involves interactivity in that the viewer is required to provide information that is not actually present in the work—from ellipses in literary narration to "missing" parts of objects in painting—and to move their eyes around a pictorial composition, or to move their entire body when experiencing sculpture and architecture. In *The Language of New Media* he writes: "When we use the concept of 'interactive media' exclusively in relation to computer-based media, there is the danger that we will interpret 'interaction' literally, equating it with physical interaction between the user and the media object (pressing a button, choosing a link, moving the body), at the expense of psychological interaction."[16]

Manovich finds such a mechanically reductive interpretation of "interactivity" to represent "just the latest example of a larger modern trend to externalize mental life."[17] He does not expand upon this idea but it merits further consideration, and brings me to the second definition of interactivity offered by my computer based dictionary—that pertaining to "society."

10) The invention of the Czechoslovakian director Radúz Činčera.

11) Directed by David Wheeler, interactive CD-Rom and DVD were both released in 1998.

12) Jenny Wong, "What's the future of interactive cinema?" in *Se7en Magazine*, no. 7 (August 2008), online at http://se7enmagazine.com/film/50-global/169-whats-the-future-of-interactive-cinema.html

13) Steve Gaynor, "Being There," online at http://fullbright.blogspot.com/2008/07/being-there.html

14) The essay is still accessible online at http://umintermediai501.blogspot.com/2008/03/art-power-and-communication-by-alexei.html

15) Lev Manovich, *The Language of New Media* (Cambridge: MIT Press, 2001), p. 55.

16) *Ibid.*, p. 57.

17) *Ibid.*

In an essay published just before the World Wide Web was invented in 1990, I describe everyday life in the "developed" world as taking place in "an image saturated environment which increasingly resembles the interior space of subjective fantasy turned inside out."[18] The arrival of the Web vastly accelerated what Manovich characterizes in his book of 2001 as the "trend to externalize mental life." The meaning of an image is largely a product of its relations with the other images with which it may be consciously or unconsciously associated. Today, we move through an environment of virtual images in which the processes of association have become increasingly automated. For example, if I go to a *YouTube* website to search for a particular clip, I will be offered not only the clip for which I am looking (assuming I am successful) but also a column of thumbnail images of other clips that the programme believes are related to my search. Clicking on any one of these will again summon not only the selected clip but a further column of apparently aleatory alternative choices. I may quickly find myself far from my original point of departure. To immediate appearances it may seem that a spontaneous "drifting" of associations has taken place analogous to the type of free movement of thoughts in, for example, daydreaming. In reality, a computer programme has formed a chain of associations between images from a database on the basis of key searchwords ("metatags") attached to those images—in effect replacing "free association" with bound association. Nevertheless, such mimicking of spontaneous human mental processes may produce the uncanny impression of an auxilliary intelligence at work, forming associations on my behalf and *in my place*. It seems that the distinction between interior and exterior associative processes is no longer valid, and that—to the extent that it imitates "primary process" thinking—the Internet now represents a form of *prosthetic unconscious*[19] as well as a form of prosthetic memory.

An unremarkable yet significant fact about the automatic associations made by *YouTube* is that they frequently intercept contents derived, directly or indirectly, from the mass media. The Internet is only the latest development in a more general process of the externalisation and industrialisation of memory that began in the 19th century—most significantly with sound recording, photography, film and television—and which led to the emergence of massive new global industries in the latter half of the 20th century. Bernard Stiegler has described how these "media" industries—film, television, advertising, video games and popular music—now produce an "ecology of the mind" (*écologie de l'esprit*) which: "rests upon the industrial exploitation of [...] consciousnesses [...] endowed with the bodies of *consumers* [...] [which] are *degraded* by this exploitation just as may be certain territories or certain animal species."[20] Starting from questions of the "technic," Stiegler arrives at much the same concept of "mental ecology" that Félix Guattari had previously arrived at from his own point of departure in the psychoanalytic. Guattari speaks of a "colonisation" of the unconscious by means of what he calls the "media-based imaginary," arguing that market values and relations have not only penetrated the economic, social and cultural life of the planet, but have also infiltrated the unconscious register of subjectivity. It would follow that we may expect to find highly disparate cultural practices that are nevertheless structurally determined in common by hegemonic beliefs, values and relations of free market capitalism in fundamental ways of which their practitioners may be unaware. In his book of 1999 *La barbarie douce: La modernisation aveugle des entreprises et de l'école* Jean-Pierre Le Goff describes the "discourse of modernisation" that since the 1980s has spread from its origins in corporate management practices to all aspects of the life of society.[21] Sounding the leitmotifs of "new technologies" and "globalisation" this discourse posits a world of perpetual and accelerating change with no purpose, and no sense, other than that dictated by the blind mechanisms of its own internal necessities—what Le Goff calls a "machinery of insignificance." "Soft barbarism" invokes a cultural revolution without end, an incessant overturning of ways of living, working, acting and thinking, such that in both their personal and professional lives individuals are called upon to give a perpetual account of their "autonomy" and "responsibility," to give continual proof of their fitness for service by showing themselves to be "motivated," "reactive" and "participative." Le Goff gives the example of a book, *L'Entreprise individualisée*—published in 1998 by the Institute of Management of Électricité de France et Gaz de France (EDF-GDF)—which presents the essentials of the new managerial ideology. In pursuit of "modernisation" it is proposed to liberate the individual from direction from above, from "obedience [to] hierarchical [...] paternalism," in order to "inculcate the spirit of initiative and innovation" demanded in the fast-moving global business environment. To this end employees must be encouraged "to think and act as if they were autonomous entrepreneurs"[22]—must be encouraged, we might say, to "take a seat in the much-coveted director's chair." In this and in other ways the prevailing discourse of "interactivity" in computer arts is structurally homologous with that of modernising management in the *subject* that both interpellate: a mechanically functionalist individual—unmarked by gender, sexuality, age, race or unconscious; a rational-instrumental entity called upon to exercise continual interactive "free" choice within the constraints of a predetermined environment over which he or she has no control.

We may perhaps rescue the idea of "interactivity" from the bleak spectre that Deleuze named the "society of control" if we admit that

18) Victor Burgin, "Paranoiac Space," in *In/Different Spaces: Place and Memory in Visual Culture* (Berkeley: University of California Press, 1996), p. 121.

19) In technical Freudian terms I am speaking here of the "descriptive" rather than "structural" meaning of "unconscious."

20) Bernard Stiegler, *Philosopher par accident* (Paris: Galilée, 2004), p. 74.

21) Jean-Pierre Le Goff, *La barbarie douce: La modernisation aveugle des entreprises et de l'école* (Paris: La Découverte, 2003), pp. 19–21.

22) All quotations *ibid*.

interactivity in visual art is more than one thing, and that even within the sphere of "new media art" the word is variously used. For example—purely at the cybernetic level—there is what we may call the *reactive* sense of "interactivity," when the "machine" (a symbiotic combination of hardware and software) responds to changes in its environment and displays these in some form or other—for example, as when variations in the number of people occupying a public square causes lights to change colour on the façade of a building. Again, there is the *transformational* sense, where the machine accepts input in one form—for example, video images of objects—and outputs the information in another form—for example sentences. Or again, there is the *substitutional* sense, as when clips from a database are inserted at random into a more or less fixed schema of placeholders—for example, recurring scenes in a narrative loop may "repeat" with variations of dialogue or point-of-view. Or there may be combinations of all of these, or other types of database-dependent machine operations. What "interactivity" means may also differ greatly between specifically different institutional settings where—even accepting the emphasis of "interactive media art" on *physical* activity—we are presented with very different corporeal experiences, in addition to different types of subject interpellation and psychological and machine interactivity. Roland Barthes confesses that as much as he may go to the cinema to see this or that movie he also goes for the darkness of the auditorium.[23] The necessary precondition for the projection of a film is also "the color of a diffuse eroticism." Barthes remarks on the postures of the spectators in the darkness, often with their coats or legs draped over the seat in front of them, their bodies sliding down into their seats as if they were in bed. He notes how the light from the projector, in piercing the darkness, turns the spectating subjects into *objects* of specular fascination, as the beam "illuminates—from the back, from an angle—a head of hair, a face." Barthes feels that his body has become "something soporific, soft, peaceful: limp as a sleeping cat."[24] These languid attitudes of spectators in the movie theater—voluptuously abandoning themselves to immersion in a film—are very different from those expected of visitors to a panoramic immersive environment, who may be outfitted with head mounted displays (HMDs), or special glasses, and may be required to operate a motorised platform, a remote control or some other piece of equipment. Where narrative enters, as Marie-Laure Ryan observes in her comprehensive book *Narrative as Virtual Reality*[25], there is a fundamental incompatibility between physical interactivity and immersion—such that "interactive immersion" becomes an oxymoron. This incompatibility is fully resolved only in the limited case of vehicle control simulators, in which there is a simultaneous one-to-one mapping of the real world setting—the cockpit, or cabin, and the instruments of navigation—upon the virtual environment.

Yet another very different setting is the Internet, which provides the de facto conditions for democratic popular art forms based on the historic example of cinema but with amateur and professional artists enjoying equal access to the means of production and distribution. Video mashups are the most widely encountered of such forms, with the remixed Hollywood film trailer the most popular genre. Many trailer mashups handle the trailer form with great fluency, most often to lampoon box-office hits. Other mashups provide new image-track accompaniments to popular songs. Such productions provide further anecdotal evidence to support the Guattari/Stiegler scenario of the colonisation of popular consciousness by the products of the industrial mass media,[26] and it is notable that many other non-Internet forms of interactive "new media" also take their contents from mainstream film and television. The Internet, of course, also offers a variety of other moving image practices. For example, the professional filmmaker Véronique Aubouy is currently assembling her participative Internet work *Le baiser de la Matrice*. Each participant uses a webcam to film her or himself reading a page from Marcel Proust's *À la recherche du temps perdu*. Aubouy's ambition is to bring together readers from 246 countries. At the time of writing she has realised nearly 40% of the project, with about 65 hours of recorded material. Although she refers to her project as a "film" it may seem we are very distant from conventional cinema. Nevertheless I find myself thinking of a scene from Miloš Forman's film *Taking Off* (1971) in which the popular hit song "Let's Get A Little Sentimental" is performed by a succession of different young women—each singing a line of the song, or sometimes just one word, from its beginning to its end. The spaces of the Internet endlessly reverberate with the echos of remembered films.

~

Towards the end of the first century of cinema, digital technologies not only dramatically enhanced existing forms of spectacular mass entertainment—most conspicuously in the area of special effects—they also facilitated what Chris Marker has described as a "cinema of intimacy, of solitude, a cinema elaborated in a face-to-face with oneself, that of the painter and the writer."[27] Such a cinema now occupies a place, albeit marginal, in the setting of the traditional movie theater (one may think, for example, of the diaristic works of Alain Cavalier) and may be finding a place on the Internet in the emerging environment of free online video editing tools and mashup productions. Other forms of "painterly" and "writerly" moving image practices are being elaborated in art galleries and museums, and I now want to describe what I see as the overall *specificity* of my own works in these settings. Although what I have to say is derived primarily from my own practices, these have enough in common with those of other

23) Barthes, *op. cit.*

24) All quotations *ibid.*, p. 104.

25) Marie-Laure Ryan, *Narrative as Virtual Reality* (Baltimore: Johns Hopkins University Press, 2001).

26) A process that Hans Magnus Enzensberger described some 30 years before the arrival of the Internet; see "The Industrialization of the Mind," in *The Consciousness Industry* (New York: Seabury, 1974 [1962]).

27) Cited by Raymond Bellour, "La querelle des dispositifs," in *Art Press*, no. 262 (November 2000), p. 49.

artists to offer a picture of a general *type* of approach to the projected image, and written and spoken text, in the gallery setting.

The setting of the gallery is specifically different from, for example, either the theatrical setting of cinema or the domestic setting of television. Different artists take account of the gallery setting in different ways. For about two decades now, visitors to art galleries have encountered a wide range of works that make more or less direct reference to cinema—from works that manipulate existing footage from mainstream films to works by artists who make their own films in order to isolate and explore cinematic conventions: casting, mise-en-scène, camera movements and so on. The *New Oxford American Dictionary* from which I took my definition of "interactivity" defines the meaning of the word "cinematic" as "relating to motion pictures" and "having qualities characteristic of motion pictures;" the dictionary gives the example *"the cinematic feel of their video."* While many video and film works by artists shown in galleries have a "cinematic feel" in this sense, I think of my own works as *uncinematic*. It seems to me that "cinematic" gallery practices, for all their differences, presuppose or interpellate the spectator as a subject of *knowledge*. For example, it is assumed that the viewer knows cinema, and may know cinema better having experienced the artist's work. A subject of knowledge is also assumed in cinematic documentaries made by artists for exhibition in galleries, where the knowledge offered is of the social and political world. My own audiovisual works in the gallery interpellate not a subject of knowledge, but a subject of the *signifier*. I hope that what I mean by this will become clearer in the course of my remarks.

In the gallery an audiovisual work occupies a more or less darkened space, usually empty of furniture, where viewers normally enter and leave at indeterminable intervals. Audiovisual time in a gallery setting is therefore dual. Although it is possible to enter a movie theater after the film has begun and leave before it ends it is normally assumed that the duration of the film will coincide with the duration of the spectator's viewing of it. In the gallery it is normally assumed that these two times will *not* coincide. Most works made for the gallery are therefore designed to loop, with a seamless transition between the first and last frames of the material. With a peripatetic viewer and an indeterminate viewing time the conditions of spectatorship of a projected image in an art gallery are closer to those of painting than to cinema; the relation to a gallery work is one of repetition, or more accurately reprise, and the ideal viewer is one who accumulates her or his knowledge of the work, as it were, in "layers," much as a painting is created.[28] The idea of repetition occurs differently in different discourses, and may be considered from a variety of disciplinary points-of-view. Music offers some analogies in, for example, the *da capo* and *ritornello* forms. As the musicologist Marianne Massin writes: "[T]he *da capo* indicates that one must resume the performance of the score either from its beginning of from some appropriate sign. It therefore implies the reiteration of the same. However [...] the reprise does not produce the identical. Auditory memory [...] gives another dimension to the second audition. Keeping the memory of the first audition, it transfigures it."[29]

The *ritornello* is a repeated instrumental sequence that lends itself to differing specifications according to historical period and geographical location. For the sake of simplicity I shall return to the audiovisual for my example. Alain Robbe-Grillet's film of 1963 *L'Immortelle* is structured throughout by visual *ritornelli*. For example, in his "ciné-roman" version of *L'Immortelle*—which preceded the film and is effectively a shooting script for it—the description of shot number 23 begins "Exact reprise of shot number 9."[30] Transfiguration in the *ritornello* is not only a matter of memory but of a changing context.

The non-coincidence of the duration of the audiovisual material and the time of viewing suggests that the elements that comprise the material should be equally weighted and autonomously significant. For example, the opening sentence of the voice-over script to a recent work I made for a gallery in Cologne reads: "The major museums are all close to the station, which is by the cathedral so I cannot get lost." This sentence establishes that the speaker is a stranger to Cologne, there to visit the museums, and it also states a material fact about the city. So far, I might be writing a short story. However, although this is the "opening sentence" of my script it is not necessarily the opening sentence for the visitor to my installation, who may come and go at any time. A specific requirement of the voice-over text therefore is that it be written so that any sentence may occupy the position of "first" sentence, just as any image may be the first image. This equality of status between elements has something analogous to "description" in the classic distinction between *description* and *narrative*: the elements that make up a description may in principle be arranged in any order in time, whereas the elements that compose a narrative obey an invariable sequential order.

Characterised by recursivity and the absence of hierarchy between elements, the spatio-temporal structure of an audiovisual work specific to a gallery setting is closer to that of a psychoanalytic session than a narrative film. The French psychoanalyst Monique David-Ménard has emphasised the *discontinuity* of time in psychoanalysis, a discontinuity, which is "the correlate of the mode of access, always fragmentary, to the productions of the unconscious that make the transference possible."[31] No part or

28) Repetition as a mode of spectatorship was established early in the history of cinema, in the "continuous programming" that allowed spectators to remain in their seats as the programme of (typically) newsreel, "short" and main-feature recycled. See Annette Kuhn, *An Everyday Magic: Cinema and Cultural Memory* (London: Tauris, 2002), pp. 224–225.

29) Marianne Massin, "L'Emploi de la musique dans Nietzsche's Paris. Un da capo Nietzschéen," in Nathalie Boulouch, Valérie Mavridorakis and David Perreau (eds.), *Victor Burgin: Objets Temporels* (Rennes: Presses Universitaires de Rennes, 2007), p. 143. In the opera seria of the Baroque period it was in fact expected that in the performance of the da capo section of an aria the singer would embellish the reprise with improvised vocal ornaments.

30) Alain Robbe-Grillet, *L'IMMORTELLE ciné-roman* (Paris: Minuit, 1963), p. 28.

31) Monique David-Ménard, "Éclats de temps et récits fragmentaires en psychanalyse," in Jacques André, Sylvie Dreyfus-Asséo and François Hartog (eds.), *Les Récits du Temps* (Paris: puf, 2010), p. 107.

detail of the material produced in an analysis is considered *a priori* more significant than any other, all elements are equally potential points of departure for a chain of associations. Temporality in psychoanalysis is also characterised by *reiteration*, for example in the symptomatic phenomenon of the "compulsion to repeat," and the therapeutic principle of—in the title of one of Freud's essays—"Remembering, Repeating and Working-Through."[32] What I have referred to as the *ritornello* in audiovisual works has its analogies in such psychical mechanisms as *deferred action*, in which a previously anodyne event may become traumatic when recalled in different circumstances, or in the unconscious determinations of the sense of *déja vu* and the *uncanny*. As Monique David-Ménard observes, "The present exists but only the past insists."[33] The spacing of isolated autonomous elements in a work allows the possibility that viewers may see what is present to perception not only through the recollection of previous elements of the work but also through their own personal memories and fantasies.

Meaning in psychoanalysis emerges mainly by way of the associative mental processes that construct the dream—which, Freud emphasises, is to be understood not as a unitary narrative but as a fragmentary rebus. The "primary processes" of the dream-work—*condensation, displacement, considerations of representability* and *secondary revision*—are those of the unconscious in general. The psychoanalysts Jean Laplanche and Serge Leclaire have described the "words" that compose unconscious discourse as "elements drawn from the realm of the imaginary—notably from visual imagination" and describe the "sentences" formed from these words as "short sequences, most often fragmentary, circular and repetitive."[34] Such minimal sequences are typical of the reiterative fractional chains that form unconscious fantasies and daydreams. As Laplanche and Jean-Bertrand Pontalis note, when Freud speaks of unconscious fantasy, "he seems at times to be referring to a subliminal, preconscious revery into which the subject falls and of which he may or may not become reflexively aware."[35] Audiovisual works composed for the specificity of the gallery setting will typically take precisely the form of "fragmentary, circular and repetitive" short sequences, in response to which the viewing subject as *subject of the signifier* may come into being on a möbius band of impressions and associations. Time here is centrifugal and centripetal rather than linear, a time of shifting perceptions and associations around a perpetually displaced moment. The audiovisual work best fitted to the specificity of the gallery setting may aspire to the condition of, in the words of the narratologist Jean-Jacques Lecercle, "a temporal crystal that assembles the totality of time in the intuition of the instant."[36]

The painter Pierre Bonnard said that he wished the experience of his pictures to have something in common with the instantaneous experience of first entering an unfamiliar room—one sees everything at once, and yet nothing in particular. What I want to add to Bonnard's purely optical picture is the fleeting concatenation of impromptu thoughts one may have at that moment, from purely personal associations to what I have elsewhere referred to as the "granular-perceptual" manifestation of the political—a mutable aspect of our everyday reality on an equal perceptual basis to the changing light, an aching knee, a distant sound or a regret. In classical rhetoric, *parataxis* is the name given to the juxtaposition of disparate elements, the relations between which are not given but must be inferred. The organisation of the cinematic heterotopia is paratactical, as is that of the Internet; the presentation of elements in a psychoanalytic session is paratactical, as is a dream. The form of organisation of materials in the type of work I have called "uncinematic" is also paratactical. Roland Barthes complained that, at the cinema, you are not permitted to close your eyes. Gaps, absences and silences are integral to paratactical organisation. Places where "nothing happens"—where you may close your eyes, follow individual trains of associations—are fundamental to what I think of as the "uncinematic."

To speak of the participation of the viewer in the creation of the work is to return to the issue of "interactivity." The word "interactive" has come to be most widely understood in the computer science sense of software-controlled exchanges between humans and machines. Although it is legitimate to argue for a different understanding of the term, it may be best to use a different word altogether if computer science connotations are to be avoided. In the early days of media theory Marshall McLuhan distinguished between "hot" and "cold" media. A hot medium is rich in detail and leaves little information to be provided by the audience. A cold medium gives little information and leaves much to be filled in. McLuhan writes: "Hot media are [...] low in participation and cool media are high in participation or completion by the audience."[37] The word "participative" might therefore seem an alternative to "interactive" in relation to the type of "cool" medium I have described. McLuhan's conceptual framework however is that of communications theory, in which a "receiver" either unambiguously receives or "completes" a preconstituted "message" from a "sender." To avoid both computer science and communications theory connotations we might better consider the word "con-

32) Sigmund Freud, "Remembering, Repeating and Working-Through. Further Recommendations on the Technique of Psycho-Analysis II" [1914], in *The Standard Edition of the Complete Works of Sigmund Freud*, ed. by James Strachey et al. (London: The Hogart Press and the Institute of Psychoanalysis, 1953–74), Vol. XII, pp. 145–156.

33) David-Ménard, *op. cit.*, pp. 121–122.

34) Jean Laplanche and Serge Leclair, "The Unconscious: A Psychoanalytic Study," in *Yale French Studies*, no. 48 (1972), p. 162–163.

35) *Ibid*. "Topographically," the fantasy may be conscious, preconscious or unconscious. It is encountered, says Freud, "at both extremities" of the dream in the secondary elaboration of the dream as consciously narrated, and in the most primitive latent contents. The daydream is somewhere between the two.

36) Jean-Jaques Lecercle, *Trame et filigrane, Annales de l'Université de Savoie*, no. 16 (1993); cited in Catherine Mari, "Tell-Tale Ellipsis in Colum McCann's *Everything in This Country Must*," in *Journal of the Short Story in English*, no. 40 (Spring 2003), pp. 47–56.

37) Marshall McLuhan, *Essential McLuhan* (New York: Basic, 1996), p. 162.

templative"—which tends today to be associated with passivity, but which once implied active interpretation. The etymology of the word "contemplate" is in the Latin verb *contemplari*—"to look attentively, thoughtfully"—and the Latin noun *templum*, a "place for observation." In classical antiquity the templum was a precisely delineated space and time set apart for the observation of auguries—which is to say, for the interpretation of enigmatic signs. Typically, in antiquity, the boundaries of the templum, and of the temple that might be built there, would be delimited by the natural field of vision directed towards a space between two trees—a scene we may assimilate to that of a modern viewer in relation to a painted or projected image and its framing edge. The idea that this relation is "contemplative" in the sense of requiring interpretative activity on the part of the viewer is well expressed in Marcel Duchamp's remark: "paintings are made by those who look at them." The viewing subject proposed here is in a symmetrical relationship with the artist as described by Julia Kristeva. In a 1980 interview Kristeva is asked how her conception of the artist differs from the traditional idea of a "subject who speaks in the work." She replies that to say that the artist "speaks" in the work is to suppose a subject that exists *before* the work, however: "[...] the practice in which [the artist is] implicated extends beyond and reshapes subjectivity. There is, on the one hand, a kind of psychological ego, and on the other, there's the subject of a signifying practice. [...] The work of art is a kind of matrix that makes its subject."[38]

Appearing in English translation only, the interview with Kristeva was published in *Partisan Review* in 1984, the same year in which William Gibson published his science fiction novel *Neuromancer*, with its prescient vision of the multidimensional "cyberspace" he named the "Matrix." My abrupt and otherwise arbitrary passage from Kristeva to Gibson here is sanctioned only by the "primacy of the signifier."

However, for all that the juxtaposition may be strictly irrational it quite plausibly suggests the nature of the symbolic space in which the subject now *takes place*—not least, the subject of the political process. In a Lacanian view the subject emerges "in the wake of the signifier." In the Saussurean context from which the term derives, the "signifier" is unambiguously the *material* part of the sign. However, as the speed and complexity of digital information processing has transformed the space and time in which the subject emerges so it has changed the signifier. We may ask what type of mutating subject of the political process is now emerging in the wake of the *virtual* signifier.

A certain cinema has died, but the movie industry flourishes and in the interests of clarity we might do best to reserve the word "cinema" for the products of this industry. I began by invoking André Bazin. Raymond Bellour observes that for Bazin the cinema was an impure art "because it drew on all the other arts while offering only reality."[39] However, Bellour continues: "might cinema paradoxically gain in purity to the extent that its most active truth becomes that of its apparatus? Forever singular ... in relation to all the apparatuses ... that travesty and mimic it today, it is at once more surrounded and more alone than ever … in its henceforth minority splendour."[40] Bellour's remarks foregrounding the specificity of the apparatus were made some eight years ago in an article in the journal *Art Press* entitled, precisely, "La querelle des dispositifs." With symptomatic incomprehension, the parallel English text in the journal translates this as "Battle of the images." The elision or suppression of the issue of specificity in general—and that of the *apparatus* in particular—has allowed some critics and curators to claim that certain artists are somehow "reinventing" cinema. It is not the historical vocation of artists to reinvent cinema, but they unavoidably work in its shadow. We are all subjects formed in the wake of cinema, citizens of the cinematic heterotopia which is today the condition and the site of a variety of extra-cinematic practices. It is not the *specific* work of the artist to seek new forms of cinema, whether interactive or not, nor to elaborate either a cinema of intimacy or of the documentary film form. It is rather, within the shifting horizons of the cinematic heterotopia, to elaborate the possible forms of the uncinematic.

38) Julia Kristeva in conversation with E. H. Baruch and P. Meisel, translated by Margaret Waller, published (in English only) in *Partisan Review*, Vol. 51, Issue 1 (1984). Reprinted in Ross Mitchell Guberman (ed.), *Julia Kristeva Interviews* (New York: Columbia University Press, 1996), p. 16.

39) See Raymond Bellour, *op. cit.*, p. 52. In French it is "puisqu'il s'inspirait de tous les autres en offrant seul la réalité".

40) *Ibid.*

Thomas Morsch

# Permanent Metalepsis

*Pushing the Boundaries of Narrative Space*

"There it is, our 1.33 to 1 rectangle, it will tolerate precious little tampering with at all."
*Hollis Frampton*

"Ah, there you are. I've hardly seen you this episode."
*Alan Shore/James Spader to Denny Crane/William Shatner in* Boston Legal, 2.13

## I.

Episode sixteen of the third season of *The O.C.* (2003–2007) begins with a voice-over by one of the protagonists, Summer Roberts (played by Rachel Bilson), who simultaneously appears on-screen. Regular viewers who are familiar with the series would find this to be stylistically out of place: Although it is a typical narrative technique used in many television series, the voice-over is not a stylistic standard of *The O.C.* The initial aside becomes an even greater disruption when Summer's friend Marissa (Mischa Barton) enters the room, pauses and surprisingly can also hear the voice from off-screen. The mystery of the voice is solved when Marissa asks Summer for an explanation: Summer walks over to the stereo, stops the replay of her recorded voice and explains to Marissa that, as demonstrated by the many television series she has seen, a voice-over makes your life seem "more dramatic and meaningful." As she points out, even April on *The Valley*, the fictional teen soap that is repeatedly referenced in *The O.C.*, has a voice-over.

This scene is an ironic commentary on standard narrative conventions in television. It calls attention, for a brief moment, to the means employed by the narration. This moment in *The O.C.* is reminiscent of *2 or 3 Things I Know About Her* (1967), Jean-Luc Godard's exercise in Brechtian estrangement technique. Since the sound of the voice-over spoken by Godard himself appears to be aligned with the camera perspective, it conveys an impression as if the whispered comments and questions from off-screen were located within diegetic space and as if the fictional characters can hear the voice-over. This results in a certain indeterminacy regarding the diegetic or non-diegetic status of the director's voice.[1] It may be that the same effect, intended by Godard to be politically progressive and anti-illusionist, amounts to no more than inconsequential ironic play in *The O.C.* Yet from a purely formal perspective, the similarity between the two cases is undeniable.

The phenomenon encountered here can be described as a type of process, as the transgression of a boundary—the boundary between the diegetic and the non-diegetic world. As an authorial and extra-diegetic voice, Godard penetrates the diegetic space and resonates within it insofar as the fictional characters are capable of hearing the voice of their narrator, or rather—since it is the voice of Godard—the voice of their (implicit or explicit) author and director. There is a narratological concept that captures this transgressive technique, first characterized by Gérard Genette in the early 1970s, and which he placed once again at the center of a recent monograph: metalepsis.[2] In the following, I hope to show two things: one, that the concept of metalepsis is suited to place a number of quite heterogeneous aesthetic phenomena in a common theoretical context, and two, that the concept of metalepsis, once transposed into the sphere of audio-visual popular culture, turns out to harbor a potential that is not evident in a strictly narratological concept. This potential becomes most evident, as I hope to show, when the figures of metalepsis are construed against the background of film theory, specifically in regards to the unity and closure of narrative space.

Gérard Genette picks up the term "metalepsis" from the rhetorical tradition and transposes it onto narrative phenomena. This results in a shift of focus from "authorial metalepsis," whereby authors rhetorically descend to the level of the characters that they create, toward "narrative metalepsis," which can take a number of different forms.[3] Originally occupying a marginal place in Genette's foundational study of narratology, the term has been increasingly taken up over the past ten years and has in the course of this reception become subject to interpretations that go beyond Genette's definition. A number of recent publications attest to the vitality of the debate over this concept within literary studies,[4] which so far has only

1) "Godard does not claim to be a character in the action, yet the characters on the screen sometimes seem to hear him. This uncertainty as to diegetic or nondiegetic sound sources enables Godard to stress the conventionality of traditional sound usage." David Bordwell, Kristin Thompson, *Film Art: An Introduction*. 4th Ed. (New York et al: McGraw Hill, 1993), p. 312.

2) Gérard Genette, *Narrative Discourse*. Trans. Jane E. Lewin. Foreword by Jonathan Culler (Oxford: Basil Blackwell, 1980); Gérard Genette, *Métalepse. De la figure à la fiction* (Paris: Seuil, 2004).

3) See Genette, 1980, *Narrative Discourse*., pp. 234–235; Karin Kukkonen, "Metalepsis in Popular Culture: An Introduction," in Karin Kukkonen, Sonja Klimek (eds.), *Metalepsis in Popular Culture* (Berlin/New York: de Gruyter, 2011), pp. 1–2.

4) See among others Brian McHale, *Postmodernist Fiction* (London: Routledge, 1987); David Herman, "Toward a Formal Description of Narrative Metalepsis," in *Journal of Literary Semantics*, Vol. 26, Issue 2 (1997), pp. 132–152; Klaus W. Hempfer, "(Pseudo-)Performatives Erzählen im zeitgenössischen französischen und italienischen Roman," in *Romanistisches Jahrbuch*, Vol. 50 (1999), pp. 158–182; Bernd Häsner, *Metalepsen: Zur Genese, Systematik und Funktion transgressiver Erzählweisen*. Ph.D thesis, Freie Universität Berlin (2001). www.diss.fu-berlin.de/2005/239/index.html; Debra Malina, *Breaking the Frame: Metalepsis and the Construction of the Subject* (Columbus: Ohio State University Press, 2002); Monika Fludernik, "Scene Shift, Metalepsis, and the Metaleptic Mode," in *Style*, Vol. 37, Issue 4 (Winter 2003), pp. 382–400; Genette, 2004, *Métalepse*; Marie-Laure Ryan, "Metaleptic Machines," in *Semiotica*, Vol. 150, Issue 1 (2004), pp. 439–469; John Pier, Jean-Marie Schaeffer (eds.), *Métalepses. Entorses au pacte de la représentation* (Paris: EHSS, 2005); Manish Sharma, "Metalepsis and Monstrosity: The Boundaries of Narrative Structure in *Beowulf*," in *Studies in Philology*, Vol. 102, Issue 3 (Summer 2005), pp. 247–279; Werner Wolf, "Metalepsis as a

been occasionally applied to audio-visual media.[5]

In *Narrative Discourse*, Genette characterizes metalepsis as the transgression of a boundary between different levels of narration, brought about by a narrative act.[6] Examples of metaleptic events include the entering of an author or extra-diegetic narrator into the diegetic universe or the escape of fictional characters from a painting, a book or a film. Since none of this is possible in reality, it is clear that Genette is thinking of narrated events and thus of the transgression of boundaries established by the narration itself within a text. With regard to film, this immediately brings to mind an example frequently cited in this context: Woody Allen's *The Purple Rose of Cairo* (1985),[7] in which one of the characters of a film-within-a-film descends from the screen into the reality occupied by Cecilia (Mia Farrow).[8] When we watch this film at the cinema, the actor does not actually descend from the screen; the boundary between reality and cinematic text remains untouched.[9] Understood in this way, the concept of metalepsis identifies an intra-diegetic structure, a particular type of narrative construction, albeit one that can take different forms. Genette explicitly reserves the term for a number of different sorts of transgression, so that his foundational text already initiates an open series of metaleptic phenomena capable of being further extended in the course of subsequent scholarly debate. All of Genette's examples share this transgression of a shifting but "sacred boundary" between the *narrating world* and the *narrated world*.[10] The transgression affirms this boundary just to the extent that its breach remains implausible. Even though *The Purple Rose of Cairo* may articulate the viewers' desire that the boundary of the screen be suspended for them as well, the unlikelihood of the transgression and the irritation that it causes in the reader or the viewer only serve to confirm, in Genette's view, the stability of that boundary.

In Genette's conception, metalepsis is not yet the narratological "killer app" that one might hope for.[11] This might partly explain why met-

Transgeneric and Transmedial Phenomenon: A Case Study of 'Exporting' Narratological Concepts," in J. C. Meister (ed.), *Narratology Beyond Literary Criticism: Mediality, Disciplinarity* (Berlin/New York: de Gruyter, 2005), pp. 83–107; Sonja Klimek, "Metalepsis and its (Anti-)Illusionist Effects in the Arts, Media and Role-Playing Games," in Werner Wolf (ed.), *Metareference Across Media. Theory and Case Studies* (Amsterdam/New York: Rodopi, 2009), pp. 169–187; John Pier, "Metalepsis," in Peter Hühn et al. (eds.), *Handbook of Narratology* (Berlin: de Gruyter, 2009), pp. 190–203; Werner Wolf, "Metareference across Media: The Concept, its Transmedial Potentials and Problems, Main Forms and Functions," in Wolf, 2009, *Metareference*, pp. 1–85; Kukkonen and Klimek, *op. cit.*

5) Jean-Marie Schaeffer, "Métalepse et immersion fictionelle," in Pier and Schaeffer, *op. cit.*, pp. 247–261; Erwin Feyersinger, "Diegetische Kurzschlüsse wandelbarer Welten: Die Metalepse im Animationsfilm," in *Montage/AV*, Vol. 16, Issue 2 (2007), pp. 113–130; Jörg Türschmann, "Die Metalepse," in *Montage/AV*, Vol. 16, Issue 2 (2007), pp. 105–112; Jean-Marc Limoges, "Quand Mel dépasse les bornes: d'un usage comique de la métalepse chez Brooks," in *Humoresques*, no. 28 (2008), pp. 31–41; Jan-Noël Thon, "Zur Metalepse im Film," in Hannah Birr, Maike Sarah Reinerth, Jan-Noël Thon (eds.), *Probleme filmischen Erzählens* (Münster: LIT Verlag, 2009), pp. 85–110; Erwin Feyersinger, "Metaleptic TV Crossovers," in Kukkonen and Klimek, *op. cit.*, pp. 127–157; Jean-Marc Limoges, "Metalepsis in the Cartoons of Tex Avery: Expanding the Boundaries of Transgression," in Kukkonen and Klimek, *op. cit.*, pp. 196–212; Keyvan Sarkhosh, "Metalepsis in Popular Comedy

alepsis emerged as a distinctive object of reflection in literary studies in the late 1990s. In the intervening years, the only notable contribution comes from Brian McHale,[12] who shows that metalepsis is among the favored aesthetic devices of postmodern literature. McHale also emphasizes the paradoxical character of metalepsis, by likening it to the "strange loops" that had been at the center of Douglas Hofstadter's best-selling book, *Gödel, Escher, Bach: An Eternal Golden Braid,*[13] and which were represented there by the Möbius strip and by the lithographs of M.C. Escher. "Strange loops" establish paradoxical relationships between the different levels of a hierarchically ordered system, and should be distinguished from the device of *mise en abyme.*[14] Metalepsis not only places part and whole, lower-order and higher-order levels, in a mirroring relationship, like the device of *mise en abyme*, but it also lets each pass over into the other in a paradoxical manner not amenable to the logic of "realism." In Genette's literary examples, this paradoxical relationship is brought about through an act of transgression, through

Film," in Kukkonen and Klimek, *op. cit.*, pp. 171–195; to some extent also Genette, 2004, *Métalepse*.

6) Genette, 1980, *Narrative Discourse*, p. 234. The performative slant of Genette's description of metalepsis as the result of an action (on the part of the narrator) will turn out to be relevant to the further discussion.

7) See Genette, *Métalepse,* 2004, p. 60; Thon, *op. cit.*, pp. 89–90; Kukkonen, *op. cit.,* p. 17.

8) Following the terminology proposed by John Pier we may call this an instance of "ascending metalepsis," since the metaleptic transgression amounts to a transition to a narrative level with a higher degree of reality. This is the case even though both levels (the film-within-the-film entitled *The Purple Rose of Cairo* and Cecilia's reality) are part of a single cinematic fiction (*The Purple Rose of Cairo*). By contrast we have a "descending metalepsis" when, for instance, the narrator steps down into the fiction and thus to a level that has, from his perspective, a lower degree of reality. Narratological debates tend to center around such terminological differentiations and attempts at categorization and definition, but they are secondary to my argument here. See John Pier, "Métalepse et hierarchies narratives," in Pier and Schaeffer, *op. cit.*, pp. 247–261.

9) There is not sufficient space here for a detailed discussion of the numerous metaleptic "gimmicks" for which especially the B-picture director William Castle (1914–1977) is known and which are specifically aimed at transgressing the bounded reality circumscribed by the screen: the presence of medical personnel at a screening, skeletons flying through the cinema and electrified seats meant to – literally – shock the audience, all belonged to the repertoire of Castle to whom John Waters has devoted an enthusiastic essay, Joe Dante an affectionate homage (*Matinee*, 1993), and Jeffrey Schwartz an award-winning documentary (*Spine Tingler! The William Castle Story*, 2007). The attempts of avant-garde and experimental cinema to transcend the screen are too numerous to be individually named here. See John Waters, "Whatever Happened to Showmanship?" in *Crackpot: The Obsessions of John Waters* (New York: Vintage Books, 1987), pp. 14–23.

10) In the original French text, Genette speaks of a "frontière mouvante mais sacrée entre deux mondes: celui où l'on raconte, celui que l'on raconte" (Gérard Genette, *Figures III* [Paris: Seuil, 1972], p. 245). The fact that Genette was at this point still uncertain about the definition, range, and scope of the concept is reflected in the shifting semantics of (at first) "levels" and (later) "worlds" as that whose frontiers are being transcended. The latter term was taken up especially by the "possible worlds" theory in literary studies (see Marie-Laure Ryan, "Possible Worlds in Recent Literary Theory," in *Style*, Vol. 26, Issue 4 [Summer 1992], pp. 528–553). The unstable semantics already hint at a certain metonymic flexibility of the concept, which will be central to my argument.

11) Fludernik (2003) provides a systematic overview of the different types of metalepsis that are found in Genette's examples.

12) See McHale, *op. cit.*

13) Douglas Hofstadter, *Gödel, Escher, Bach: An Eternal Golden Braid* (New York: Vintage Books, 1989 [Orig. 1979]).

14) Hempfer, *op.cit.*, p. 180.

the transition from one narrative level to another. These considerations yield a "minimal definition"[15] of metalepsis as "a usually intentional paradoxical transgression of, or confusion between, (onto-)logically distinct (sub)worlds and/or levels that exist, or are referred to, within representations of possible worlds."[16]

The focus on intra-diegetic events—events "within representation," as Wolf writes—remains even when the concept of metalepsis is sharpened so as to capture a specifically paradoxical phenomenon. Consider how in various episodes of the show *Glee* (2009–), Sue Sylvester (Jane Lynch) makes reference to herself as a representational subject, for example when she complains that she has just been mocked "in slow motion" ("Bad Reputation," 1.17), or when she explains in a voice-over that to simply say the word "Madonna" aloud "makes me feel powerful—even in voice-over" ("The Power of Madonna," 1.15). These are instances of paradox, since Sylvester moves back and forth between ontologically different levels, but the paradox remains at the level of representation, since this transgression—here in the form of a rhetorical reference—is a transgression on the part of the character, Sylvester, not on the part of the actress, Jane Lynch.[17] The paradoxical nature of metalepsis emerges more clearly in cases where boundaries are transgressed ontologically rather than rhetorically.[18] The Comedy *Hellzapoppin'* (H.C. Potter, 1941) serves as a classic example, and is also commented on by Genette in a monograph that attempts to transpose the original literary concept of metalepsis to other media.[19] In *Hellzapoppin'*, film—a medium that rests on technical reproduction—dreams of itself as a performative art. The metaleptic construction of the film is not limited to the fact that the characters Ole Olsen and Chic Johnson make constant references to "this film": They also interact with the projectionist of the film they are in, for example by asking him to rewind the film so that corrections may be made to a prior event. Conversely, the projectionist (at the higher-order level of reality) influences what happens in the film (and thus at the fictional, lower-order level of reality). At one point he chooses what is visible in the frame, as though the exposed filmstrip did not already fix this. The intra-diegetic level of film projection also affects the level of fiction in other ways. Thus, the film roll becomes dislodged within the projector so that the space between the frames comes to be located in the middle of the image, severing the bodies of the characters at the torso, who strug-

15) Kukkonen, *op. cit.*, p. 10.

16) Wolf, 2005, *Metalepsis*, p. 91. There is no space here for a critical examination of the possible worlds theory of literature on which this definition is based. But from an analytical point of view it appears questionable to extrapolate from the information provided by a piece of fiction, and the events presented in it, to an entire "world" and thus to a theoretical construction that is no longer analytically anchored to the text itself. It seems more useful to restrict the semantics of world construction to those fictions for which the completion of a world is in fact an aesthetic goal. For instance, Jeffrey Sconce regards the cumulative and complex television series of recent times as an aesthetic form whose narrative strategies tend to rely on cultivating a distinct "world" within which the respective story is embedded. Jeffrey Sconce, "What If?: Charting Television's New Textual Boundaries," in Lynn Spigel, Jan Olsson (eds.), *Television After TV. Essays on a Medium in Transition* (Durham: Duke University Press, 2004), p. 95.

gle within the image to become whole again. There is also a blending of two logically and materially separate fictions: as a consequence of the mistaken insertion of a roll of film from a Western, the protagonists of *Hellzapoppin'* now have to run for cover from flying bullets. This mishap corrected, Olsen and Johnson then find themselves redoubled and facing their own respective selves in the image, asking their alter egos to exit the film. The basis of the film's numerous metaleptic maneuvers is the imaginary possibility of an intervention in what is already fixed by technology. What brings about the various metaleptic entanglements is the impossible simultaneity of the temporally separate levels (or worlds) of recording and projection. This leads to paradoxical consequences within the film, because the film-within-the-film is simultaneously finished (previously recorded) and yet still alterable.[20]

The example of *Hellzapoppin'* allows for additional conclusions. For one, the film demonstrates how the transposition of metalepsis from the literary to the audio-visual realm complicates the basic concept and multiplies its possibilities.[21] This is exemplified by the fact that in *Hellzapoppin'* the cinematic images, which after all serve not as the objects but as the media of representation, figure by turns as film, as film-within-a-film and as projection-within-a-film—and all this within a projected film. Whereas Genette thought of the metaleptic boundary transgression as a determinate event, the ontological abyss of the cinematic image blurs that boundary and thereby also its transgression.

Secondly, by staging undramatic and playful transgressions between different levels, *Hellzapoppin'* draws attention to the fact that those levels are constructions on the part of a viewer who is applying "realist" or common-sense categories to artificial works of fiction.[22] Ontolog-

17) After all it would be something quite different if Jane Lynch were to make reference to her own appearance in the series in the context of a DVD audio commentary.

18) The distinction between rhetorical and ontological metalepsis was introduced into the debate by Marie-Laure Ryan. She attributes discovery of the rhetorical type of metalepsis to Genette, and of the ontological type to McHale. She defines them as follows: "Rhetorical metalepsis opens a small window that allows a quick glance across levels, but the window closes after a few sentences, and the operation ends up reasserting the existence of boundaries. This temporary breach of illusion does not threaten the basic structure of the narrative universe. [...] Whereas rhetorical metalepsis maintains the levels of the stack distinct from each other, ontological metalepsis opens a passage between levels that results in their interpenetration, or mutual contamination. These levels, needless to say, must be separated by the type of boundary that I call ontological: a switch between two radically distinct worlds, such as 'the real' and 'the imaginary,' or the world of 'normal' (or lucid) mental activity from the worlds of dream of [sic] hallucination" (Ryan, 2004, "Metaleptic Machines," pp. 441–442).

19) Genette, 2004, *Métalepse*, p. 66.

20) This simultaneity is reflected in the spatio-temporal simultaneity of *histoire* and *discours* that Klaus Hempfer presents as a characteristic feature of metaleptic and to that extent (pseudo-)performative narration, in which the narrative act presents *itself in process*. Hempfer, *op. cit.*, p. 165.

21) This is also shown, for example, by Jean-Marc Limoges in his text about metalepses in the animated films of Tex Avery (Limoges, 2011, "Metalepsis"). On metalepsis in animated films see also Feyersinger 2007, "Diegetische Kurzschlüsse".

22) Monika Fludernik articulates this as a critique of narratological theories of metalepsis: "The critical impasse that is here seen to rear its head is additionally aggravated by the insight that the ontology of narratological levels exists only in the mind of readers and critics. It is

ical and narratological levels or worlds come into existence only when we construe a narration, an image, a film, or some other type of fiction in the light of our everyday assumptions, instead of identifying them as artificial constructions in which the laws of reality are suspended. Notice how in *Hellzapoppin'*, boundary transgressions take place only from the perspective of the viewer. Unlike *The Purple Rose of Cairo*, where the hero's descent from the screen creates a public sensation, this film does not thematize its events as violations of realistic assumptions at all—they simply happen.

Thirdly, the comedic context of the metalepses in *Hellzapoppin'* points to the indefensibility of the long-standing assumption that metalepses are in principle transgressive and therefore subversive.[23] Metalepses are neither a specifically postmodern stylistic device, whose reach would be restricted to the corresponding genres, nor do they necessarily have anti-illusionist effects. Depending on context and on how they are deployed, metalepses may instead serve to enhance and stabilize fiction.[24] Metalepsis should therefore be thought of in the first place as a formal device (and, by extension, as an aesthetic strategy) whose function, force and effect need to be ascertained anew from case to case.[25]

Fourthly, the redoubling of the characters in *Hellzapoppin'*, who through the projectionist's error are suddenly confronted with their own respective selves, exemplifies a general metaleptic aspect of film as well as of other audio-visual media, which becomes especially manifest in the two-fold role of the body. With the exception of animated films and abstract experimental films, every film incorporates pieces of reality.[26] Filmed landscapes, cities, buildings, and places always have a double status in fictional films: on the one hand they serve as fictional locations; on the other hand they enjoy a material existence outside the film that invades the film they are part of.[27] The same holds for the body of the actor, who in the viewer's eye always belongs to two different worlds: he is always at once (for example) "James Bond" and "Sean Connery" (if not the real person, then at least a public persona outside the fictional world of the film). This double status can be taken up and put to narrative use within the film. Thus Jean-Marie Schaeffer,[28] in his analysis of the ending of *The Great Dictator* (1940), claims that in his final speech, Chaplin exits his role and switches over to the persona of Chaplin. In cases of this sort, the gen-

a fiction based on realistic presuppositions about heterodiegetic and especially authorial narrators. Narrative levels or narratological boundaries are erected by recourse to commonsensical realistic scenarios that have been metaphorically and perhaps metaleptically applied to narratological theorizing. It is only in relation to a strong commitment to a realistic or pragmatic narratology, firmly based on the story/discourse distinction, that the concept of metalepsis can be fruitfully discussed as a metaphoric crossing of taken-for-granted (but really artificially imposed) theoretical boundaries." (Fludernik, *op. cit.*, p. 396) While I share Fludernik's approach of resisting realist assumptions as a foundation for analyzing and theorizing fictional works, what follows from this, in my view, is not so much skepticism regarding the concept of metalepsis (to which Fludernik, in line with narratological orthodoxy, gives an overly narrow construal). What follows, rather, is the need to incorporate the fundamental artificiality of fiction into the concept of metalepsis itself, instead of using metalepsis as a narratological wild card whenever the discursive nature of fiction clashes with everyday expectations and realist assumptions.

eral metaleptic *potential* of the actor's body is condensed into a metaleptic narrative *procedure*. Attention to the role of the body also reveals that, in the context of the audio-visual and performative arts, metalepsis cannot be understood (as it has been in literary studies) as an exclusively representational phenomenon, since the double status of the body (and thereby the metaleptic devices based on it) transcends the boundaries of representation itself.

Before I turn to some further examples, I would like to mention a final point that arises from taking a closer look at *Hellzapoppin'*. The play that is being staged here, involving both the physical space of the cinematic image and the—albeit intra-diegetic—metaleptic crossing of intra- and extra-filmic space, has the effect of drawing attention to the specifically spatial dimension of metalepsis, which is already implicit in the semantics of boundary crossing, and which extends to the metaphoric terminology of "levels" and "worlds." Thus, there is a close relationship between spatiality and narrative, which film theory in particular has sought to explicate.

The rectangular shape of the screen does not allow for manipulative interventions (at least *prima facie*, that is to say, disregarding the experiments of Expanded Cinema and related strategies), nor does—according to Hollis Frampton's remark quoted at the beginning of this article—the rectangular image frame. The *material* boundary of the screen is therefore simultaneously a *narrative* boundary. In his writings, Stephen Heath[29] emphasizes the dependence of cinematic narrative on the category of space, and thus the spatiality of cinematic narration. The unity and coherence of narrative space,

23) See, for instance, Malina, *op. cit*. Despite overwhelming evidence to the contrary, Malina clings to the thesis that metalepses destroy the coherence of a work and that they constitute acts of aggression against the subject deconstructed by metaleptic procedures.

24) See Fludernik, *op. cit.*, p. 392; Klimek, *op. cit*.

25) Thus Jean-Marc Limoges correctly points out what is true not only of metalepsis but also of other self- and meta-referential procedures: "Two formally identical self-reflexive devices may at times break and at other times maintain the audience's aesthetic illusion." Jean-Marc Limoges, "The Gradable Effects of Self-Reflexivity on Aesthetic Illusion in Cinema," in Wolf, 2009, *Metareference*, p. 391.

26) In his monograph on metalepsis, Genette offers a parallel argument with respect to fiction in general: "En vérité, la fiction est, de part en part, nourrie et peuplée d'éléments venus de la réalité, matériels et spirituels. [...] Tout fiction est tissée de métalepses." (Genette, 2004, *Métalepse*, p. 131). Even though this is correct, it is still the case that audio-visual media are moored in external reality in a qualitatively different way than other fictional media. Moreover it seems more useful to reserve the concept of metalepsis for specific *procedures* and aesthetic *strategies*, instead of hollowing it out by extending it indefinitely "de la figure à la fiction."

27) Kracauer placed this property of film at the center of his film theory. Siegfried Kracauer, *Theory of Film. The Redemption of Physical Reality* (New York: Oxford University Press, 1960). See on this property of audio-visual media as sources of metaleptic procedures also Feyersinger, 2011, "Metaleptice TV Crossovers," p. 149. From this observation, Schaeffer (2005) infers a general dynamic tension, within film reception, between immersion in the mimetic world and a representation of reality. However, following Genette (see footnote 26), Schaeffer's thesis is not restricted to film; a similar oscillation is said to hold for non-cinematic forms of fiction as well.

28) Pier and Schaeffer, *op. cit.*, pp. 247–261.

29) Stephen Heath, "Narrative Space," in *Questions of Cinema* (London/Basingstoke: Macmillan, 1981), pp. 19–75.

which a film must first establish in the face of the ruptures affected by cuts, correspond to the spatial unity of the framed cinematic image whose limits are set by the screen, as well as to the psychological coherence of cinematic perception established by the space of the cinema itself, whose darkness isolates the viewer from external reality. Film, according to Heath,[30] is based on the creation of a stable position within this spatial structure. This stable structure finds expression in the perspectival orientation of the image. Not only is perspective itself a symbolic form[31]; there also exists an intrinsic relationship between perspectival and narrative space, which has been identified by Rosalind Krauss (writing with a critical intent and from a specifically modernist viewpoint) as follows: "Perspective is the visual correlate of causality that one thing follows the next in space according to rule." This spatial arrangement corresponds to the causal succession of events in a narrative, "and within that temporal succession—given as a spatial analog—the 'meaning' of both space and those events was secreted."[32] Thus, space and narration depend on each other: Just as perspectivally organized space constitutes an order that corresponds to the order of narrative causation, a narrative serves to focus cinematic space into a unified stage, a stable object there to be viewed.[33] In this way film theory has established allegorical interrelations between narrative space, cinematic space and the physical space of the cinema. They mirror each other due to their common function of constituting a unified space of significance, which alone allows for a film to be 'readable.'

## II.

The characterization of spatial conditions just offered does not fit the medium of television even in cases where the latter takes up the generic narrative conventions established by cinema. Television may in many respects be thought of as releasing the cinematic apparatus from its inherent limitations. The sheer temporal extension of serial narratives, which belong to the core business of television, explodes the framework to which cinematic narration is subject. But no less does the greater currency of metaleptic devices testify to the increased flexibility and permeability of narrative boundaries in television compared to the boundaries that constitute the narrative space of cinema. In keeping with my line of argument so far, the metaleptic permeation of the televisual text is of a predominantly spatial nature, aiming to transcend the boundaries of the symbolically or materially configured spaces of television.[34]

To some extent this is already evident in cases where the previously mentioned metaleptic potential of the actor's body is made to unfold in the context of specific aesthetic procedures. In the Nickelodeon children's show *Clarissa Explains It All* (1991–1994), which is an example of the intensification of fictional immersion through metalepsis, the main protagonist Clarissa Darling (Melissa Joan Hart) is precariously located on the divide between the intra-diegetic and the extra-diegetic levels. On the one hand, she forms the center of the fictional world, and in this respect she occupies the same level as other characters, such as her family and her friend Sam. On the other hand, she constantly steps outside the fictional world and takes control of the discourse by directly addressing the viewer and talking with them about what is happening. Diagrams, displays of writing, photographs, computer simulations, and other graphical elements shown on-screen supplement her spoken words. Clarissa produces these graphics as discursive elements that cannot be construed as part of the fictional world in any realistic sense. What we encounter here is a type of metalepsis that is not uncommon in the performative arts: the breaking of the fourth wall, which has come to form the aesthetic core of this series. Here it takes the form of a constant intra-diegetic crossing of the boundary between *histoire* and *discours*, both through the direct address of the viewer and through the use of graphical elements, with Clarissa functioning as a mediator between the two levels. What remains in place is the boundary separating the intra-diegetic from the extra-diegetic or extra-textual world, for even in her role as a discursive authority the integrity of the character "Clarissa Darling" is upheld rather than being diffused into the identity of her impersonator, Melissa Joan Hart. In any case, the direct address of the viewer tends to strengthen their relationship to the main character and their participation in her world, rather than calling into question the fictional world. Yet at the same time, the story becomes a function of discourse; its independence vis-à-vis the narration is negated.[35]

David E. Kelley's show *Boston Legal* (2004–2008), on the contrary, uses metaleptic elements to put pressure on the boundary between fiction and extra-textual (as well as inter-textual) reality. Although this was not originally part of the show's conception, an accumulation of metalepses can be seen between two of the protagonists, Alan Shore and Denny Crane, who make reference to their extra-textual existence as the actors James Spader and William Shatner: Denny / Shatner describes himself as "the star of the show" and notes that he received an Emmy (2.9); Alan / Spader complains that he has hardly seen Denny in the course of a certain episode (2.13), and points out to Shirley (Candice Bergen) that they should kiss, since they are in a "sweeps" episode (2.27); Alan is warned by his secretary not to get involved with a woman named Chelina, since she is only a guest star (2.23); in the episode "New Kids on the Block" (3.2), Alan greets some new characters with the words "Welcome to Boston Legal," and Denny is puzzled that the newcomers were not yet there for the season premiere; in the final episode of the third season, Denny says to Alan, "till next season," to which Alan replies, "I can't wait to see what we do

30) *Ibid.*, p. 26.

31) Erwin Panofsky, *Perspective as Symbolic Form* (New York: Zone, 1991 [Orig. 1927]).

32) Rosalind Krauss, "A View of Modernism," in *Artforum*, no. 11 (September 1972), pp. 50–51.

33) Thus Heath writes that the cinematic image rests on the continuous negation of space in favor of a specific place, a signifying scene of action (Heath, *op. cit.*, pp. 39 and 53).

34) One could find additional striking examples of this by including non-fictional television formats. In what follows I will rely on fictional television series alone.

35) This corresponds to one of the types of metalepsis that Fludernik identifies in Genette (see Fludernik, *op. cit.*, p. 388).

next" (3.24)—and so on. The metaleptic references repeatedly allude to the varying time slots of *Boston Legal* over the course of its five year run at ABC, and thus to the institutional context of the show, as well as to William Shatner's role as Captain James T. Kirk in the Star Trek universe, and thus to the inter-textual aspects of the show that are owed to the identity of one of its actors. These rhetorical rather than ontological metalepses—to take up Marie-Laure Ryan's distinction[36]—might also be characterized, following William Nelles,[37] as "epistemological metalepses," since their distinguishing mark seems to lie in the fact that the fictional characters possess a certain "impossible knowledge" of their own fictional status, and are therefore able to reflect and comment on their mode of existence as television characters played by actors.

The two examples just cited, which mainly rely on the metaleptic potential of the actor's body, are yet surpassed in this respect by the sitcom *It's Garry Shandling's Show*, which rests entirely on a metaleptic construction: in the person of Garry Shandling, actor and character are reflected onto one another in such a way that the boundary transgression is barely observable as such. Correspondingly, the dramatic space of the show is spread out across several diegetic levels: "When typical pro-filmic elements are shown intentionally, as in *It's Garry Shandling's Show* (1986–1990), where Garry Shandling is established as both a character and an actor commenting on the fictional aspect of the show, then they gain a diegetic status of their own, effectively pushing diegetic elements to an embedded hypo-diegetic level. In *It's Garry Shandling's Show*, the image of an actual (pro-filmic, extra-diegetic) studio signifies a fictionalized (diegetic) studio that signifies a (hypo-diegetic) living room. However, this narrative shift does not change the internal hierarchy of these levels. The fictionalized studio is still extra-diegetic with regard to the central story world. *It's Garry Shandling's Show* constantly shifts between its narrative levels that are conflated within the same filmic image."[38]

Even though the diegetic levels can still be logically distinguished from each other, their metaleptic entanglement has reached such a degree that what is at the center of the viewer's experience is not so much the difference bridged by way of boundary-crossing, but rather the intermingling of all available levels of fiction and reality. But even with respect to this particular sitcom the result stands that metalepsis does not as such have a transgressive or critical character.[39] Instead its effects depend on its use in a particular situation.[40]

## III.

The television series considered so far suggest that the discourse of television may be less dependent on stable identities, and they certainly show that metaleptic destabilization can be compensated for by the duration and depth of the relation that serial narrations establish between a viewer and a fictional world.[41] But the analysis of metalepsis as a transgression of spatial boundaries, be they between "levels," "worlds" or "texts" leads to yet another type of metalepsis, which is characteristic of current television. The erasure of the boundaries of fictional space that is accomplished in *Boston Legal*, *Clarissa Explains It All*, and *It's Garry Shandling's Show* by aesthetic means is also encountered at the institutional, technological and discursive levels. The delimitation and framing of the narrative that is needed in order to constitute a space of significance is undone by technological means, insofar as the fictional world of the show spills over into a variety of media formats.[42] In other words: the creation of narrative and spatial unity and coherence that lies at the basis of the process of signification in film comes to be in tension, in the context of television, with the boundary-dissolving tendencies of the televisual text. This concerns the latter's spatio-material arrangement, dispersed across a diversity of media, no less than the modularization of the narrative, which contains elements belonging to quite different degrees of fiction and reality. These kinds of boundary-crossings follow, in more than just a metaphorical sense, the procedure of metalepsis. Of course there exist some closed fictional spaces in television, just as there are films aimed at the systematic transgression of such spaces. Nevertheless it is fair to say that this metaleptic tendency—not only in symbolic and aesthetic respects, but also with regard to the material, technological and institutional dimensions—is far more typical of the medium of television than it is of film.

This tendency is nowhere more apparent than in the series *Lost* (2004–2010), where the questions of space and its unity also arise at the story level. The spatial dimension is constantly present as a structuring moment of the narrative itself, both through the necessity of exploring a foreign space—which follows the logic of computer games and of reality TV formats like

36) See note 18.

37) William Nelles, "Stories Within Stories: Narrative Levels and Embedded Narrative," in *Studies in the Literary Imagination*, Vol. 25, Issue 1 (Spring 1992), pp. 93–95.

38) Feyersinger, 2011, "Metaleptic TV Crossovers," p. 149. With respect to the example of the studio space it should be mentioned for the sake of completeness that the fictional apartment in the sitcom is modeled after Garry Shandling's real apartment. This has the effect of undermining the hierarchical arrangement of fictional levels that Genette takes for granted, since the setting of the fictional level with the "lowest degree of reality" (the scene of the series-within-the-series) corresponds to the "highest level of reality", insofar as it is taken from the extra-textual, real existence of the actor Garry Shandling.

39) This would require, first and foremost, the existence of fixed and stable boundaries that are a matter of consensus between the author and the reader or viewer (see Turk, *op. cit.*, p. 87)—an assumption that is not warranted under the current media and cultural conditions.

40) One example for the fullest use of the critical potential of metaleptic structures may be the live episode broadcast on the evening of the 1988 presidential elections, where Shandling announced—contrary to fact—that the democratic candidate Michael Dukakis had won the election against George H.W. Bush.

41) Jeffrey Sconce rightly sees this as a special quality of television vis-à-vis film: "What television lacks in spectacle and narrative constraints, it makes up for in depth and duration of character relations, diegetic expansion and audience investment." Sconce, *op. cit.*, p. 95.

42) With reference to the teen soap *Dawson's Creek*, Brooker speaks of an "overflow" of the text that he regards as typical of television and the culture of convergent media. Will Brooker, "Living on *Dawson's Creek*. Teen Viewers, Cultural Convergence, and Television Overflow," in *International Journal of Cultural Studies*, Vol. 4, Issue 4 (December 2001), pp. 456–472.

*Survivor*[43]—and through the fact that the protagonists' sphere of action is narrowly confined. The loss of spatial and temporal unity that afflicts *Lost* and its protagonists reflects the loss of narrative coherence that results from the transformations of what is still called "television" but has long ceased to be reducible to the apparatus and the set of institutions that were originally signified by that term. Television series such as *Lost* have by now come to be at home in a number of different media, and the narrative tends to be split up into ever more "modules." Therefore, narration constantly crosses spatial and media boundaries. At the same time, the various modules are more than just parts of a whole: they protrude one into the other and mutually complement and comment on each other. The spatio-medial dispersion of the televisual text not only calls into question the unity of narrative space but also the structured succession of events, which is normally determined by the narrative itself. Beyond what is provided by the "core text," the viewer enjoys a certain temporal and chronological autonomy in drawing on secondary and supplementary narrative modules.

The properly metaleptic character of this narrative modularization arises above all from the fact that a certain number of modules present the boundary between fiction and reality as permeable. Consider, for example, the alternate reality game (ARG) *The Lost Experience*, which was placed between the first and second season. The continuation of a narrative in a different medium is not unusual in the current media environment, and is not as such a metaleptic procedure. It becomes metaleptic when there is a spill-over from the narrative into material reality: there are websites for the Hanso Foundation and the Dharma Initiative; one can purchase a book by a fictional author who died in the crash of Oceanic flight 815 ("Bad Twin," a critical engagement with the doings of the Hanso Foundation); the Hanso Foundation placed advertisements in national newspapers disputing the contents of the book, to which there was in turn a public reaction by the publisher—and so on. Koch,[44] Brooker,[45] Johnson,[46] and others have documented these fluid metaleptical transgressions, the "overflow of television fiction into geographical reality,"[47] and have read them as indicators of a new aesthetics of television. Thus Johnson writes: "Ultimately, *Lost* strikes a unique relationship between fictional storytelling and 'reality'."[48] Yet from the perspective taken in the present essay, *Lost* also appears as an extension of metaleptic aesthetics. The aesthetics here take on a new quality, which renders it emblematic of the current state of the medium. Johnson points out that the removal of a fiction's boundaries is motivated above all by economic considerations:

"*Lost*'s attempts to spill its narrative institutions into the space of the everyday [...] are part of a much larger historical trajectory of dispersing the television world into other texts and experiential contexts. [...] *Lost* continues a historical trajectory of pervasive, divergent, hyper-diegetic textuality that allows narrative spaces to spill into the spaces of the everyday, but it does so in ways specifically adapted to a shifting television economy; an economy in which the economic viability of lavish narrative programming has come into question and opportunities for sponsor participation in the story world have become increasingly advantageous. [...] Ultimately, *Lost* represents the dissolution of boundaries between diegetic space and the space of consumption, allowing narrative, promotion and advertising to overlap."[49] But whatever the logic of production that gives rise to this development, its effects are certainly aesthetic ones.

In *Lost*, the metaleptic movement occurs not only as a spilling over of fiction into reality. *Lost* is typical of current television also in the specific way reality crosses into fiction.[50] The text, viewer and authors all participate in this. The mystery plot of *Lost* unfolds in a complex and allusive way that makes reference to numerous books, theories, real persons, etc. It encourages the viewer to step outside the fictional space and consult secondary sources to gather further information that is ostensibly needed (or at least useful) for a proper understanding of the story, and to then return to the fiction armed with those reality-based clues. In other words, *Lost* suggests a "forensic" mode of viewing,[51] focusing on every minute detail and comparing it with the information gathered from extra-fictional sources. The construction of the text and the mode of uptake on the part of the viewer establish a two-way metaleptic relation between fiction and reality. This metalepsis also has quite a material, technological aspect: when television shows are being watched from a DVD or as downloads on a computer screen, forensic viewing takes the form of metaleptic switches between different "screens" and "windows."[52] Just like the transgression of boundaries be-

43) Derek Johnson, "The Fictional Institutions of *Lost*. World Building, Reality and the Economic Possibilities of Narrative Divergence," in Roberta Pearson (ed.), *Reading Lost* (London/New York: I.B. Tauris, 2009), pp. 31–32.

44) Lars Koch, "Previously on *Lost*," in Sascha Seiler (ed.), *Was bisher geschah. Serielles Erzählen im zeitgenössischen amerikanischen Fernsehen* (Cologne: Schnitt, 2008), pp. 40–53.

45) Will Brooker, "Television Out of Time: Watching Cult Shows on Download," in Pearson, *op. cit.*, pp. 51–72.

46) Johnson, *op. cit.*

47) Brooker, *op. cit.*, p. 56.

48) Johnson, *op. cit.*, p. 31.

49) *Ibid.*, pp. 35–46.

50) Elsewhere I have described the mutual transgressions of fiction and reality by reference to political television series, without however drawing on the formal concept of metalepsis. Even though the entanglement of fiction and reality functions in several different ways in the series discussed there (*24*, *Battlestar Galactica*, *The West Wing*, *K-Street*, and *The Wire*), the removal of the boundaries of political space analyzed there can be placed in relation to the structural metalepsis of serial television that is my topic here. See Thomas Morsch, "Representation, Allegory, Ecstasy—Fantasies of the Political in Contemporary Television Series," in Christoph Dreher (ed.), *Auteur Series. The Re-invention of Television. Autorenserien. Die Neuerfindung des Fernsehens* (Stuttgart: Merz & Solitude, 2010), pp. 200–249.

51) See Brooker, *op. cit.*, pp. 61–70; Jason Mittell, "*Lost* in a Great Story: Evaluation in Narrative Television (and Television Studies)," in Pearson, *op. cit.*, pp. 128–30.

52) See on this M. J. Clarke: "[...] the ideal perspective to see these programs is a decentered one that keeps one eye on the on-air series itself and the other on a computer screen viewing an episode guide or a wiki entry, simultaneously juggling a wealth of minute visual details and character backstories, both explicitly shown and implicitly suggested." M.J. Clarke, "*Lost* and Mastermind Narration," in *Television & New Media*, Vol. 11, Issue 2 (March 2010), p. 126.

tween levels and worlds, the transgression of boundaries between screens and windows implies shifts between spaces of significance and between technologically, epistemologically and discursively distinct logics. Both the content and the conception of the show drive viewers from the "center," the broadcasted episodes, to the "peripheral" media where they seek additional and supplementary information that can easily turn into the main object of attention. The numerous secondary formats that *Lost* has generated in various media only add to this tendency.

A final point concerning the metaleptic aspects of *Lost* as well as of contemporary television culture leads us back to the historical origins of the concept of metalepsis: that is to say, to the phenomenon of authorial metalepsis in the rhetorical tradition, which served as the starting point for Genette's reflections. *Lost* is marked by a strong authorial presence, which manifests itself both in symbolic and literal ways. The show's mystery plot is primarily based on the device of hiding a series of clues within the narration that cannot be fully explained as elements of the fiction itself, but point to a diegetic level that tightly steers the flow of information available to the viewer. Occurrences of the mysterious numbers that seem to determine Hugo's existence are no more explicable by reference to the level of fiction than the appearance of an anagram for "flash forward" is on a sign for the "Hoffs-Drawler Funeral Parlor" in episode 2.23, where for the first time flashbacks give way to a flash-forward. The level of *discours* persistently proves more powerful than the level of *histoire*, a level at which the characters possess only very limited agency. An authorial entity noticeably interjects the fiction.[53] In a manner that is typical of metaleptic structures, here fiction is displayed as a dependent variable, determined by discourse. The presence of an authorial entity outside the fiction draws attention to the features of the narrative construction itself, which becomes an object of fascination in its own right. At this point my considerations regarding metalepsis meet with Jason Mittell's description of an "operational aesthetics," which he regards as characteristic of the particular form of narrative complexity found in serial narratives.[54] Explaining his own older thesis specifically with regard to *Lost*, he writes: "I argue that one of narrative complexity's chief pleasures is an 'operational aesthetic' that calls attention to how the machinery of storytelling works as an additional level of engagement beyond the story world itself. *Lost* is exemplary of this operational aesthetic at work—we watch the series not just as a window into a compelling fictional universe, but also to watch how the window itself works to distort or direct our line of vision. Watching a series like *Lost* demands dual attention to both the story and the narrative discourse that narrates the story, with particular pleasures offered exclusively at the level of a story's telling."[55]

The fact that it is precisely the most passionate fans that devote equal forensic interest to the story and the diegesis, confirms once more that immersive experience, suspense and an empathetic relation to the characters are not at odds with self- and meta-reflexive forms and with an analytical view of diegetic discourse.

What I have said so far concerns the perceptible presence, in the text, of an implicit author who represents a "diegetically ambiguous entity" that cannot be clearly placed either within or outside the world of the story.[56] But there is also a tendency in current televisual culture towards an increased presence of the extra-textual, real author. By this I mean not just the return of authorship in television: the growing significance of the writer-producer, the fact that the shows of quality television are marketed as "auteur series"[57] and that "auteurism" has come to infiltrate the imaginary and the self-descriptions of televisual production collectives.[58] The proliferation of author-centered paratexts on DVDs and of audio commentaries, interviews, and regular podcasts has given authors a tangible presence in the discourse of television. Not only in DVD features about the work process in the "writer's room," authorship has become a veritable public performance which reverberates in television culture. Especially with regard to the previously mentioned multiplication of formats and forms of expression within the serial universe, the author serves the important function of integrating and guaranteeing the coherence of the many heterogeneous elements.[59]

The horizon against which its viewers take up a series is partly formed by the communicative interventions of the author. By now there are designated lines of communication connecting authors and fans. Authors such as Joss Whedon, Ronald D. Moore, Carlton Cuse, and Damon Lindelof are known for following and reacting to fan communication on Internet forums, a practice that profits from the temporal proximity between production and reception that is characteristic of television. The production of television series follows a very rigid time schedule, with conception, writing process, shooting, and broadcasting following each other in close succession. This way, authors are in a position to react to criticism from the fan base within a reasonably short time frame.

In the case of *Lost*, the considerable public visibility of the authors was in part the result of

53) It is at least questionable whether one does justice to the special case of authorial presence in *Lost* by speaking, as Clarke does (following Wayne Booth), of an "implied author," as the implied author is part of *every* fiction. *Ibid.*, p. 128f.

54) See Jason Mittell, "Narrative Complexity in Contemporary American Television," in *The Velvet Light Trap*, no. 58 (Fall 2006), p. 35.

55) Mittell, 2009, "*Lost* in a Great Story," pp. 130–131. Mittell is right to cite the final episode of the third season, which suddenly allows us a glimpse into the future, as an example of such an operational aesthetics.

56) Clarke, *op. cit.*, p. 127.

57) Christoph Dreher (ed.), *Auteur Series. The Re-invention of Television*, *op. cit.*

58) See Denise Mann, "It's Not TV, It's Brand Management TV. The Collective Author(s) of the *Lost* Franchise," in Vicki Mayer, Miranda J. Banks and John T. Caldwell (eds.), *Production Studies. Cultural Studies of Media Industries* (New York/London: Routledge, 2009), p. 105.

59) A look at the parallel world of superhero comics, especially the *DC* universe, might show how important coherence, continuity, and unbroken sequences in a multi-format narrative are for both the producers and the fans. Thus the disappointment of many *Lost* fans about the lack of consequences that the events of the alternate reality game had for the following season.

a crisis of confidence. By the third season, the show was faced with doubts on the part of fans concerning the meaningfulness of the plot. An increasing number of fans were worried that the authors had no idea where the journey was headed, and that they were developing the series as they went along.[60] The authors responded by assuring that they were in fact executing an over-arching master plan. Against this background, the flash-forwards in the final show of the third season may be seen as a way for the authors to answer the criticisms directed at them. Here they appear to be anticipating the ending of the series by offering an answer to the question that had so far seemed to constitute the central question of the plot: will the survivors of Oceanic 815 succeed in leaving the island? Interpreted in this way, the flash-forwards are a clear authorial gesture by which the communication surrounding the series is taken up within the series. Thus, metalepsis has become a basic element of televisual discourse even at the pragmatic level of production.

The narratological device of metalepsis has served us as a guide for assembling a number of important examples and phenomena of serial television culture. The spatial and medial dispersion characteristic of current television turned out to be its signature feature, especially as contrasted with the closure of material and semantic space to which cinematic forms of expression were shown to aspire. Metaleptic figures, just like the operational aesthetics of television identified by Mittell, bring about a constitutive schizophrenia on the part of the viewer, an oscillation between heterogeneous perceptual levels and spaces of signification. This schizophrenia is something that cinema has quite literally dimmed out along with the light in the screening room. To avoid assimilating televisual reception to a pathological condition, one should perhaps speak of *modular* rather than of schizophrenic perception as having become typical of television. In contrast to cinematic perception, this novel form of perception can no longer be coherently described in relation to well-defined textual elements or in correspondence with a regimented *dispositif*. The authorial metalepsis that permeates the fictional worlds of television is in conflict, so to speak, with the unregulated metalepses of perception that result from the technological, temporal, spatial, and media-related splitting of fictional coherence.

Modular perception is not simply a quantitative multiplication of forms of experience across different media, but rather a qualitative transformation in the aesthetic experience of series. Narrative and non-narrative, intra- and extra-diegetical, textual and extra-textual, fictional and real aspects are blended together to yield synergetic effects that are not entirely predictable. Television cultivates a modular and transversal way of viewing for which metalepsis has become the standard mode of textual configuration and aesthetic expression. Just like the pleasurable addiction to which continuing series and their temporally unbounded fictions give rise to, the metaleptic movement between

60) See Clarke, *op. cit.*, p. 124.

different modules, levels, and worlds belongs to the specific forms of pleasure developed by television in contrast with cinema. These qualitative changes in reception become significant for the perception and experience of other media to the extent that television and television series acquire increasing aesthetic and economic importance within current media culture. Due to the growing relevance of serial and televisual forms of expression, the transformations of reception and experience witnessed in the field of television series also bear on other media. What happens *in* the television series, *with* the television series and—in front of a television, computer or mobile phone—*in the face of* the television series is, in the long run, likely to affect the reception of other types of media as well.

*Translated by Felix Koch*

Gertrud Koch

# What Will Have Been Film, what Theater?

*On the Presence of Moving Images in Theater*

Arguments about the affinities and differences between film and theater have existed since the very beginning of film. What remains uncontested is that there is an eclectic relationship between film and the arts that is inscribed in its genealogy: painting, sculpture, music, stage design, novels, dramas, variety shows, dance, and song are all components that have been absorbed by film. Conversely, "the cinematic" as an aesthetic operation has become a stylistic component in other genres, for instance the novel. Along with the critique of essentialist positions that metaphysically affirm qualities as supra-historical entities, the question of media-specific particularities, or even of the status of the paragon of the arts, has been deemed obsolete. It has, however, been newly posed for film, for cinema, due to the technical shift within production that has called for a distinction between analogue and digital images. But even in less significant points, the question of the specificities of the various arts and their genres has arisen once again. Only now in the corrected version: The question "*What* is film (theater, music, etc.)?" becomes "*When* and *where* and *how* is film (theater, music, etc.)?" Film *is* onstage, quite obviously; on René Pollesch's stage, for instance, and Christoph Schlingensief used his films within his own theatrical productions, just to mention two prominent directors. What is important to me in the following is less about demonstrating that film and theater interweave, but more about developing criteria, by means of a few examples, of how this interweaving is achieved and how it changes our aesthetic perception in the process; when live performances by actors/singers are synchronized with projected moving images.

For theater, the visual is tied to the scenographic. In antiquity and the Renaissance, scenography designated the process of creating perceptual spaces in a general sense, which were distinguished from the painting of illusion: "It is significant that the earliest Terence illustration that shows a street scene with foreshortened 'mansions' can be found in the Venice 1545 folio and that the part of Serlio's *Architettura* which deals with perspective in the theater was printed during the same year. However, it must be remembered that 'décor en perspective' appeared elsewhere at a considerably earlier date and that the first occurrence of these Vitruvian antecedents is generally considered to be the staging of Ariosto's *Cassaria* in 1508, although at that time the illusion in depth was created through a backdrop painting of a receding landscape and not by means of a constructed scenery which allowed the performance to take place 'in it' and not merely in front of it. This is of course rudimentary information in any sound history of Italian scenography, as would be a standard account of the contribution of such scenic artists and architects as Serlio, Palladio, and Peruzzi."[1]

Coming from this tradition, then, scenography is meant to produce spatial representation. In scenography the location of a scene is developed as the location of an action, with exits and entrances, as *stage design*. Scenography functions as a kind of architectural choreography. In a certain speculative way, one could perhaps say that scenography developed these aesthetic operations that create an environment for an actors' actions: a sculptural object that enables a pictorial framing of events in the plot and denotes space. Scenography ties the acting onstage to pictorial ideas of the world in which it plays. Like props and costumes, it creates the tangible for a merely imagined, acted world. The space of the stage thus closes into a space of illusion. In certain dramas, the play is divided into acts, as sections, as scenes; in some they are described as a tableau. Even the terminology refers to the connection between an event in the plot and a pictorial realization of the world in which it is found. In this spatial pictorializing of a world of temporally subdivided actions, the hearing and seeing of the actor becomes concentrated into *one* world. The perception of this event is set up in many modes: I hear the footsteps behind the door, I am afraid along with the actor, etc. A complex correlation between text and image occurs, and it is here that we begin to sense a first, faint analogy to film. Admittedly, in film the relationship is reversed. Scenography can be thoroughly saturated in reality by landscape shots, for instance, or in an urban canyon in New York, and in its material presence it can fuse the actor of the performance into the fictional closing of an "automatic world projection" (Cavell).

Film introduces a technically produced illusion as a medium of fiction, which isolates the spectators both temporally (the event has already occurred) and spatially (the spectators are not at the shooting *location,* but see a technically produced image of something that happened in their absence). It is this twofold distance that makes it possible for the spectators to immerse themselves in the represented world, a world that lies beyond their own possibility for agency.

The difference, which is supposed to make all the difference between theater and film, is, according to the thesis shared by most people, that theater is acted out in a spatio-temporal copresence between the actors/singers, etc., and the spectators. Film, on the other hand, like all technically conveyed media, does require a copresence of performance and spectators, but is not a play; the live action that was played out in front of the camera is the past and can no longer be the present. The theatrical plays establish an interaction between actors and spectators, while film relies on a mechanical projection as the condition of its performance. This reliance lacks freedom of interaction, precisely

1) Bodo L. O. Richter, "Recent Studies in Renaissance Scenography," in *Renaissance News*, Vol. 19, Issúe 4 (Winter 1966), pp. 346–347.

because it is only an inanimate technical event, and thus is void of that very dimension of critical distance that makes theater a medium of the tragic for Christoph Menke. In the conditions of its performance, a theatrical play keeps to an Aristotelian unity of space and time by integrating the spectator into the space and course of the play. On the other hand, as the argument goes, film should not be misunderstood as real presence. Rather, and here I quote Christoph Menke, film is "the medium of an elevated, intensified presence, which comes to be in the undifferentiated melding of actor and person, of who is performing and who is being performed."[2] What is lacking here is the ironic distance between a play and a non-play, between showing and doing, which defines tragedy as a play; the tragic is shown as an involved, dependent practice, but in a play it is independent of its own requirements. Thus the seemingly paradoxical logic arises that the playing of tragedy, its performance, refers the tragic to a practice other than its own, and is therefore not tragic in and of itself; instead it becomes aesthetic. Tragedy is the aesthetic sublation of the tragic in a play. Inasmuch as film is not a play in the execution of real time, and is therefore lacking the performative freedom that becomes the condition of resonating tragedy, film becomes a medium of fiction, which can simultaneously do both more and less than theater.

At this point we must ask where the immanent procedural logic lies, which continually produces more and more theatrical productions that explore the difference between film and theater in complex exchanges between spatial and temporal modes. The question is then: "What does film become when it appears in the space of theater?" or "Does theater create its own cinema, and if so what kind?" The answer will presumably be different based on the vantage point from which the question is asked: cinema or theater. For doubtlessly there are also efforts within cinema that are steeped in admiration of theater, and have made it a central location of cinema. There are innumerable films set in theatrical milieus or that have stage actors as their protagonists: for instance, the many backstage musicals such as *42nd Street* (Lloyd Bacon, USA, 1933), melodramas like *All about Eve* (Joseph L. Mankiewicz, USA, 1950) or *Todo sobre mi madre* (Pedro Almodóvar, Spain, 1999), or films such as Alain Resnais's *Smoking/No Smoking* (France, 2003) and comedies like *To Be or Not to Be* (Ernst Lubitsch, USA, 1942), etc. Many of the films that implement a theatrical stage within a film narrative can be understood as attempts to present the fascination of theater using exactly the premise described at the beginning; that of a play in real time before physically present spectators; a play, however, that usually turns away from the stage and becomes a play of things which occur differently than in the theater. In a lucid lecture, Miriam Hansen has drawn our attention to the opening sequence of Max Ophuls's *Liebelei* (1932) in the Vienna Opera House, in which the technical media of transmission used in the plot meld with the performance of Mozart's *Entführung aus dem Serail* on the stage, and thus two levels of "play" come into effect.[3] The technical reverse of the opera is also the playing field for the Marx Brothers in *A Night at the Opera* (Sam Wood, USA, 1935), in which the plot of Verdi's *Il trovatore* is artfully braided together with the threads of what's going on backstage, until something happens that one must imagine, along with Stanley Cavell, as "[using] the power of film to achieve the happy ending in which the right tenor gets the part, the film concluding triumphantly with the opera's most famous, ecstatically melancholy duet."[4] In the end, then, there is a *happy ending*; the triumph of the film reconstructs the opera. The performance of the opera becomes the happy ending of the film. It was a privilege for cinema to link up with other, older art forms according to the motto: "Bella gerant alii, tu felix Austria nube. Nam quae Mars aliis, dat tibi diva Venus."[5] The competition of the arts, a rivalry that runs through philosophy and art theory since Plato, seems to be reconciled in the medium of film. Film and cinema eclectically incorporate older media, much like the *Gesamtkunstwerk*, which originated at the same time.

Conversely, the question arises about what has become of film and cinema in view of exogamy, for quite obviously it is not only the technical equipment that has left its imprint everywhere. It can hardly be overlooked that above all, theater has co-opted the technically produced moving image. For this reason, in the following, I am initially concerned with explaining *how* film is found onstage. I will draw on suggestive productions that originated, or at least have also been performed on Berlin stages, without making any claim to have an overview of the entire scene of recent theater. I will therefore restrict myself to four productions from spoken and musical theater, by means of which I wish to show how and whether new constellations have arisen from the perspective of the moving image, which redefine both theatrical and cinematic space, and which alter the temporality of both.

### I. CHRISTOPH SCHLINGENSIEF, *JOAN OF ARC—SCENES FROM THE LIFE OF ST. JOAN*

In Christoph Schlingensief's staging of Braunfels's opera *Joan*, he draws on films that he shot previously in India.[6] Projected partly on transparent scrims, and partly on the bodies onstage,

2) Christoph Menke, *Die Gegenwart der Tragödie* (Frankfurt am Main: Suhrkamp, 2007), p. 126.

3) Miriam Hansen, "Max Ophuls and Instant Messaging: Reframing Cinema and Publicness," Perspectives on the Public Sphere: Cinematic Configurations of "I" and "We" (Conference) Berlin, 23–25 April 2009; published in this volume.

4) Stanley Cavell, "Nothing Goes without Saying: Reading the Marx Brothers," in *Cavell on Film* (Albany: State University of New York Press, 2005), p. 186.

5) "Blest Austria, though others war, for thee the marriage vow. Through Mars let others hold their realm, by Venus's favour thou." Thus was the dynamic marriage politics of the Habsburgs characterized in a bon mot that draws on a myth from Ovid.

6) The premiere of Schlingensief's staging of the opera *Jeanne D'Arc – Szenen aus dem Leben der Heiligen Johanna*, which Walter Braunfels had composed in 1938–1942, was held at Berlin's Deutsche Oper on April 27, 2008. Due to Schlingensief's illness, it was partly prepared by his team in close consultation with the director. Text and music by Walter Braunfels, based on the trial records. Musical direction: Ulf Schirmer; idea, conception: Christoph Schlingensief; staging: directorial team, based on notes by Christoph Schlingensief. With Marry Mills (Johanna), Morten Frank Larsen (Gilles de Rais), Lenus Carlson (Herzog de la Trémouille), and others.

they demand constant attention, not only because the moving images attract the eye, but because the people in the film are staring out into the audience. This is "appealing" in a certain sense in that these gazes overlay the bodily presence of the singers onstage. The oversized close-ups of the stark stares of unknown persons in the opera house refer to a world in the off-space of the theatrical space, opening its fourth wall.

The presence of the absent thus leads to a heightened experience of something real—invading the space with the play. The cinematic illusion takes on an ambiguous role with its scenery and events, really proceeding over the course of the play, within the aesthetic illusion of the opera staging. The visual presence of the film overshadows the visibility of the theatrical space, which is nonetheless part of the staging. Quite obviously this is a case of two conflicting poetics that enter into a tense relationship. Both imply different forms of presence and absence, from which the intensity of the aesthetic experience accrues, the sensual and cognitive involvement of the spectator.

## II. HEINER GOEBBELS, *ERARITJARITJAKA: MUSEUM OF SENTENCES*

This perplexing and captivating example of an underlying interlocking of illusive effects and the aesthetics of theatrical presence is a work from the musical theater of Heiner Goebbels, *Eraritjaritjaka: Das Museum der Sätze* (2004).[7] The play is based on texts by Elias Canetti, which are recited by the actor André Wilms and accompanied onstage by the Mondriaan Quartet. The set plays with the model of a house, the front wall of which closes the stage off at the back, which is then used as a projection screen. Right from the beginning André Wilms is followed by a cameraman who pursues the actor as he is coming down from the stage, crossing the auditorium and the foyer and getting into a taxi, until finally he reaches and disappears behind an apartment door. Then we see him in the apartment preparing food, etc., watching television and pursuing other activities, reciting Canetti and accompanied by the music onstage. A clock in the kitchen jarringly shows the real time of the performance. Towards the end, the front wall of the house gains transparency and we see that the presumably distant apartment into which Wilms vanished is the rear side of the stage set. In the end, then, it becomes clear that the performance is based on the creation of an illusion, which causes the spectator to ponder, over the whole course of the performance, how the old Aristotelian dramaturgies of the unity of space and time were here simultaneously called into question and fulfilled: Was Wilms ever really gone, or instead always playing just behind the

7) *Eraritjaritjaka: Das Museum der Sätze*, premiere: Théâtre Vidy, Lausanne, Switzerland, April 20, 2004. Words by Elias Canetti. With André Wilms and the Mondriaan Quartet. Music by Shostakovich, Mossolov, Lobanoc, Scelsi, Bryars, Ravel, Crumb, Bach, and Goebbels. Composed and directed by Heiner Goebbels; stage and lighting design: Klaus Grünberg; costumes: Florence von Gerkan; live video: Bruno Deville; sound: Willi Bopp. Co-produced by Théâtre Vidy Lausanne with schauspielfrankfurt, Berliner Festspiele, T&M-Odeon Theater Paris. Materials on the production, including the libretto with the Canetti texts, can be found on Heiner Goebbels's website.

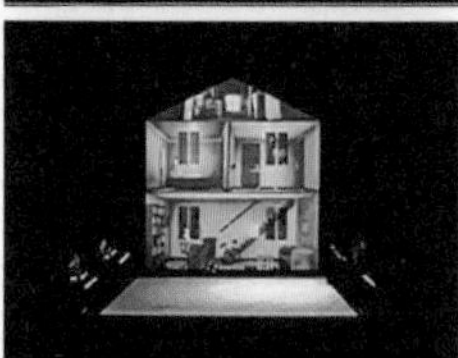

*Joan of Arc – Scenes from the Life of St. Joan*, composed by Walter Braunfels, directed by Christoph Schlingensief, Deutsche Oper Berlin, premiere April 27, 2008.

*Eraritjaritjaka: Museum of Sentences*, composed and directed by Heiner Goebbels, premiere: Théâtre Vidy, Lausanne, Switzerland, April 20, 2004.

wall? Was all this projected live onto the front wall (as the theater specialists believed), or was Wilms indeed not gone during the performance, and we saw a pre-recorded film to which the music merely played live synchronously (as the film specialists believed)? Do we see, then, what is there to see? At any rate it was impossible during the ongoing performance to be able to reconstruct exactly when each theatrical and / or cinematic illusion was produced and how; it was only clear that the aesthetic tension was produced by constructing an illusion, an illusion that lay in the production of a presence, which in one way or another was experienced as a semblance. By means of a video recording of one performance and a direct question to Heiner Goebbels, it was possible to clarify the puzzling appearance: It was an impenetrable interweaving of theatrical and cinematic illusion, which had combined the real time mode of theater and live projection with the completed production time of film. To achieve the fragility of the illusion, it was precisely the short video of Wilms's trip in the taxi through Berlin (or any other site of performance) that was prerecorded. While this was being projected, Wilms had the time to get back onstage from the foyer unnoticed, where he was then projected as he played from the set of an apartment in a direct projection on the front wall. In Aranda, the language of an aboriginal tribe in Australia, "Eraritjaritjaka" means something like "a great longing for what has been lost."

### III. RENÉ POLLESCH, *JFK*

The physical space of the theater has been turned into a movie theater.[8] On the screen, which completely covers the stage, we see the credits for the performance, followed by a cut to a close-up of a woman with a microphone, who appears as a reporter or an emcee or a guide / narrator in a puppet theater or a film narrator. While the camera pans back, the microphone and the actor holding it as a "soundman" become completely visible and the space of the stage is opened up. "J: I have very mysterious neighbors. Very often they stand around in front of doors holding a manuscript in their hands, as if they were about to go in, or they are lost in thought, they smoke another cigarette, they have every intention of leaving this place out of sheer impatience, holding a suitcase. I visit them sometimes. They stand before the threshold, seemingly hesitating, but this has nothing to do with me. Or they stand in front of one or the other open doors and suddenly a wall pops up where they actually assumed that I was."[9]

"As if they were about to go in" is the cue which sets the camera into motion. The camera is thus simultaneously introduced and confirmed as a medium of fiction ("as-if") and a shift is made, from staging direct address as a medium of theater into one of absorption. Now things are moving, the play, the piece, the film, now suddenly the fourth "wall" "pops up" in place of theatrical address; the camera takes over the function of the fourth wall, showing us the backstage area as a set from the living world, a space in which something happens.[10]

And furthermore, the camera shows us the "wall" as a real set. It immediately becomes a metaphor for the imaginary "fourth wall," which separates the world within a play on the stage from the audience. After about the first six minutes, the curtain, the surface of the live projection, is finally raised and the actor is now seen standing onstage. We see the set and the space of the stage. The interlocking of moving image, space of the stage, and space of speech/sound is worked out in great detail, and it is by no means easy to separate all the multimodal perceptions from one another. In the end, the space of the stage that we can see into is the space that is referentially projected onto the screen—and in a certain way the moving images here are offered up as variations on bodily proportions. There are bodies and faces of actors, which pop up now and then from the two-dimensional close-ups into physical, living figures over the entire one-hour duration of the performance. The scale of the actors' bodies underscores the play given that the stage and the screen are presented in various sizes. The large screen becomes smaller over time, but continues to show moving images from backstage at the upper edge of the stage, while the visible parts of the stage appear foreshortened by the stratification of the various backgrounds. Thus, taken as a whole, a dynamic of formats is developed that undermines any functional certainty in the sense of "whenever x happens, medium y is used" (for instance, drama=close-up, etc.).

#### IV. RENÉ POLLESCH, *THROW AWAY YOUR EGO*

In *Schmeiß Dein Ego weg* the "fourth wall" becomes an agent of the scenography.[11] The thematizing of theater and cinema as different modes of implementing the "fourth wall," which was latent in earlier works by Pollesch, is now developed into a discourse about the "old" theater and the wishes and needs that were associated with it; they are potentially still waiting behind the "fourth wall" for their entrance, for their embodiment. However, only the soul is projected where the bodies are, outside and inside are poles of irritation: "M: You know, Miss Peterson, we're blind, we can't see anything. I'll tell you a tale. You must have heard of the

8) *JFK* by René Pollesch. Directed by René Pollesch; set and costumes by Janina Audick; video by Marlene Denningmann; dramaturgy by Juliane Koepp. With Judith Hofmann, Felix Knopp and Katrin Wichmann. Thalia Theater, Hamburg, May 9, 2009; Deutsches Theater, Berlin, December 19, 2009.

9) Quoted from the manuscript of the text, distributed by Rowohlt Theater Verlag.

10) Here, I am consciously drawing on Michael Fried's terminology, who occasionally applies it to the difference between film and theater. While merely using his terminology does not replace an extended discussion of Fried's position, I am doing so in order to refer to a wider debate. See Fried, "Art and Objecthood," in *Art and Objecthood: Essays and Reviews* (Chicago: Chicago University Press, 1998), pp. 148–172.

11) *Schmeiß Dein Ego weg* by René Pollesch, premiere: Volksbühne, Berlin, January 12, 2011. Dir. René Pollesch. Set and costumes by Bert Neumann. Chor. direction by Christine Groß. Camera by Ute Schall. Lighting by Frank Novak. Dramaturgy by Aenne Quiñones. Perf. Margit Carstensen, Christine Groß, Martin Wuttke. Chor: Jeremias Acheampong, Tim Fabian Bartel, Sarah Gailer, Silvana Schneider, Irina Sulaver, Marlon Tarnow, Marcus Tesch, and Paula Thielecke.

fourth wall? I'm sure of it! It was something that didn't even exist up to a certain point in time. It was more of a term for something that didn't exist at all. People talked about something and called it the fourth wall, meaning that it actually didn't exist. Do you understand so far? Yes, I see you do. How nice. What can I compare it to? Something that doesn't exist, but that can oddly become a body… That's it! Maybe like the portrayal of souls in traditional painting."[12]

The "figure of speech" of the "fourth wall" is taken literally and embodied. When the spectator enters the auditorium, there is a wall visible onstage, which continues into the décor of the auditorium, sealing off the space where the curtain normally hides the stage from the audience. This blocked off space is broken up by a projection from the "inside" to the outside of the "fourth wall." Video is projected from backstage onto a surface resembling a bull's eye in art deco style or an old fashioned picture frame, until one of the panels of the "fourth wall" enters. At the same time, an actor appears through the stage corridor in a cloud of dust, which runs in front of the "fourth wall." The scenographic pattern is similar to many earlier works by Pollesch: the stage is divided horizontally by a wall that creates a backstage space, from which video is projected on screens that are placed at various spots in the auditorium or onstage. In front of the wall a narrow strip is kept free for entrances and the acting that occurs outside the backstage box. The box-like character of the backstage area is underscored when the whole space is projected from a bird's eye view onto the front side of the "fourth wall," and actors in white clothes perform the letters of the word "love" with their bodies on this rectangular image. Text, image, music, and video are an arabesque representation of the semantic machinery of theater, beyond the old mimesis of acting and nonetheless within the paradox of representation.

#### MORE OR LESS EVIDENT CONCLUSIONS

The four examples briefly sketched out here use film and video in different variations:

The *first* variation (example I) projects films that come entirely from the outside and were produced independent of the theatrical production. They are foreign bodies in the truest sense of the word, and their impressions are due entirely to their foreignness. The gazes that are directed into the opera house from the close-ups theatricalize the film precisely because they jump over the "fourth wall" of the stage and refer the audience to an utterly absent world. This world nonetheless has much more of a reality effect than the performance does, with which the film is not synchronized, neither in terms of time or space except of course that the projection is chronologically synced with the performance onstage. It is a model of simultaneous sequencing, inasmuch as both performances take place at the same time, but the modes of film and theater are sequentially contrasted with one another.

The *second* variation (example II) works with the difference between theater, film and video

12) Quoted from the manuscript of the text, distributed by Rowohlt Theater Verlag.

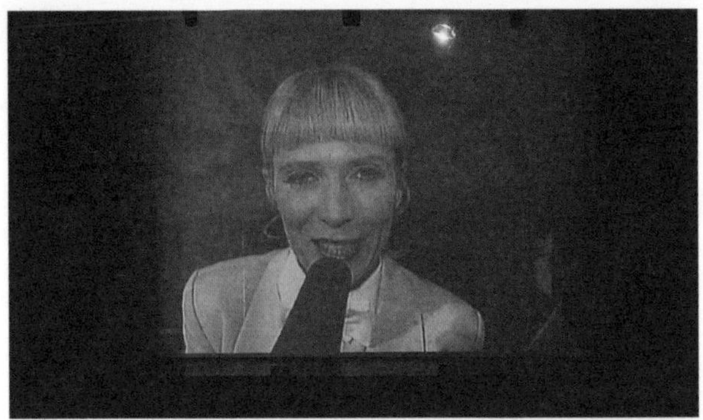

*JFK*, written and directed by René Pollesch, premiere: Thalia Theater, Hamburg, May 9, 2009.

*Throw Away Your Ego*, written and directed by René Pollesch, premiere: Volksbühne, Berlin, January 12, 2011.

projection in terms of a synthesized integration, which as a whole produces a meta-fiction in which the illusionary qualities of the three media are interwoven.

The *third* variation (examples III and IV) works within a spatial and temporal continuum, in which video projection and the space onstage are imagined as intersections of perspective. The video projection becomes a medium to convey the simultaneity of spaces, which are staged as merely withdrawn from perception, but not absent from it, either in space or time. They become viewing spaces, which, constituted from off-camera and on-camera, turn into image spaces. In this mode of projection, video becomes a scenographic spatial image, which also makes use of simple film-related forms such as the scale of bodily sections in close-ups, bird's eye perspective, etc. The stage thus becomes cinematic, as the crucial relationship between inside / outside, which is a central topos in many of Pollesch's works, shifts into a camera relation between on / off-screen. Therefore, a sequential mode of projected image space and the scenographic space of the stage is opened up.

What did theater lose to the movies or at the movies? Is it the "fourth wall," which is now reinserted onto the stage, and which proves to be the film screen, or the capacity of fictional illusion? Using the examples of contemporary theater, it can be shown that the aesthetic of illusion, as it is associated with film, is no antiquated technology of deception for the lower tiers of mass art. It rather shifts into the center of a poetics that refers to the experience of the dynamic qualities of the horizons of space and time. The video camera acts on its own, and is thus an agent in the sense of the old actors' theater; it takes part in a live performance which is based on the spatio-temporal co-presence of camera / man / woman with the actors onstage.

Therefore, the theater becomes much more than a simple extension of a venue for screening films—the poetics of film aesthetics intervene in the space of the theater and the live performances of video can also be understood, in the sense of Expanded Cinema, as an extension of film by which the dualism of theater and film is undermined.

*Translated by Daniel Hendrickson*

Simon Rothöhler

# Where Film Drops Off

*Michael Mann's High-Definition Images*

The question of what makes an image a film image—an object that belongs to the realm of cinema—has always been characterized by an inevitable superimposition of taxonomic operations and aesthetic distinctions. Following the profound multimedia diffusion of film, we are now facing a visual culture in which moving images from heterogeneous sources constantly blend with each other; they are routinely sampled, remixed, and given new communicative functions. This is exacerbated by the fact that cinema itself is working faster and faster to swallow up all kinds of related or competing images, implementing or translating them through film aesthetics. The intensified transfer among diverse audio-visual media has made it much more challenging, however, to determine the origins and classifications of technologically created moving images.

For this reason alone, the "special image," as Serge Daney dubbed it,[1] has multiplied and can now be called up in various media configurations. Even apart from the (primarily Internet-based) practices of appropriation, the film image today has several media identities; it has been dispersed to such an extent that it becomes increasingly implausible to define the institutionalized perceptual *dispositif* known as the cinema as its "home." "Cinema" is merely one of several modes of displaying the film image. With regard to reception and production aesthetics, the film image is, of course, involved in a continual process of exchange with all the other image-worlds that border it: it appears on strongly reflecting notebook displays and on smartphone screens smeared with fingerprints; it can be a huge picture beamed onto a home theater screen, but it has also become portable and is often just a mouse click away from other streams of visuals: it is merely one desktop window among several others. At the same time, it can, without further ado, pick up on Web aesthetics and on visual forms which, genealogically speaking, might have belonged to the worlds of television, video games, art, and so forth. It is in this context that Janet Harbord refers to the resulting crisis of definition of an academic discipline whose understanding of the moving image is constitutively bound up with an institutionalized film practice that caught on after the relatively non-standardized, 'multimedia' phase of early cinema: "Film scholarship has concerned itself with the identification of moments in which stability oc-

1) Quoted by Christa Blümlinger, "Ein Seismograph in der Landschaft der Bilder," in Serge Daney, *Von der Welt ins Bild. Augenzeugenberichte eines Cinephilen* (ed. and trans. Christa Blümlinger, Berlin: Vorwerk 8, 2000), p. 12.

curred, transformation slowed, and film was consolidated by the formalized rituals of the cinema."[2]

The diagnosis—that the formerly privileged film image belonging to the cinema has spread into a less differentiated zone (which Daney still wanted to distinguish by calling it "the visual")—is certainly applicable in many ways. For film studies it delineates several new areas of research: decoding the evolution of images during a phase of destabilization (as far as the nexus of cinema-screen-celluloid is concerned); analyzing the phenomenological aesthetic differences among various types of images; undertaking a comparative study of screens which would arrest the images at different points during their circulation, freezing them, as it were, in different aggregate media states. At the very least, however, film analysis under today's conditions has to be flagged as *dispositif*-specific—and not just when it is about overarching questions of reception theory, like Laura Mulvey's model of "delayed cinema."[3] Analyses that deal with material aspects can no longer avoid accounting for and reflecting upon the kind of media configuration of 'film' they refer to.

In contrast, large portions of the debate that has now arisen around "digital cinema" do not even bother to confront their fixation on ontological theorems with, for example, the specific difference between post-neo-realist DV documentaries and contemporary CGI practices. Film theoretical discussion of 'post-photographic' images still tends to be conducted in a rather lopsided manner, from the position of computer-generated "images ex nihilo"[4] (David Rodowick), while ignoring the existence of 'analog' precedents for many 'digital' practices (from photo-montage to retouching to the composite image) and other complex continuities.

Keeping these implications in mind, I would like to examine a specific phenomenon within the continuum of digital film aesthetics: the (digitally reproduced) high-resolution video image, which has been in use for some time now in the production of American mainstream cinema. During the past decade high-definition has asserted itself as a "digital capture" system in two main areas: pure special effects imagery (aside from fully computer-gen-

2) Janet Harbord, *The Evolution of Film: Rethinking Film Studies* (Cambridge, UK: Polity Press, 2007), p. 3.

3) Laura Mulvey, *Death 24x a Second: Stillness and the Moving Image* (London: Reaktion, 2006), pp. 144–196. For Mulvey, the new kinds of reception brought about by a 'progressive' digital media culture alter the ways in which the spectator experiences the hegemonial time of the film diegesis through an individual *time shifting*, liberating the "cinematic punctum" and leading, in general, to the expansion of the position of the "pensive spectator." Here, Mary Ann Doane has justly offered an objection, not only because Mulvey's "delayed cinema" somewhat prematurely establishes, at long last, the feminization of audiences and separates the new forms of filmic stasis from the coordinates of sexual difference. Doane points out that the individualization of film experiences through portable, flexible media technologies definitely converges with the "new spirit of capitalism" as decribed by Boltanski/Chiapello: "The acceleration and propagation of individualized ways of consuming images coincides with historically specific changes in commodity capitalism. [...] Commodification no longer strives to produce homogeneity—in its objects and consumers—but thrives on heterogeneity." Mary Ann Doane, "Review: Death 24x a Second: Stillness and the Moving Image," in *Screen*, Vol. 48, issue 1 (Spring 2007), p. 117.

4) D. N. Rodowick, *The Virtual Life of Film* (Cambridge: Harvard University Press, 2007), p. 104.

*Public Enemies* (2009, Michael Mann)

erated sequences, we may think of the high-speed photography in films such as *Inception* [2010, cinematographer: Wally Pfister] or *Sherlock Holmes* [2009, cinematographer: Philippe Rousselot]; in both cases, Panavision's Phantom HD camera was used) and as a means of making video look like 35mm film (for instance, in aesthetically rather unremarkable comedies such as *Click* [2006], *Superbad* [2007], or *Grown Ups* [2010]—all shot entirely with a Panavision Genesis camera). Philip Rosen has referred to the latter practice as a "digital mimicry" of the "photographic" tradition of film.[5]

In the high-budget segment of the American film industry, however, some authorial positions can be discerned which engage more specifically with the aesthetic difference of high-definition. Along with Steven Soderbergh (*Che: Part One / Che: Part Two* [2008], *The Informant* [2009]) and David Fincher (*Zodiac* [2007], *The Social Network* [2010]), Michael Mann is the preeminent figure in this context. Mann has worked with two directors of photography (Dion Beebe, Dante Spinotti) and two HD systems (Thompson Viper, Sony CineAlta) to produce three films (*Collateral* [2004], *Miami Vice* [2006], and *Public Enemies* [2009]) which open up the most aesthetically complex experimental field. In the following, I wish to address these three works in order to make some observations on the HD image as a "special case" in digital film aesthetics.

### I. IN THESE SHADOWS: HD AS NIGHT IMAGE

Working with cinematographer Emmanuel Lubezki, Michael Mann began using an HD camera for the introductory sequences of his biopic *Ali* (2001) and also employed it in the CBS series he produced, *Robbery Homicide Division* (2002). His first work to be entirely organized around the high-resolution video aesthetic, however, is *Collateral*, an urban thriller that takes place at night and in which Los Angeles literally plays itself. The storyline revolves around a series of contract killings—a pretense for moving through an urban landscape after dark, which is the actual protagonist of the film. The unity of time and space is condensed into the course of one night. The film ends in gray, at dawn, when the city extracts the killer from itself by means of a public transit vehicle, driving him, as it were, to a well-deserved death.

With its enormous depth of field, high-definition is the technology of choice for the nighttime outdoor photography in *Collateral*: filmed on location with as little artificial lighting as possible, these sequences trace the polymorphous experience of light in Los Angeles. Most of the interiors, however, were shot on 35mm film with a Panavision Millenium camera—although it was only used for interiors that were not 'exteriors in disguise,' i.e. scenes in which the illuminated night projects deeply into the interior (in the taxi, or the palatial glass office building at the end of the film). The nighttime images were recorded on two different cameras, a ViperFilmStream by Thompson and a Sony CineAlta. The latter had not been fully developed at the time the film was shot and was mainly used to show the moving taxi from the outside. In the passages where *Collateral* reverts to 35mm—the club sequence, for instance, where tests had shown that the saturation effects of blacklight were difficult to manage—the film material was altered in post-production to approximate the HD look as closely as possible, especially with regard to the economy of contrast in the images. Within certain boundaries, therefore, there are ways for celluloid to mimic digital film; remediation is not a one-way street, as Bolter/Grusin demonstrated, with reference to the "desktop" aesthetics of contemporary newspaper layouts.[6]

As a night image, the highly light-sensitive or light-receptive HD image develops almost encyclopedic traits; as an expanded, hyper-photographic device for storing light, it collects numerous forms and colors of artificial, urban illumination: rays of headlights and streetlights, neon signs, spotlights, public and private lighting systems—all captured and dispersed into the California coastal fog caused by cold water streams in the Pacific, mainly on summer nights. But it is not only from the viewpoint of climate that nighttime L.A. appears to be filmed more specifically than ever before. Mann and Beebe present the city as if it were an organism that awakens at twilight and burns out in the wee hours of the morning.

The fact that *Collateral* seems to glide into and out of the night in a uniquely organic manner is a direct consequence of Mann's radical decision to forego a different sort of artificial light: film light, i.e. the directional lighting used on a set. For the exteriors in particular, the director's motto was, "Make the fill light the key light." Whenever the main characters, played by Tom Cruise and Jamie Foxx, interact with the outside urban space, there is no directional light; the visual space is structured by found, pro-filmic sources of light. Thus, the stars' bodies remain visible, but often as a secondary attraction, because, despite the de-saturation during post-production, a multimedia, color-drenched spectacle of light takes place all around them.[7]

Apart from the controlled 'explosions of color,' it is the precision of details and a new depth of focus that take the HD image beyond

5) See Philip Rosen, *Change Mummified. Cinema, Historicity, Theory* (Minneapolis: University of Minnesota Press, 2001), pp. 301–350. From today's vantage point, it is hard to dispute the notion that the perfect mimicry of photo-realistic conventions constitutes the actual purpose of "digital film." But it is also possible to understand the current photographic restrictions on digital images as a provisional, intermediary state of remediation, in the sense of the media evolution theory proposed by Bolter and Grusin. See Jay David Bolter, Richard Grusin, *Remediation: Understanding New Media* (Cambridge: MIT Press, 1999).

6) See Bolter and Grusin, *op. cit*, p. 49.

7) This does not apply to the taxi interiors, according to Paul Cameron, who replaced Dion Beebe after three weeks of shooting (because of Beebe's "creative differences" with Michael Mann): "We'd light beautiful night exteriors that looked amazing and natural and had so much detail, but when we went in for the close-ups, we had to overlight the actors to reduce the noise on their faces. On the monitor, it looked horrible and incredibly overlit. […] It was a constant battle between what looked good on set and what would look good at the film-out every weekend." Quoted by Bryant Frazer, "How DP Dion Beebe adapted to HD for Michael Mann's *Collateral*," in *Film & Video*, August 2004 (www.studiodaily.com/filmandvideo/searchlist/How-DP-Dion-Beebe-adapted-to-HD-for-Michael-Manns-Collateral_4680.html).

the photo-realist standards of visibility in film. Full of contrast and variety, palm trees are silhouetted in front of a nuanced, dark gray and purple night sky. In the areas where 35mm registers a deep, rich black, HD reveals a world full of different shapes and shadows. "These cameras have an enormous range at the very low end of the sensitivity curve. At the bottom end of the curve, where film drops off or picks up a lot of grain, these cameras sort of kick in."[8]

As in Abbas Kiarostami's *Ten* (2002), for instance, the city in *Collateral* is consistently portrayed from the perspective of the automobile. The movement of the taxi motivates a montage of urban visuals, weaving together the space in terms of genre dramaturgy and aesthetics. Unlike *Ten*, however, *Collateral* is not so much about driving by and collecting particular public spheres; it does not build up any sort of social space, but instead uses video cinematography to create spatialized light sculptures. The HD image of Los Angeles is not 'true to life' or 'congruous'; rather, the city is revealed as an aesthetic presence. Even the water-spotted windshield of the taxi produces its own visual pattern of attraction—as viewed from within the car, it is like a sheet of graphic design, adding texture to the sea of (neon) lights outside. Occasionally, a kind of reversible figure emerges: HD's enormous depth of field, celebrated in numerous shots that gauge the canyon-like streets, can also turn into a flat plane, 'sucking' the city onto the dirty windshield and re-scaling the cinematic space to the intimate, chamber-sized dimensions of a taxi / container.

~

*Miami Vice,* an adaptation of the 1980s television series of the same name, is also based on images captured by the Thompson Viper. In many respects, it is a further escalation of HD visuals. The film elaborates on the centrifugal effect of the HD image: its increased responsiveness to the unique aesthetic logic of disparate, profilmic light sources, and its artificial translation of nighttime gray zones. Two years after *Collateral*, Mann finally allows Beebe to let the video image 'get out of hand,' deliberately driving it to extremes of color, contrast, and texture—by using deep focus sequences in broad daylight, for example, or by exposing visual noise effects during night shots (almost programmatically so in the first sequence, on the high rise) which implicitly refer to the lack of grain in digital images, their lack of photo-chemical 'mobility' and 'warmth.' Here, the comparably compact, localized, and aesthetically coherent image of L. A. at night in *Collateral* gives way to a heterogeneous flush of HD images, changing as seamlessly from the tropical, fluorescent nighttime views of Biscayne Bay to the spectacle of light and color that is Ciudad del Este to the sedate surfaces of Geneva's financial district, as it does between the visual technologies and screens that often fill the frame: mobile telephone displays, speedboat speedometers, radar, night vision goggles, surveillance monitors.

*Miami Vice* almost never calms down; it contains almost no aesthetic or narrative gestures that are not broken off, suspended by a fast, contingent cut or by linkages that do not seem

8) Dion Beebe, *ibid.*

to be rooted in the dramatic or narrative logic. In accordance with the genre, the high-speed editing attaches itself to high-tech vehicles, coupling fast boats with convertible sports cars, Lear jets with helicopters, while the continually new HD image, always moving in a different direction, burgeons out in abrupt amplitude. The direct dynamic of the action genre—the movement of an undercover operation, the criminal investigation in the image and *via the image*—dissolves into kinetic particles, pausing only for brief moments to generate an identifiable vector. In HD, it is difficult to focus or direct a film's kinetic energy (the product of movement in the image, camera movement, and editing rhythm), because these kinds of images are specifically responsive to detail, creating autonomous visual islands which draw attention to themselves and tend to resist motion. Again and again, the viewer's gaze gets stuck on high-resolution marginalia and is torn away from the visual movement or from narrative engagement.

In *Miami Vice*, this logic of aesthetic disintegration, which takes place on various levels, is *structural*—mainly because Mann and Beebe do not take advantage of homogenizing post-production options, as they did in *Collateral*. Instead, they emphasize the dissonances, the moment of dispersion. (The decidedly low-tech, anti-baroque realism of the sound design, characterized by the material effects of various communication media and by the flat, echoing aesthetic of the shoot-out sequences, plays a similar role—but this is a different matter.)

~

Under 'post-cinematographic' conditions, the HD image also has various media identities. While no one would contest the fact that, as Hollywood movies, *Collateral* and *Miami Vice* are works of cinema, their specific high-definition aesthetic did not actually appear there, or only in the vestigial form of 'celluloid mimicry,' since neither film was projected digitally (for purely pragmatic, distribution-related reasons, 35mm prints had to be shown—most cinemas were not yet equipped for digital projection). Apart from highlighting the fact that "digital cinema" is not just a production category, this also points toward an epistemological problem in film studies: visual analyses need to be geared to the specific media in question and can no longer tacitly assign the role of the privileged image to projected 35mm film (thus implying that all other identities of the image are derivative). The specifics of the HD images discussed in this article can actually only be seen in a completely digital reception mode; for instance, if a Blu-ray disc is used in combination with a 'Full-HD' screen or projector (producing a resolution of 1920 pixels wide by 1080 high) within a home theater setting or when a 'traditional' cinema screening is based on the 2K format (similar to 1080p) or the enhanced 4K format (4096 × 2160 pixels). When considering Michael Mann's HD films, the phenomenological differences between something like 35mm film-out and a digital projection are so significant that, basically, we are talking about two different images.

During production of *Collateral* and *Miami Vice,* the final transfer back to film (for the purpose of creating the 35mm release prints) was anticipated by a digital projector that Mann and Beebe had re-configured to simulate the lower-contrast, but 'warmer' texture of celluloid. The relative instability of today's image-objects and the question of the 'valid' image become even more interesting, if we remember that HD-compliant hardware also produces its own unique effects. The equipment that makes up the standard 'home theater' of today (a HD screen and a 1080p player) tends to play back any sort of image, regardless of how it was captured, in a visual mode specific to HD. This means that the best-scanned Blu-ray of a Murnau film (or an upscaled DVD) seems far more 'de-celluloided' than any previous media transfers (such as film to TV). Most HD projectors and screens, therefore, offer a "cinema mode" playback option, a set-up which softens the contours of the digital image (often regarded as too 'cold') and suspends the 'hyperrealism' of HD. This soft focus, a backward operation from the perspective of the media historian, is an example of 'digital mimicry,' simulating the visual norms of the old cinematic medium which the conventions of film perception still insist upon.

### II. PERIOD PICTURE: HISTORY IN HIGH RESOLUTION

In a certain way, *Miami Vice* accentuates the specificity of the HD image as a 'post-classical' one, adding its centrifugal force to the list of options for blockbuster cinema and demonstrating, instance by instance, how the most capital-intensive filmic practice can be accelerated, fragmented, and de-semanticized via digital aesthetics. At first glance, *Public Enemies* seems to revert to the classic format, without any sort of deconstructive impetus. The period picture replaces the digitally 'perforated' action mode; the intensified night-image gives way to the construction of a high-resolution representation of history. At its heart, the film's historical subject is the Depression era and the dawning of a police state in the 1930s, when the FBI was constituted by instrumentalizing and promoting the story of John Dillinger and other fabricated 'public enemies' in order to convince the American people of the need to expand the authority of this federal institution.[9] But it is precisely the confrontation between the HD image and the aesthetically conservative parameters of the classic period picture with its "annexation of the past" (Kracauer)[10] which makes *Public Enemies* a complex film—not just with, but also *about*, this 'new' image.

For their frayed, melancholic epic about a serial killer, *Zodiac,* David Fincher and his cinematographer, Harris Savides, had already used the Thompson Viper to capture images that would create a historical diegesis. In the process, however, they systematically moved HD in the direction of 'film,' underplaying the specifics of high-resolution visual spaces and textures. "Should a movie look like film or like something else? It's subjective. The Viper does give the images an almost hyper-real quality that might work for this particular film. However, I also tried to go against that look a bit because *Zodiac* is a period film, and the audience has some impression of what [the 1970s] looked like. The colors, tones, and designs of that period—as documented in the photography of

Stephen Shore and William Eggleston—became our bible. [...] But if you have a synthetic image like the Viper's—which reminds me a bit of the vivid, colorful look of a cibachrome photo—you're taken right out of the story. I wanted to give the image a patina, to remove the newness."[11] Inasmuch as it is digitally reproduced, the 'newness' in *Zodiac*, despite all efforts to attain a 'historical' look, is still evident—in the night scenes, for instance, but primarily in the depth of field and sharpness of detail whenever the offices of the *San Francisco Chronicle* come into play (for the historically meticulous set designer, even the pen on a distant desk could become a problem).

*Public Enemies* is diametrically opposed to *Zodiac* in terms of aesthetics; even though it was put together with comparable HD technology (a Sony camera, the F23, instead of the Viper), it does not strive for the patina of film as a visual seal of reassurance and historicism. Savides's statement leads us to believe that he and Fincher reverted mainly to those signifiers which, from the perspective of media history, have become the hegemonic representatives of the era in question: signs that are perpetuated as such in every instance of their iteration, even an ever so delicate one; precisely because of this, they trigger immediate recognition and can be combined to achieve a representative "look."

~

The HD images in *Public Enemies* are full of period detail, researched and assembled with all the accuracy of a high-end production: 'history' reconstructed via carefully prepared, 'authentic' locations, costumes, hats, matchboxes, shoelaces, paving stones, street lamps, shop signs, and other elements of set design. The hand-held camera frequently captures these elements in extreme close-ups, using abrupt pans and zooms. Dynamic, restless, driven, it traverses the sets, sweeping across the period details instead of exhibiting them in measured long takes. On this level, Mann and Dante Spinotti consistently dispense with the common vocabulary of the period picture, which normally allows the viewer's gaze to rest on the 'historical items'—the capital invested in their reconstruction.[12] Instead, we get a 'nervous' aesthetic involving the permanent scanning of material: very close to the textures, the fabrics, but with a sense of distant tangibility; rushing forward momentarily, but not evoking the stable tableaus and haptic sense of 'period,' a past feel-good space.

The primary effect of this type of historical HD image is its tendency to override the repre-

9) The film is based on Bryan Burrough's *Public Enemies: America's Greatest Crime Wave and the Birth of the FBI, 1933–34* (New York: Penguin Press, 2004).

10) Siegfried Kracauer, *Theorie des Films* (Frankfurt am Main: Suhrkamp, 2005), p. 138.

11) Harris Savides, quoted in David E. Williams, "Harris Savides, ASC, and Director David Fincher Plumb the Depths of Human Obsession with *Zodiac*," in *American Cinematographer*, April 2007 (www.theasc.com/ac_magazine/April2007/Zodiac).

12) Here, Philip Rosen maintains that the logic of reception of film referentiality in general is built upon the exposure to/perception of diegetic details, especially when it comes to historical films that establish and insure their version of the past by specifically "rationali[zing] [...] the detail." See Rosen, *op.cit.*, pp. 147–200.

sentational conventions of film (i.e., any kind of semiotic shorthand that would signify 'the 1930s' or the 'Depression' or simply 'back then'). The hyperrealist aesthetic pushes the veil of 'filmic' patina aside; its evocation of presence (an often noted aspect of the HD image) translates into an expressly 'anti-historic' manner of evoking the past, turning it into a presence past. Precisely because of its distance from the dominant media coding for this past, *Public Enemies* is, as a historical representation, remarkably unstable and provisional. Digital reception can provide an irritating experience of presentness, enabling the audience to intuitively sense what these old-fashioned cars, steam locomotives, and rough tweed fabrics would have felt like when they were ultra-modern and contemporary, that is, the high-tech and high fashion objects of their time. In part, this intense sort of contemporary sensation is surely also a product of sheer 'newness,' of the encounter with a high-resolution cinematic image whose properties—the 'non-filmic' sharpness, for instance—are mostly known from the screens installed in art museums, as in the latest HD works by Omer Fast and other artists.

Aesthetically speaking, the HD image is not without risk for the genre of period pictures. On the one hand, because the routine use of time-capsule images (such as William Eggleston's photographs) is constantly disautomatized and on the other, because the digital expansion of the visible zone threatens to break the hermetic seal of the fictional narrative space. To put it in very pragmatic production terms, a newly visible background detail that is not a period detail can stand in opposition to the historical claims made by the diegesis (cars from the wrong period, or an undisguised streetlight intruding on the picture). There is also the possibility that a specific 'insistence of the profilmic' may become manifest. It seems to be harder for the HD image to endow the given or constructed world of objects with fictional meaning, to deliberately format them so that they perform their diegetic duties. The audience sees a great many things far too precisely, just 'as they are' (or is not yet used to seeing certain phenomena with such utmost clarity, such as the pores of an actor's skin) that it cannot but feel it is witnessing a kind of re-enactment, a play that actors clad in historical costumes are putting on for the camera. Accordingly, the tense relationships between the image and the world become all the more obvious in a genre that is required to lend a stable historical signature to the profilmic givens.

It is primarily during the finale of *Public Enemies* that attention explicitly shifts to the status of different kinds of images. *Miami Vice* had shown a lot of interest in meta-forms and self-referentiality, albeit in a much more 'postmodern' manner—as a subtle discourse on the proliferation of digital imaging technologies and the multiplication of screens and displays. The film's self-reflexive nature is evident in the way it highlights the instrumental functions of technologically created images and their ubiquitous presence in practices of surveillance and deception. In *Miami Vice*, they are part and parcel of a game of intelligence and counter-intelligence that sets out to follow the virtual movements of money and the actual movements of illicit drugs—an effort that must ultimately fail since such images, it seems, can never be more than the visual simulation of transparency. In this sense, *Miami Vice* can be seen as a war film that relies on global capitalism's visual weapons, such as Jesus Montoya's Bloomberg TV routine or the picture puzzle screen casino run by his paranoid underling Yero. And even the AWACS technology that is omnipresent not just in the war on drugs is duped when two Lear jets are flown so closely together that they appear as a single object on entering the radar screen.

Near the end of *Public Enemies*, there is an almost 'mental' sequence: John Dillinger on a summer afternoon, flooded by sunlight, strolling through a Chicago police station—right under the noses of the police. Here, *Public Enemies* and *Miami Vice* share for a moment an understanding of the image-as-instrument, to the extent that the logic of police surveillance and identification is associated with practices of eidetic fixation. Elegant and barely camouflaged, Public Enemy Number One moves through the offices of a special commission named after him, but none of the officers notices the primary object, as if he were a ghost. He saunters past—and looks at—the walls of the investigation bureau which are covered with photographs of many other public enemies. The photos don't need to be stamped "deceased" in order to be immediately interpreted as pictures of the dead. The fact that the police cannot identify Dillinger—who is, at this moment, quite literally, a *dead man walking*—has less to do with the baseball game they are avidly following on the radio than with the fact that they have, for years, pursued a media fabrication, a strategically launched 'icon': the relatively unreferenced image of a phantom.

Dillinger's encounter with himself as a police photo culminates in a change of perspective (with a built-in foreshadowing of death)—one medium's view of another. The HD image outlines the diegetic mug shot, feeling out the paper it is printed on and, through this gesture, emphasizing the different material qualities of both media, the aesthetic distance that separates them.

At the end of the film, however, it becomes clear that, in terms of reflecting upon images, *Public Enemies* is not primarily interested in the differences between photography and film—a re-entry of the older medium in the younger, for example[13]—but instead, wants to build a relationship between the HD image and the 35mm film image. From the viewpoint of high-resolution video, 35mm film is an antecedent medium to be looked back at, as if looking into the mirror of media history. The mirror reflects a kindred, yet unfamiliar image. Seen this way, HD is the first type of digital moving picture in which the classic, celluloid-based film image can be isolated and excluded as something Other, something historical.

~

13) See Raymond Bellour, "The Pensive Spectator," in *Wide Angle*, Vol. 9, Issue 1 (January 1987), pp. 6–10.

On July 22, 1934, John Herbert Dillinger was shot on the street, in front of the Biograph theater in Chicago, right after he had seen MGM's production of *Manhattan Melodrama* (1934), a film about a man whose bigger-than-life motto helps him decide against a life in prison and in favor of the electric chair: "Die the way you lived, all of a sudden, that's the way to go."

Mann and Spinotti translate this highly improbable, yet undisputed historical fact into a special piece of visual dialogue. They use the full range of HD lighting and depth of field in order to establish the street in front of the movie theater as the final setting, before initiating a parallel action that will lead to Dillinger's death. Melvin Purvis (Christian Bale) and his FBI agents, including the designated assassins Charles Winstead, Clarence Hurt, and Herman Hollis, are located outside, on the street/stage; Dillinger and Anna Sage, the woman who betrayed him, are inside, in the Biograph theater.

The HD camera registers all the details of the historical cinema—the box office, the movie posters, the swinging doors—and then proceeds to the interior, escorting Dillinger to his meeting with an image that was new and contemporary in 1934 and is now historical, the image of Hollywood cinema during the studio era. From a certain distance, we see the ornamental borders around the screen; then *Public Enemies* presents us with the credit sequence of *Manhattan Melodrama*, which was already designed as a form of re-mediation: the raising of a theater curtain. The HD image increasingly narrows its frame now to encircle the image of classical cinema, moving closer and closer towards the spaces and faces of old Hollywood. Finally, Clark Gable, William Powell, and Myrna Loy fill the entire frame and in the high resolution video image the unstable grain of the celluloid image becomes clearly visible—a vibration deep inside the projected film, something that cannot be captured, an indeterminate thing, not a pixel.

Almost gingerly, Mann intervenes in the image of *Manhattan Melodrama*, slowing it down and enlarging it, exposing its aberrant material quality. At the same time, however, he ties this intervention—a found-footage film within a film, Mann's version of a work by Martin Arnold—back to Dillinger's gaze, the gaze of an audience member who can foresee his own end for a second time: sudden death, as prefigured on the screen. Johnny Depp and Clark Gable are joined together in a series of shots and counter-shots, an impossible exchange of glances which transcends the ontological boundary between screen and image: two men with thin moustaches, two portraits of gangsters who, from this moment on, belong together in the history of cinema.

In the HD image, the cinematic image is shown as historicized; it becomes the object of longing, a stand-in for the aesthetic difference in the continuum of all images in Hollywood history. Having said that, the new image does not keep the old one at arm's length. Recording it digitally, the new image also seeks contact with the old one; it shares the identification inscribed in Dillinger's gaze: Johnny Depp's view of Clark Gable, an imaginary axis that runs through the history of the Hollywood star system, linking two eras of American cinema.

A film that reconstructs an old genre in a new image (which is not only 'new' because it articulates different things, but also because it shifts, loosens, and digitally reconnects old gestures, movements, faces, codes, and the dramatic twists and turns of the gangster film), *Public Enemies* is a traditionalist project. It doesn't necessarily look for disruptive effects, but for alternative translations of a generic formula such as the period picture. In this context, it almost seems programmatic that Dillinger's death in slow-motion was one of the few sequences filmed not digitally, but with a Kodak Vision camera, in Super 35mm. It is a 'real' celluloid movie death—and, once again, a difference in media, which under the appropriate conditions of reproduction and reception, can be regarded as a clearly marked leap into another type of image, a gesture of incorporation, or a reference to the lingering existence of an old visual prototype which is simultaneously preserved, overridden, and transcended by a film that works with a new prototype.

*Translated by Allison Plath-Moseley*

Ute Holl

# Cinema on the Web and Newer Psychology

"... il finit par entrer en résonance
avec le monde de future..."

*Chris Marker,* La Jetée

Watching films on the Internet, one of the most popular ways to experience cinema today, has changed many aspects of how cinema is perceived. Looking at it in terms of power structures, it has changed the *dispositif*, the availability and perception of images, the way in which the apparatus disposes of the subject, body and mind, skin and bone and of the ways of seeing. In trying to grasp the effects of online cinema, the problem remains in using anachronistic terminology to describe new experiences. Much has been written on how the notion and practices of the archive have been changed by online cinema; or the notion of time in cinema, or the notion of the public and private, as well as on the perception of images in different formats. These formats range from tiny handheld monitors to large home movie projections, all of which modify the impact of a picture to which, as we know, there is no original. I will instead focus on another aspect of online cinema, its psycho-physical impact and the way it organizes behavior towards the world. In order to challenge the ready-at-hand notion of participatory cultures and underline the concept of behavior as a transmission between human beings and apparatus, I will return to an earlier text that found corresponding elements between cinema's logics and models of human perception. It was conceived of in March 1945, in a moment of political hope and confidence based on filmic realism and enlightenment: Maurice Merleau-Ponty's lecture to film students at the *Institut des Hautes Études Cinématographiques* in Paris.[1] The notions of behavior and being in the age of cinema, which mediates between apparatus and humans, changed radically. In the same way, I will argue, the special habits attributed to audiences or rather *users* of online cinema might also be regarded as virtues, as a new form of perception albeit of old films. In examining the relation between the Internet and cinema's mind, this essay sketches out the framework for an audiovisual unconscious 2.0.

The aesthetics of cinema on the Internet cannot simply be compared with or adapted to the models and terminology of traditional cinema perception. Old cinematic forms of optical deception differ fundamentally from the intricacies of virtual perception on the web. This is expressed by the fact that the classic cinematic *dispositif* has not only been characterized as a motionless gaze at projected light in the dark of a movie theater, but much rather as a way time is construed in transforming stroboscopic light flashes into duration and producing an impression of movement that leaves our perception unaware of this synthesis.[2] The old form of cinema, when it burst into the minds of modernity, was described as a technical organization of mental operations, such as attention or memory through filmic technologies,[3] and thus as a "dynamization of space" and "spatialization of time."[4] It has been described as a way of dynamiting, fragmenting space and time and thus paving the way towards recognizing an optical unconscious in our "prison worlds," as Walter Benjamin put it.[5] And cinema was conceived of as a new form of collective perception.[6] Considering the fact that the Internet is definitely the most advanced form of a collective mind, the temporal and spatial effects of online cinema might be even more complex. Historical cinema has been understood as a form of externalized perception relating to a network of gazes, glances, visions and points of view. In comparison, the network of viewpoints in new cinema is even more intricate. In order to determine differences between old and new forms of cinema, it might be wise to ignore questions of cinema's essence, and to begin with examining the different kinds of behavior that are provoked by cinematic forms.

## BEHAVIOR ON THE MARGINS OF IMAGINATION

Rather than simply conceiving of online cinema as a virtual film-and-video store, it could be regarded as a new and unprecedented miscellany of forms of perception; creating new and unprecedented social formations. It seems impossible to narrow the notion of online cinema down to digitized forms of feature films. Instead, all of the remakes, remixes, replays, data mash-ups and moshings, that are more or less inspired by classic cinema, have to be taken into account since they are part of what would be understood online as cinema. Online cinema continues to emerge as people are uploading, broadcasting, tagging, searching for, rating, watching, downloading, observing and reloading films and clips; in other words, users can participate, in intended or unintended ways. Online cinema is an activity

1) Maurice Merleau-Ponty, "The Film and The New Psychology," in *Sense and Non-Sense* (Trans. Hubert L. Dreyfus and Patricia Allen Dreyfus, Evanston: Northwestern University Press, 1964), pp. 48–59. The first German translation and interpretation of the text by Frieda Grafe (*Filmkritik* 11/1969, pp. 695–702) had a decisive influence on German film theory and criticism in the 1970s.

2) See Mary Ann Doane, *The Emergence of Cinematic Time. Modernity, Contingency, the Archive* (Cambridge: Harvard University Press, 2002).

3) Hugo Münsterberg, *The Film: A Psychological Study. The Silent Photoplay in 1916* (New York: Dover, 1970).

4) Erwin Panofsky, "Style and Medium in the Moving Pictures," in *Transition*, no. 26 (1937), pp. 121–133.

5) Walter Benjamin, "The Work of Art in the Age of its Technological Reproducibility: Second Version," in *Selected Writings, Vol. 3, 1935–1938* (Cambridge: Harvard University Press, 2002), pp. 101–133.

6) Walter Benjamin, "The Work of Art in the Age of its Technological Reproducibility: Third Version," in *Selected Writings Vol. 4, 1938–1940* (Cambridge: Harvard University Press, 2003), p. 264: "[...] an object of simultaneous collective experience, as architecture has always been able to do, as the epic poem could do at one time, and as film is able to do today."

rather than a passive state of perceiving. Simultaneously, these activities alter and transform the material they visualize and the perception of its viewers as users. Feedback relations established between virtual imaging and imagination best describe the aesthetics of online cinema. Cinematic time on the Internet is constructed and condensed through imaging activities. Times of observation are warped and looped. With online cinema, time does not simply progress, but rather expands like the universe, in all directions, differentiating its structures while its meshes are set. In March 2010, *YouTube* announced, "24 hours of video uploaded every minute."[7] Through repetition and combining on the web, each one of these images resonates in the other. Online cinema exceeds individual control, or at least requires surfing those superior forces and incalculable waves of information. As a familiar time-structure passes and passes out, being on the Internet and watching films changes our behavior; its social component remains subliminal for the time being.

From the perspective of analog media, Internet aesthetics are coined through a perception of iterations, recursions and reprises. This is especially true of online cinema—its surfaces and montages, practices and procedures, its distribution. There is always something being repeated and reenacted, and more often than not what we see is just a different version of the same thing. The more we focus on the emergence of new forms—spaces, audiences or new forms of reception—the more we have the old ones staring back at us. Online cinema repeats the structures of early cinema, and has done so from the very beginning: montage of attractions, very short formats, and an open, variable programming.[8] But online cinema also reprises early television structures and programming, it is reminiscent of the structure of home movies, the project of Do-It-Yourself, as well as restaging the videotape and the structure of waves and vibrations inherent to it.[9] Online cinema resumes all of the experimental and amateur film movements, and their plans for politicizing art; it produces avant-gardes everywhere, since there is no first or last, no beginning or end on noded screens. Digital cinema can simulate, mix and blur material traces of all kinds of film formats, forge scratches and overexposures, imitate video dropouts or tape defects. Any reference to the source material is unreliable, because indexicality remains a second order relation between algorithms. While its political gestures are grossly aestheticized, Internet art remains to be politicized, perceived as a social way of seeing; beyond the individual, beyond the self-assured subject.

Since our own behavior and that of others is intertwined, we can no longer insist on a centered subjective viewpoint, but have to look at phenomena from the corner of the eye, as Hans-Jörg Rheinberger insists, from the margins of attentiveness, from where "the place of absorption" is located.[10] Only by moving along the verge of vigilance can we trap cinematic attention as our own. The commercial Internet confuses attention with ranking. It distinguishes center from periphery, what is important from insignificance, and it does this by quantitatively measuring attentiveness. Internet values are created through logics of the hit parade and the stock exchange. Instead, by being methodically inattentive, by working with "moderate dishevelment,"[11] we might discover a medium beneath a message—and, as Jean-Luc Godard put it, a medium beneath the desires.[12] Thus we may find a popular road to film's unconscious 2.0.

### OLD CINEMA AND NEW PSYCHOLOGY

In 1945 Maurice Merleau-Ponty in his lecture "The Film and the New Psychology" explained how, from a phenomenological perspective, the world and desires are closely entangled when watching film.[13] In his neuropsychological investigations on the structure of behavior during the 1920s and 30s,[14] which he connects to the laws of *gestalt* psychology, Merleau-Ponty assumes that a new psychology has to deal with effects of a visual field, drawing audiences into it as if under a spell. This action of the visible could simply be called *image*, but it is an image that emerges from forms of behavior and relationships. The act of perceiving basically creates homogeneity of this field, according to the *gestalt* rules of figure and ground, of proximity, similarity, simplicity, closure, repetition. There is no longer a simple view of the world as the subject is automatically drawn into this entanglement of intention, sight and sound, but rather a way of interlacing things with the dynamics of affective structures. "When I perceive something, I do not think the world; it organizes itself in front of me,"[15] writes Merleau-Ponty, referring to a joint procedure in apparatus and mind. Relating cinema experience to the laboratory work of *gestalt* psychology of his time, Merleau-Ponty shows that cinema refutes the Cartesian division between *res cogitans*, as mind, and *res extensa*, as the physical, and he shows that human beings—simultaneously perceivers and those being perceived in the drama of the world—do not think or decode this world, but rather behave within it in direct relation to other people and things. Watching a film also means presenting consciousness as "thrown into the world, subject to the gaze of others and learning from them what it is."[16] The relationship to others is not

7) www.youtube.com/t/press_timeline.

8) See Joost Broeren, "Digital Attractions: Reloading Early Cinema in Online Video Collections," in Pelle Snickars, Patrick Vonderau (eds.), *The YouTube Reader* (Stockholm: National Library, 2009), pp. 154–165.

9) See Maurizio Lazzarato, *Videophilosophie. Zeitwahrnehmung im Postfordismus* (Trans. Stephan Geene and Erik Stein, Berlin: b_books, 2002). Lazzarato explicates the vibrational model he describes for video formats through a modulation of time in duration, according to Bergson and Deleuze. "The *video image derives its movement from the vibrations of the material; it is this vibration proper.* Video technology is a modulation of currents and the video-image is the relationship between these currents." (p. 66, translated from German.)

10) Hans-Jörg Rheinberger, *Iterationen* (Berlin: Merve, 2005), p. 67 (translated from German).

11) Max Delbrück, in a letter to his friend, Salvador Luria, dated 1948, quoted in Rheinberger, *op. cit.*, p. 66, as "*gemäßigte Schlampigkeit.*"

12) Jean-Luc Godard, *Histoire(s) du Cinéma*, F/CH 1988–98.

13) See Merleau-Ponty, *op. cit.*, p. 51.

14) See Maurice Merleau-Ponty, *La Structure du comportement* (Paris: Presses Universitaires de France, 1942); published in English as *The Structure of Behavior* (Trans. Alden Fisher, Boston: Beacon Press, 1963).

15) Merleau-Ponty, 1964, "New Psychology," p. 51.

16) *Ibid.*, p. 58.

regulated by introspection and empathy, but by a common bond of views, visual fields and behavior, which cinema produces and simultaneously renders visible—in a close-up, for instance, or in a long-focus lens.[17] Cinema theorists after Merleau-Ponty were also interested in the idea of external constellations as emotional issues.[18] What is interesting about cinema in terms of the Internet and a newer psychology is not its ability to store or distribute images, but rather its way of generating fields of perception as socially linked spheres.

In his lecture to future filmmakers, Merleau-Ponty did not mention that phenomenological as well as cinema perception, which "make us *see* the bond between subject and world, between the subject and others, rather than to explain it,"[19] do not simply stage a peaceful coexistence on a visual plane, but instead create relationships of difference. On the field of vision, the subject is, as Lacanian film theorists have repeatedly shown, subjugated to the gaze of the other.[20] Unlike Jean-Paul Sartre, though, Merleau-Ponty did not regard these encounters of two gazes as fatal battles on common ground, but as a fissure in the fabric of the world, something that generates instability between seeing and being seen, between visible and invisible fields, and hence creates new relationships. The chiasmus of sight and image in the age of technical media is a blind spot at the intersection of subject and *dispositif*: if this blind spot comes into view, it disturbs the stability of the subject.[21] For online cinema, the film's single fissure turns out to be an endless series of relays. Bonds between "subject and world," "subject and other" prove to be manifold and oscillating relationships.

During the 1920s and 30s, new psychology and the perception of cinema went hand in hand; psychologists could be filmmakers, and filmmakers, psychologists.[22] At the end of his lecture, Merleau-Ponty himself is taken aback by the coincidence of perception theories and cinematic *dispositif*, asking, "why it is that precisely in the film era this philosophy [i.e. phenomenology] has developed,"[23] detecting in it a world view shared by philosophers, psychologists and cineastes. Cinema and perception, or the self and the world, constitute each other in a reciprocal manner, forming loops of feedback.

In the 1940s, the idea of processing sensory data and feedback behavior in holistic fields of perception was not just a matter of cinema theory, but also an issue of experimental science. In a cybernetic experiment conducted in the same year that Merleau-Ponty gave his paper, a kinesthetic animal was implemented with sensomotoric loops that simulated nervous action. It was named "Palomilla" and it could behave either as a moth or as a bedbug. Its photosensitive chip could perceive an amount of light from a lamp in its environment and transform it into voltage, setting a tiller in motion that would steer a motor. Depending on how the tiller was programmed, the electrical animal would either move towards the light, or away from it. In a field of more or less light, Palomilla seemed to behave according to her perception, in a sophisticated way beyond simple patterns of reaction. Here, behavior turns out to be a notion assumed by the observer of the system. In a second experiment, Palomilla's steering movements could be exaggerated, over steered, and then appear as over- or hyperactive. This dysfunctional behavior flabbergasted neurologists because it exactly simulated forms of neurological pathology, purpose tremor or Parkinsonian aberrations—as notions of the observers.[24]

In cinema, motor movements are reduced while reactions, even physical ones, are part of the perception.[25] The feedback behavior between sensory organs and reactions is, in the old cinema *dispositif*, turned inward, toward the internal circuits, into emotions, shivering, overheating, sweat, and tears, which are monitored in the laboratory of a cinema of humors and fluids. Film rhythms as rhythms of light and sound, of energy, as we know them from the old forms of cinema, are, in new cinema, recombined with motor activity to create completely different dramaturgies. While old cinema, in its plush seats and surroundings, tries to reduce noise and disturbances in order to focus the audience's attention on the screen, online cinema is notoriously perceived in passing, over the shoulder, on trains and tubes, in motion, blending many different distractions into its visuals and environment. *YouTube* videos precisely blur the boundaries between image and frame, motion and background, levels and meta-levels, inside and outside, so that the site of perception becomes ambiguous.[26] In the images of online cinema, space is nothing but a

17) According to Merleau-Ponty, this is also true for the organization of sounds in cinema, which he discusses in terms of the radio montage—not the inscribing gramophone—, although, unlike his contemporaries Cage or Schaeffer, he explicitly excludes noise from his considerations.

18) This includes not only phenomenological film criticism, prominently represented by such writers as Don Ihde and Vivian Sobchak, or film theory based on Lacan's model of organizing optics, which also goes back to Merleau-Ponty, but also the practice of filmmaking itself: in his self-observational film, *JLG/JLG*, Godard has (blind) actors reciting long passages from Merleau-Ponty's *The Visible and the Invisible*.

19) Merleau-Ponty, 1964, "New Psychology," p. 58.

20) See e.g., Kaja Silverman, *The Subject of Semiotics* (New York: Oxford University Press, 1984), pp. 194–236 and Judith Mayne, *The Woman at the Keyhole. Feminism and Women's Cinema* (Bloomington: Indiana University Press, 1990).

21) For more on this, see Hans Dieter Huber, "Überkreuzte Blicke. Merleau-Ponty, Lacan, Beckett, Spencer-Brown," in Antje Kapust, Bernhard Waldenfels (eds.), *Kunst. Bild. Wahrnehmung. Blick. Merleau-Ponty zum Hundertsten* (Munich: Fink, 2010), pp. 135–156. Also, the groundbreaking, brilliant study by Andreas Cremonini, *Die Durchquerung des Cogito. Lacan contra Sartre* (Munich: Fink, 2003).

22) See Kurt Lewin's wonderful home movie as experimental film for the 1929 psychology congress at Yale, *Field Forces as Impediments to a Performance*, on *YouTube*: www.youtube.com/watch?v=BeS9R4wLcgY, uploaded by the Virtual Laboratory at MPI Berlin http://vlp.mpiwg-berlin.mpg.de, one of the treasure troves of Internet cinema.

23) Merleau-Ponty, 1964, "New Psychology," p. 59.

24) See Norbert Wiener, *Cybernetics: Or Control and Communication in the Animal and the Machine*. (Cambridge: MIT Press, 1948), p. 7 and the following pages.

25) See Vivian Sobchak, "What My Fingers Knew," in *Carnal Thoughts. Embodiment and Moving Image Culture* (Berkeley: University of California Press, 2004), pp. 53–84.

26) See Albert Figurt, "The Thin Red Line Between On and Off: A (Re:)Cyclothymic Exploration," in Geert Lovink, Rachel Somers Miles (eds.), *Video Vortex Reader II. Moving Images Beyond YouTube* (Amsterdam: Institute of Network Cultures, 2011). Online version here: www.networkcultures.org/_uploads/%236reader_VideoVortex2PDF.pdf.

constantly changing topology through which we have to move, like meandering moths or bedbugs. This topology establishes perceived spaces as much as social ones.

In the light of Merleau-Ponty's ideas on older cinema, the question of a philosophical model of perception for new online cinema arises; not to verify one or the other, but in order to understand forms of behavior as they appear, in different historical times, simultaneously in neurophysiological and media-technological models.

## DIGITAL PERCEPTION

After having interviewed Jacques Derrida for a television program, Bernard Stiegler subsumed the issue of digital imagery and subsequent technical externalization of perception's logics under the trope of a *Grammaticalization of the Visible,* referring to the procedure of crushing down images to single data that can be recombined.[27] He raised this as a political problem in 1993, just as technical images had caused severe doubts about their relation to reality. Television channels had broadcast the experience of extremely unreliable pictures: images that were supposed to show targeted bombing of Baghdad in real time could not really provide any analog-based authentication. "Something has intervened—treatment as binary calculation—which renders transmission uncertain."[28]

For online cinema, which appeared much later, this kind of grammaticalization of the visible was again criticized as political deprivation. Fundamental scruples are expressed: films are not watched on the Internet, but simply read, and they are not even read as films, but as sets of digital data. "We no longer watch films or TV; we watch databases," writes Geert Lovink in his introduction to one of the first (electronic) books to deal extensively with watching films in an electronic space.[29] Stiegler again projects grammaticalization onto problems of spatiotemporal identification and archiving—and discovers Internet images to be basically organized by the surveillance principle, by providing "the development of an algorithm for automated discretization of spatial [...] and temporal [...] and spatiotemporal continuities [...] and the automated comparison of such isolated discrete elements allowing for signatures of images and searches in a body of diverse occurrences of the same type of iconic or sound information (an object, a voice, a face)."[30] While the observation is basically correct, his conclusion is strange: in this procedure, he fears "psychosocial individuation."[31] Like Merleau-Ponty 60 years earlier, both authors, Stiegler and Lovink, relate the state of media, electronic grammaticalization of the visible, to a neurological phenomenon. But when Merleau-Ponty related cinema perception to neurophysiology in his speech, this was not intended to diagnose pathological behavior—which, as a child psychologist, he would have been familiar with. While Merleau-Ponty cherished his discovery as a fortunate coincidence of human faculty and *dispositif,* the latter diagnosed a syndrome, defective behavior: *attention deficit hyperactivity disorder*. In the inability to concentrate, the fidgeter returns, in the realm of the alphanumeric. Much earlier, in Jean-Martin Charcots Parisian clinic and in the first phase of technical media practices of the 1870s, the relationship between media and psychiatric behavior was made evident through the first series of chronophotography. These created symptoms of maladies without matter, "sine materia," which suggested a relation of imitation and mimicry between the symptom and the publicly perceived: "The idiosyncratic affectation *sine materia,* the imitation of organic illness, has been described as neuromimesis."[32] The imaginary bond between media and frangible experiences of the body, as well as between media-theorists and neurologists is as old as technical media. Neuromimesis is a viable term to describe acting under the influence of an apparatus.

In the digital age, images, texts, numbers and sounds are computed at speeds that exceed those humanly perceptible, to then be transmitted onto our motor-sensory system by suitable interface technology. Every piece of digitally processed information has to take its detour via analogous, physical and, that is, material channels, before human eyes can see it, human ears can hear it and human skin feel or sense it, etc.[33] To be meticulously precise, we never watch, see or hear sets of data, but rather their physiologically perceivable effects. Still, the question of the figurativeness of digital film or television transmissions definitely contains the political aspect Geert Lovink addresses: on the Internet and on the screen we are confronted with effects of metadata, not with qualities of light and sound as they impose their force on photochemical or magnetic material; moreover, because of the speed of digital procedures, we do not have full control over these data-generating algorithms, which create images and sounds. Therefore, the political criticism Stiegler puts forward remains: "the production of metadata, whose digital concept was formulated in 1994, but whose practice goes back to Mesopotamia, had always been executed in a *top-down* fashion, by the official institutions of various forms of symbolic power."[34] Metadata limit access to cultural technologies

27) Bernard Stiegler, "The Discrete Image," in Jacques Derrida and Bernard Stiegler, *Echographies of Television. Filmed Interviews* (Trans. Jennifer Bajorek, Cambridge/UK: Polity Press, 2002), p. 149. As an addition to the transcripts of the television discussions Derrida and Stiegler conducted, this text was reconstructed out of two later lectures of Stiegler's. In this text, Stiegler emphasizes the destructive consequences of digital grammaticalization, while Derrida in his answers proves vividly interested in the deconstructive and differentiating process of discrete imageries.

28) *Ibid.*, p. 153.

29) Geert Lovink, "The Art of Watching Databases: Introduction to the Video Vortex Reader," in Geert Lovink, Sabine Niederer, *Video Vortex Reader: Responses to YouTube* (Amsterdam: Institute of Network Cultures, 2008), p. 9. Meanwhile, a second volume has made its electronic appearance. See note 26.

30) Bernard Stiegler, "The Carnival of the New Screen. From Hegemony to Isonomy," in Snickars/Vonderau, *op. cit.*, p. 51.

31) *Ibid.*, p. 54.

32) Jean-Martin Charcot, *Poliklinische Vorträge*. Bd. 1: Schuljahre 1887/88 (Trans. Sigmund Freud, Leipzig/Wien: Deuticke, 1893), p. 13 (translated from German).

33) See Wolfgang Hagen, "Die Entropie der Fotografie. Skizzen zu einer Genealogie der digital-elektronischen Bildaufzeichnung," in Herta Wolf (ed.), *Paradigma Fotografie. Fotokritik am Ende des fotografischen Zeitalters* (Frankfurt am Main: Suhrkamp, 2002), pp. 195–235.

34) Stiegler, 2009, "Carnival of the New Screen," p. 52.

that are intellectual poison to the masses. But even if applied top-down, the function of metadata and its relation to the according channels has been recognized, and can be seen today from the regions neighboring Mesopotamia where it is used to oppose the current just as well.[35]

Bernard Stiegler's objection relates to two issues: the technical and the institutional side of digital programming. Due to its slowness, the human brain and sensory equipment cannot follow operations conducted by electronic relays, and therefore cannot intervene in the programs, as long as a series of commands are running—a warning that has already been put forward by Norbert Wiener for the automated control of computed processes—a threat that might be more dangerous in the context of weapons systems and atomic power plants, if we still want to make a difference here, than it is in programming films.[36]

Jacques Derrida, in his conversation with Stiegler, reminded the latter that time and space, in technological media transmissions, has always been an artifact. Whatever medium processes and transmits an image, it will always transform the perception of all who are linked to it, and allow for new differences and differentiations to emerge. For instance, audiences watching Internet television are no longer defined by their nationality, they can watch *sans frontières*, limited only by commercial broadcasting rights; an argument that reminds us of Bertolt Brecht's radio theory, distinguishing between the possibilities of the apparatus and restrictions implemented due to political or commercial interest. Here, the virtual space of the Internet has initiated a deterritorialization of media subjectivization, as Derrida observed: "What the accelerated development of teletechnologies, of cyberspace, of the new topology of 'the virtual' produces is a practical *deconstruction* of the traditional and dominant concepts of the state and the citizen (and thus of 'the political'), as they are linked to the actuality of a territory."[37] Thus, Derrida discovered new and unforeseen possibilities for political experiences in digitized visual spaces,[38] for the alphabetization of visual illiterates as well as for political education that could counteract the laws of orthography, of imaging and the state.[39] But other frontiers remained to be crossed: that of the finite image, its frames and surfaces, and the frontier between Internet and the mind, between new cinema and new psychology.

The year 1993 marked a fundamental reterritorialization of the Internet as a whole. The president and vice-president of the United States, as part of a techno-political program, claimed the historically open architecture of the worldwide electronic information network for state politics and economic interests, making way for its commercialization. Images and Internet videos were hardly important at that time—except for diagrammatics or comics of communication theorists—but in principle, the option for commercial digital cinema opened up and marked the beginning of an accelerated flow of images.

For many years, the consequences of digital imaging did not really affect cinema or its perception. Only on surfaces and user interfaces of monitors and TV-screens did electronic images and aesthetics create unexpected effects. Old-style cinema reacted reluctantly to this. One of the first few directors to do this was Lars von Trier in his films *The Kingdom* (1994) and *Breaking the Waves* (1996). Trier programmatically broke the old logic of light waves by digitizing painting, film and video images and layering the digital surfaces through various processes of copying and converting. He was already a master of discriminating, composing, pasting and editing in discrete seriality. Rather than follow dramaturgy and acting in the old sense, the behavior of his protagonists, for instance in *Breaking the Waves*, was organized according to these new mixed media surfaces and their visibility. Just as the director went along with the surprises of unforeseen effects of landscapes composed of digital layering of film, video and painting, his protagonists had to accept their unforeseeable reactions in a synthetic world computed in technical parameters.[40] The female heroines in Trier's films, mostly victims of a joint venture of apparatus, environment and the visual pleasures of northern myths, could well be compared to the unconscious or trance-like behavior of Charcot's hysterics. The aesthetics of his films could well be called neuromimesis. After all, the strange behavior that was eventually classified as "hysteria" began to emerge in a similar constellation of new media—a new psychology emerged from the chronophotographic series in Charcot's days based on new orders of the visible. Although we learned from Palomilla that behavior is always in the eye of the beholder: the psychiatrist, the philosopher or the cinema audience.

For digital cinema, the problem or lack of materiality remains a predominant issue. Stiegler remarks that the basics of photographic ontology involving the impression of reality onto the materiality of the image—as André Bazin observed—have been lost in digital photography. Regarding a loss of memory, Stiegler states that a break in the "chain of memorial light,"[41] once based on photographic inscriptions of light onto plates, would eventually create mental images. In the digital world, indexicality no longer refers to a universal reality, but to more sets of data. Therefore, a reorganiza-

35) The first draft of this article was written in March 2011. We keep a "moderately disheveled eye" on Mesopotamian political landscapes.

36) Wiener, *op. cit.*, p. ix and p. 27.

37) Derrida and Stiegler, *op. cit.*, p. 36.

38) Derrida's *Spectres de Marx* (Specters of Marx) was published in Paris in 1993.

39) "Just as literacy and mastery of language, of spoken or of written discourse have never been universally shared, (it goes almost without saying that there have always been, not only people who can read and people who can't, but among those who can, a great diversity of competencies, abilities, etc.) so today, with respect to what is happening with the image, we might say, by analogy, that the vast majority of consumers are in a state analogous to these diverse modalities of relative illiteracy. [...] There is also, if not an alphabet, then at least a discrete seriality of the image or of images. We must learn, precisely, how to discriminate, compose, paste, edit." Derrida in Derrida and Stiegler, *op. cit.*, p. 59.

40) See also Ute Holl, "Mazzen, Fazzen, Augenjazzen," in Martin Warnke et al. (eds.), *HyperKult II, Zur Ortsbestimmung analoger und digitaler Medien* (Bielefeld: transcript, 2005), pp. 287–296.

41) Stiegler, 2002, "Discrete Image," p. 154.

tion of traces is necessary to permit automatic navigation through the "flow" or flood of images. Instead of reconstructing history in diachronics, there will be an orientation in synchronical pathways: "In the future, digital technology is going to go very far in spotting [discontinuities in a film]: in addition to planes, it will recognize *automatically* different camera movements, identical objects present in a film, recurrent characters, voices, sets, etc. It will be possible to make indices of these things, to inscribe them in temporal scales. This will allow us to navigate through the flow of images in a nonlinear fashion towards ever finer and more iterative elements, in the same way that we've been able to in books."[42] As in the dreams of the Russian avant-gardes, a technical eye substitutes the subject of cinema. However, automated seeing creates its own topologies and tropes and ultimately infects social ways of seeing.

What Maurice Merleau-Ponty, referring to *gestalt* psychology, described as the automatic organization of the world before our minds, corresponds to an automatic organization of the visible on the Internet, which follows the rules of data and algorithms. Only twenty years after Stiegler's statement, algorithms on the Internet seem to actually be able to address single sequences, images and close-ups—as well as detect faces in close-ups and other singularities quite quickly. Algorithms transform images into information, and connect pieces of information to the imaginary. Although this is an experience completely different from the old form of watching film, there are filmic aspects to this: the increasing supply of film-images on the web, even if in fragmented formats and subverted versions, allows us to finally read books on cinema: we no longer have to remember or imagine shots, montages or framings, instead we can watch, repeat, analyze them, and even edit, project and compare them automatically with the help of mechanical eyes. We are operating with sets of data of course; we are dealing with digitally organized forms of memory and a digitally tracked unconscious. This is not a cinematic experience in the old sense, but we are operating with images regardless.

There is a hitch, though, to this broad notion of an image. As opposed to the old analog media, which raised the ontological question of what an image is, images on the Internet provoke the operational question of what an images does. Images, still or moving, as well as written works on cinema connect through different traces on the web and are fed back into a new experience of cinema. The audience on the web does not actually see or watch, but becomes entangled in algorithmically formed visible worlds. It is, itself, observed, traced and led into their meshes through the paths of other gazing users of films and film clips. For old cinema models, especially the Russian avant-garde, the entanglement of the human eye and cinema apparatus produced an impassionate political eye, which does not get hung up on narratives or celebrities, when it is simply supposed to decipher images. The entanglement of the human eye and digitized sight seems to produce an equally intelligent way of seeing: even the historical eyes of old-school film scholars are seduced by the logics of the web and instead of thinking in shots, cuts and montages, they begin to write in terms of accumulations, transitions, series, and clusters.[43] Yet, while the phantasm that machines can read and reproduce images without limitations is far from reality,[44] an imaginary thing, which works and gives feedback on the basis of algorithms, has arrived.

All common practices of online cinema occur within the parameters of coding and decoding, reading and rewriting data, but the procedures of transforming them into images, its aesthetics, have yet to be discussed. Users and hackers employ the organization of these sets of data as material for painting, in turn creating new visuals out of aleatoric interventions into data structures and compression codes. Thus, these visuals raise questions about the structure of the imaginary and figurativeness, just like Cézanne once raised the issue in the era of old new media.[45] Hacker aesthetics, such as datamoshing, form images from the logics of digital processes and compressions. Those pictures appear as transformations between bits of information, between the lines, between the digital data set and its analog effects. To be perceived, these images require a form of "moderate dishevelment," watching on the verge of vigilance, a form of systematically distracted attention or sloppy observation. Seeing from the corner of the eye, seeing algorithmically produced, data-moshed images requires a certain amount of fidgeting, trembling and headshaking. They require perception in between familiar forms, in between two levels, since, as Tom Levin put it, in those videos "one image is haunting the other."[46] The perception of time in data-moshed videos is completely different from cinematographically synthesized time in that it evokes something visible out of ambiguities and intervals; it is a form of technically implemented, intentional inattention, which takes what is seen from the corner of the eye and then spreads it across the entire field of vision. Images like these take inattentiveness into account. The diagnosis of *attention deficit disorder* is an inappropriate verdict, since attention deficit is required here in order to see the order.

### BEHAVIOR ON THE INTERNET

Digital imaging practices on the Internet are considered, somewhat justifiably, the end of a certain visual culture and the beginning of a new kind of training to adjust to behaviors in indeterminate topologies. Just like the old cin-

42) *Ibid.*, p. 157.

43) See Thomas Elsaesser, "'Constructive Instability,' or: The Life of Things as the Cinema's Afterlife?" in Lovink/Niederer, *op. cit.*, pp. 13–31 and Elsaesser, "Tales of Epiphany and Entropy: Around the Worlds in Eighty Clicks," in Snickars/Vonderau, *op. cit.*, pp. 166–186.

44) See Friedrich Kittler, "Computergraphik, eine halbtechnische Einführung," in Sabine Flach and Georg Christoph Tholen (eds.), *Intervalle 5. Schriften zur Kulturforschung* (Kassel: Kassel University Press, 2002), pp. 221–240, and, investigating computer-aided means of searching for similarities among images Wolfgang Ernst, Stefan Heidenreich, Ute Holl (eds.), *Suchbilder. Visuelle Kultur zwischen Algorithmus und Archiven* (Berlin: Kadmos, 2001).

45) On the practice of data-moshing, see, for instance, Ute Holl, "Vom Kino-Eye zur You-Tube," in *Cargo*, no. 3 (September 2009), pp. 72–74, and more recently, Tom Y. Levin in a paper at the SHIFT Festival, Basel, 2010.

46) Levin in his paper at the SHIFT Festival.

ema, online cinema has to fulfill a social function to "establish equilibrium between human beings and the apparatus," as Walter Benjamin put it.[47] Watching films in the days of Vertov and Benjamin taught modern city dwellers, through the means of time loops, close-ups, pans, and montage, to move in environments much too fast to consciously grasp every detail, and to discover in their own behavior an optical unconscious in the perception of everyday life. Watching digitized cinema today might provide the same training and mediating effects: the web allows users—while they select, reiterate, recombine, transmit and thus produce protocols of all of those actions—to observe and record this topology and their own movements on it as symptoms of their own unconscious topology. This second order observation of one's own behavior is self-reflective and self-producing. The histories of those chains of actions and decisions on the web provide a protocol for the digital unconscious of their users and, at the same time, constitute pathways and nodes of the Internet as it emerges from the users' operations. Lovink asks, "What does it mean that our attention is being guided by database systems?"[48] alluding to the fact that, on the Internet, attention is the means to navigate and at the same time to organize the realm of images for all others. Attention, individually and collectively, uses and prioritizes pathways in the structure of the Internet. Lovink rightfully inquires into the relationship between the topological survey of electronic and that of psychological pathways, which correspond in their structure, in order to understand the impact of the web on the formation of subjectivity.[49] Films in online archives and collections are not just series of images, but attention traps, which entangle the users' desire in a network of economy. This is not just one of desires and dreams, as Jean-Luc Godard insisted, but also of simple capitalist utilization. The old logic of the "dream factory" returns in online mode: "Allowing oneself to be led by an endlessly branching database is the cultural constant of the early 21ST century. [...] Time is the Message: what we are consuming with online video is our own lack of time."[50] But the Self 2.0 is no longer just a victim of an industrial merchandizing of imaginary commodities; it is engaged.

At this point, critical theory meets Jean-Luc Godard's psychoanalysis of cinema. Right at the beginning of Godard's *Histoire(s) du Cinéma*, a work that, in retrospect, proves to be a great dry run for watching *YouTube,* long before its existence, he comments on a scene from Freud, quoting the title sequence from his own *Le Mépris* (1963): "Cinema substitutes for our gaze a world that corresponds to our desires.—*Le cinéma substitue à notre regard un monde qui s'accorde à nos desires.*" The idea that the world would *correspond to our desires*—and of course Godard will quote Merleau-Ponty later—or in plainer English, that the world would "tune into" our desires describes the uncanny alliance between media and mind, one which we have already observed as the blind spot of subjectivization. There is a fundamental distinction between Godard's laboratory and various online cinema experiments: Godard can still play his films forward and in reverse on videotape and therefore their effects are in accordance with cinematic time. Godard's process, like old analog media, especially the gramophone, is in contact with reality, not because there is some scratch in the wax surface, but because the impression of reality in analog media is produced in proportion to time, and in firm connection with it. In the beginning of the film, when Godard cites from Freud's *Interpretation of Dreams* and his account of the burning child, rolling the videotape forward and backward, he is very aware of cinematography and repeating his own memory structure as cinematic memory, as difference, desire, and repetition, "the reappearance of the perception constitutes the wish-fulfillment."[51] In the aesthetics of the *Histoire(s)* he makes clear there is no other way of investigating one's own perceptive structure than by recovering it in an outside world of images, on an external recording device, as Freud modeled it in the magic writing pad. Here, too, it is the time structure of perception that resists any sort of ontology of the image. Godard in his *Histoire(s) du Cinéma* is sitting in front of his many monitors, all of them reflecting his own face in the dark passages of the films. The users of the Internet are seemingly not interested in their simple reflection in cinematic images, but would rather have it refracted and modified by the multitude of viewers that also see and modify: in online cinema, reflection is substituted by feedback. While Godard's behavior is desire-based and self-reflective, the Internet cinema-goer's behavior has to take into account the multitude of others, even if they try to remember which film sequences were their favorites: they would not have been visible at that point, had it not been for other viewers. On the Internet the viewer cannot roll a film backwards, instead, they can copy and operate on the databases that others have produced. Instead of rolling images back and forth, faster and slower—as in the case of Godard's *Histoire(s)*—Internet cinema posits "a logic of selection and expression, competition and attention,"[52] as Jens Schröter critically notes. However, these concepts, i.e., "selection and expression, competition and attention," are not necessarily a behavioral reduction. Understood in the context of cybernetic communication or informational aesthetics, they actually proliferate the possibilities of behavior. In terms of media aesthetics, Max Bense, for example, included the concept of selection—no matter how precarious the word remains in German—in schemes of augmenting calculable possibilities, as a "selection from a repertoire," which provides references to existing operational processes. Aesthetics for Bense is a mathematical case of calculation and probability of occurrence or even—as a special

47) Benjamin, 2002, "The Work of Art: Second Version," p. 117 (italics in the original).

48) Lovink, *op. cit.*, p. 10.

49) *Ibid.*: "Why has searchability become such an essential organizing principle? Why is our personal relationship to the relational database being pushed?"

50) *Ibid.*, p. 12.

51) Sigmund Freud, *The Interpretation of Dreams*. Third Edition (Trans. A. A. Brill, New York: Macmillan, 1913), p. 446.

52) Jens Schröter, "On the Logic of the Digital Archive," in Snickars/Vonderau, *op. cit.*, p. 343.

problem of the Internet—reoccurrence: "*Aesthetic states are actually material states of specially classifiable distributions of frequencies.* Aesthetic processes are statistical-stochastic processes. Each and every statistical-stochastic process is, in principle, an aesthetic process."[53] This kind of re-materialization of algorithms corresponds to hacker-practices of intervening in databases, compression codes, algorithms, practices of remixing and replaying, and reiteration. Clearly, a part of media usage is limited to the habits of the super- or the media-market. This kind of usage alone, however, hardly describes the possible forms of visual and acoustic behavior that is possible on the Internet. Instead of lamenting a reoccurring surveillance principle, we should also consider the fact that in digital cinema on the web, psychology and cinema once again join in a common model of social perception.

Behavior on the Internet of images need not be fundamentally new. Lev Manovich, for instance, who discusses social media statistically from the viewpoint of information aesthetics, tunes his post-punk attitude back to dandyism when he proposes to waste time in the *YouTube* Arcades, when he recommends to stroll around at a tortoise's pace in front of its images, to watch a lot of boring videos in the calculable hope of eventually coming across something exciting—to practice, at any slow rate, a strategic method of hanging out on the Internet. According to Manovich, this could lead from blind user tactics to intelligent strategic behavior,[54] where behavior can be regarded as connecting a set of data to other sets of data, including those of identity proper in psychomotoric activities. This kind of behavior definitely includes the active critique of power structures, yet it does not begin by assuming a subject structured by lack and desire.

## FINIR PAR ENTRER EN RÉSONANCE AVEC LE MONDE DE FUTURE (ANTÉRIEUR)

From a phenomenological point of view, two aspects of Internet cinema are important: firstly, the reorganization and changing of image-structures through duration—even if ultra short—of viewing, and secondly, the social aspect of cinema, of establishing and transforming relationships to others—who on the Internet become a plurality, one of many, but not masses as their actions count individually. The simple relationship Maurice Merleau-Ponty assumed in his cinematic experience turns into a multifaceted resonance elsewhere.[55] Duration as well as the many-others no longer relate to a homogenous visible field, or field of vision, instead there is a topology of interconnected data and databases that combine perception into a site-less, virtual image. This topology produces a socialized field of vision somewhere in between materiality and immateriality.

Within this topology of the Internet, a new kind of film audience has emerged. It seems to believe that the old form of cinema, which, according to the Russian avant-garde, the Weimar cinema, Italian realists or Hollywood films, promised to provide a resonating worldly and public space, is in fact a strangely closed-off and socially dead space. For this new audience, images only connect to the world if computers who produce them are online and networking, producing meshes and moshes of endless afternoons. Still we find the same dynamics here that Merleau-Ponty described, only more complex. Subjectivization under the gaze of the other on the Internet turns into an attempt to capture the attention of many users through the reiteration of actions and images. Online cinema practices and their theory hardly ever discuss single images to describe cinematic qualities. Instead, an image on the web is always considered the result of connected behavior. Cinema on the web, as opposed to old forms of cinema, is a resonating space, and not just metaphorically: Wolfgang Ernst, following McLuhan, has shown that, technically all electronic images are oscillating processes in a frequency field.[56] On the web, those frequencies organize themselves as a calculable interference. This corresponds to a new model of the mind and of communication in neuropsychology. Newer neurophysiological theories of perception do not assume that "the world organizes itself in front of me," as Merleau-Ponty put it, but that it reorganizes all relationships we have with the world through minute calculations. Perceptual models of cortical activity conceptualized in psychology today seem to correspond with the perception of images on the web.

The Max Planck Institute for Brain Research in Frankfurt, returning to the laws of *gestalt* theory as previously described by Merleau-Ponty,[57] has for some years been conducting tests to explore the blurring boundaries of *gestalts* in images. New schools of psychology and neuropsychology alike, as well as media studies, by the way, which need to calculate effects of computer graphics,[58] are addressing *gestalt* questions in order to trace so-called "binding problems" in visual structures. They are examining visual areas where contradictory and complex formations do not allow for any clear decision regarding the organization of the field of vision and *gestalt*—making it impossible in those cases to decide what elements or re-

53) Max Bense, *Programmierung des Schönen. Allgemeine Texttheorie und Textästhetik* (Krefeld/Baden-Baden: Agis, 1960), p. 125 (translated from German).

54) Lev Manovich, "The Practice of Everyday (Media) Life," in Lovink/Niederer, *op. cit.*, p. 33. "In the case of social media, the unprecedented growth of numbers of people who upload and view each other's media led to lots of innovation. While the typical diary video or anime on *YouTube* may not be particularly special, enough are. In fact, in all media where the technologies of productions were democratized (video, music, animation, graphic design, etc.), I have come across many projects which not only rival those produced by most well-known commercial companies and most well-known artists, but often explore the new areas not yet touched by those who are endowed with large amounts of symbolic capital." Manovich refers to Michel de Certeau and his thesis on the functional interplay between strategy and tactics of procedures: as institutions become tactical, users become increasingly strategic in their procedures.

55) See Bernhard Waldenfels, *Topographie des Fremden, Studien zur Phänomenologie des Fremden 1* (Frankfurt am Main: Suhrkamp, 1997).

56) Wolfgang Ernst, "Takt und Taktilität—Akustik als privilegierter Kanal zeitkrischer Medienprozesse," in Derrick de Kerckhove et al. (eds.), *McLuhan neu lesen: Kritische Analysen zu Medien und Kultur im 21. Jahrhundert* (Bielefeld: transcript, 2008), pp. 170–180.

57) See Wolf Singer, "Neocortical Rhythms: An Overview," in Christoph von Marlsburg et al. (eds.), *Dynamic Coordination in the Brain: From Neurons to Mind* (Cambridge: MIT Press, 2010), p. 164. "Synchronization correlates well with elementary Gestalt rules such as continuity, co-linearity, and common fate."

58) See Kittler, *op. cit.*

gions are part of the figure and which are part of a background. This questions the coherence of a field as an image or visual field, because the information coming from the sensory organs allows equally plausible interpretations. Perception cannot make a decision; it cannot make up its mind, so to speak, and therefore oscillates for a long time between several visual states. Only slowly, after some time, will the perceiving mind decide on a specific way to structure the organization of an image or the world, and "this process of segmentation requires a considerable amount of processing time."[59]

The complex procedures of Internet perception show an ongoing and indecisive back-and-forth between visual data, frame and image, layers and levels of information before an image and a homogeneous field of vision appear. Much fluctuation, testing, and oscillating happens between data-sets, which should by no means be regarded as a loss of responsible and self-dependent thought, as Bernard Stiegler put it.[60] Instead, this kind of oscillating attention is a perceptive process that will constantly change frames, levels and parameters of approach until finally an image emerges that makes sense—or changes the mind. Perception becomes ever more complex over a longer period of time. Ambiguity is, to a certain degree, necessary. "On all processing levels the neurons react to more than just one single characteristic. They are sensitive to changes in the parameters of various dimensions of characteristics. Thus, individual cells respond with ambiguity."[61]

The ripple of leaves stirred by the wind, as it marked early cinema's perception[62] has become, as it were, the ripple of brain waves stirred by electronic images. The idea that electric pulses of nerve activity produce waves that can be analyzed according to harmonics was indeed the basis for Norbert Wiener's studies on cybernetics in human beings and machines likewise.[63] In order to find out how the brain processes the impression of a face out of large quantities of data, Wolf Singer's research group in Frankfurt might as well have played a datamoshed film to their lab cats and monkeys. The researchers observed that coherencies similar to those entities perceived according to *gestalt* logics are constituted when the brain rhythmically coordinates vibrations of various areas. "Neurons responding to the components of faces (e.g., eyes, nose, mouth) synchronized their responses when the arrangement of these components was such that the animals recognized a face; however they did not synchronize when the components were scrambled or presented in a way the animal deemed incompatible with the appearance of a normal face."[64] As the old *gestalt* theory in Frankfurt had shown approximately a century before, it is easier for shapes to emerge from fields if we who perceive the world move in relation to these fields. Constant movement is a precondition for perceiving complex *gestalt* figures, as today's supposedly fidgety children seem to know well. While Bernard Stiegler sees them as nervous wrecks in front of manipulated monitors, their behavior perfectly complies with newer psychology, which advises us to repeatedly change frames and levels of viewing through constant movements in order to make sense of the world. Observers can assume that they are not just nervous, but actually training to see out of the corners of their eyes. Norbert Wiener once suggested shaking a machine in case it did not work—and with Wiener it is justified to include animals and probably adults and children.[65] The children diagnosed with ADHD by Stiegler and Lovink might just be shaking themselves in order to distill perceivable objects out of the masses of data that make up images on the Internet. Whether this reaction is pleasant or unpleasant can hardly be determined. Getting used to new media cultures always seems to imply a lot of nausea and vertigo, as pre-cinematic experiences indicate, like those of the Hale's Tours, but also laboratory experiments with Wilhelm Wundt or Hugo Münsterberg in the service of perception theory.

Newer psychology argues that seeing and hearing are dependent on constantly changing one's situation in space. If the images of the world change, then the brain—and ultimately the mind—will alter its attitude towards the field of vision. "A cell in the primary visual cortex that is sensitive to orientational information changes the amplitude of its response not only when the orientation of a contour changes, but also when there is variation in its position, contrast or extension."[66] In a way, Merleau-Ponty's observation that a "certain philosophy" emerges "particularly in the age of cinema," could also be applied to the new psychological model and the corresponding practices of cinematic perception on the Internet. A common aesthesis between media and psychology emerges simultaneously. While neuropsychologists study irritating amounts of processed data in order to describe corresponding perceptive patterns and behavior, film perception deals with the same kind of data organization as information within online cinema, that could be considered either as images-to-be or as fragmented meta-data. The digitized brain has to make up its mind, taking its time, switching levels, before it decides which *gestalt*, background or movement can be coherently distinguished. In both historical cases, behavior is not limited to a defined space, but rather it describes the problem of an attitude within an os-

59) Wolf Singer, "Der Beobachter im Gehirn," in *Der Beobachter im Gehirn. Essays zur Hirnforschung* (Frankfurt am Main: Suhrkamp, 2002), p. 150 (translated from German).

60) See Stiegler, *Die Logik der Sorge. Verlust der Aufklärung durch Technik und Medien* (Frankfurt am Main: Suhrkamp, 2008), pp. 118–123.

61) Singer, 2002, "Beobachter im Gehirn", pp. 156–157 (translated from German).

62) See Siegfried Kracauer, *Theory of Film. The Redemption of Physical Reality* (New York: Oxford University Press, 1960), p. 31.

63) See Wiener, *op. cit.*, pp. 181–203.

64) Singer, 2010, "Neocortical Rhythms," p. 164.

65) Norbert Wiener, "Kybernetik (1948)," in Bernhard Dotzler (ed.), *Futurum Exactum. Ausgewählte Schriften zur Kybernetik und Kommunikationstheorie* (Vienna and New York: Springer, 2002), pp. 13–29. "What do we do with a machine when this kind of an accident [oscillation between two states, U.H.] occurs? First, we try to delete all of the information in the hope that the problems will not appear again with other data when the computer is rebooted. If this does not work and the error cannot be fixed, then we shake the machine..." (p. 22, translated from German).

66) Singer, 2002, "Beobachter," p. 157 (translated from German).

cillating topology in a field of vision. The difference between old and new cinema is that in a projection hall the number of others watching is known and their reactions—except in comedies—are mostly muffled, while on the web audiences consist of countless reactions, albeit deferred, shared with anonymous other users using the same programs. Only after choosing to look at, to stop, to repeat while watching films on the Internet, does the audience realize that they are an active part of a structure. The procedures involving our own subjectivization have become far more complicated in new cinema and probably require "a considerable amount of time" to process.[67]

Neurophysiology as well as media theory will have to search for solutions to describe the complexity and disparity of this new form of inattentive and distraught perception, beyond simply dismissing it as ADHD. The researchers in Frankfurt propose that localities of the brain's cortex are not simply affected by stimuli coming from the environment, but that transmissions of forms, figures, images and sounds stimulate a set of different areas in the cortex that will, depending on rhythmic resonance, form unities and coherence. Areas responding to common vibrations and their harmonics constitute or activate a coherent impression of the world.[68] It is not through localization and association, as was assumed around 1900, but through resonance in topologies, through corresponding frequencies, that a relation of mind and matter is established. This allows for perceptual worlds to be interlaced, looped and connected in feedback processes, in complex phase relations, in phase-locking loops.[69] In hypothesizing a new model of brain functions, Wolf Singer writes, "This concatenation of rhythms offers the attractive option of establishing graded correlations between neuronal assemblies of different size, thereby encoding nested relations. Such encoding is required for the representation of both composite perceptual objects and composite movement trajectories."[70]

Images, in this sense, are relational states in an oscillating space. Rhythmic and vibrational processes establish a perceptual structure, which lasts over a period of time until perception makes up its mind to find another vibrating or vibrant correspondence that is more probable. The same can be said for grasping film-like images between the logic of the web and older film formats that rely on reflected light, a defined surface, camera movements and montage. In the perception of films online, we resonate with a cinema of the future, trying to catch its vibrations beyond coherent and material images. Or, as an Australian translator of *La Jetée*, probably a surfer himself, put it for the protagonist between the times: "... he eventually caught some waves of the world to come." In this spirit of surfing, the forces and forms of film production and perception on the Internet should be observed.

*Translated by Allison Plath-Moseley*

67) *Ibid.*, p. 150.

68) "Precise synchronization of discharges is often associated with an oscillatory patterning of the neuronal responses." Singer, 2010, "Neocortical Rhythms," p. 162.

69) *Ibid.*

70) *Ibid.*

Ekkehard Knörer

# Movable Images on Portable Devices

"I, too, used to be a fanatic about such things. But… not anymore, no."[1]

*Pedro Costa*

### WATCHING MOVIES ONLINE

I will be writing about a simple thing only: the new online culture (and emerging market) of what we traditionally call movies, including the discourse around them. I do not want to define this term here; let me just say that I refer to a certain configuration of social, technical and aesthetic practices that came to be at the center of what might be called a cinephilic age; the movies with a capital M, The Movies. This is not about contemporary forms of digital image production such as cat content memes, datamoshing experiments and all the other contributions to a new Do-It-Yourself video culture on platforms from *Vimeo* to *YouTube*. Instead, my question is: What becomes of movies (The Movies) in the digital age? Clearly, the image as such is becoming digital on almost all levels and in almost all fields of image production. Producing a film with an analog camera will soon be considered an ancient and rather quaint practice. The fact that both the film image and its projection are going digital in their everyday use is and has to be implied in everything that follows.

Film museums will soon be the only places where old devices for projecting light through analog filmstrips still exist. At the same time, many film archives have already entered into a process of transferring parts of their collection to digital media. Movies have always been migrant, of course: physical copies had to be struck and sent and transported and projected and returned. This process will die out as movies, by dint of their digitization, are turned into a more fundamentally migrant art. They are no longer located and locatable in a single place. Large parts of what is considered the core of movie history have been copied into their own digital versions, on DVD, on Blu-ray and more frequently in all kinds of files that are available on purely digital online sources. These sources include commercial sites like *Hulu* and *Netflix* to file-sharing communities and streaming link ag-

1) That's what Pedro Costa said when confronted with a horrendous projection of one of his short films at the *Rencontres Internationales* festival in Berlin in July 2011. David Hudson reports, and continues: "He added that just the night before he'd downloaded an early Renoir and, even for all its splotchy pixels and the tininess of the window on his computer screen, it was a better viewing experience than many a film he'd seen at Cannes projected under the most ideal conditions." (http://davidhudson.tumblr.com/post/7196410286/im-retired-pedro-costa-repeated-last-night).

gregators of the more or less legal kind (from *archive.org* to *ubu.com* to the late *kino.to*). There is no doubt in my mind that this is changing the status of the "originals" in film museum and film studio archives. Digital copies are in the process of being struck from them so they can continue generating the future of film's history. This history however will be present in the digital copies that circulate on the Internet.

The question then is: How is the configuration of what used to be (and still is) called the movies changed by the fact that movies no longer have a place to truly call their own? The newly movable images, in their new instable homes (*YouTube*, illegal streaming sites, file-sharing communities) are confronted with new kinds of behavior, new neighbors, new formats, and an incessantly changing landscape of what is considered a moving image, of what it means to watch a m/M/ovie and/or moving images. I will briefly touch upon these new configurations, focusing first on the cinephilic, non-commercial niche, then on what seems to me the future of mainstream, commercial online movie watching practices. I will look at a file-sharing community on the one hand, and at the most likely winner of the competition for new models of valorization in this newly emerging market, i.e., *Netflix*; a corporation that is at this very moment still geographically confined to North American markets. However, with the recent announcement of the entrance into the Latin American market, this is already changing. It is my bet that the future forms of our online consumption of moving images (on TVs probably rather than computers) are already showing their contours in the business model of *Netflix*.[2]

This also means that I am not much concerned with the media theory of these changes. Or, conversely: I assume that something like "a movie" and "the movies" will continue to exist, with the accompanying discourses, practices (of watching), etc.; transformed, but still recognizable from a history that stretches back more than a hundred years, to the very beginning of the art form. To put it even more bluntly: The history of cinema and the movies will continue even after the transformation of the digital age. It almost goes without saying that along with the media, the image also changes: from emulsion to compressed digital data, from a dispersion of light to the result of an algorithm, from image to information. Much is being made of this media revolution, and what you make of it definitely depends on your theory of media. The more you see media in its technical/material aspect as determining the (psychic, perceptive) configurations of its "use," i.e., the closer you are to the Kittler school, the more radical the change that is taking place has to appear. Changes in technology, however, are never mere changes of material mechanisms or innovations that remain limited to the workings of a machine. Every change and innovation has to

2) *Netflix* has managed to act rather stupid with its attempts to separate the DVD rental and streaming businesses lately. It seems a bit more probable than before that competitors might get back in the game. This does not detract much from my argument, though: *Netflix* is working towards a model for the commercial future of moving image consumption. My guess is that this future will have to look something like what *Netflix* is offering.

be implemented and thereby appropriated by individuals and societies in order to truly assume contours as a "new thing." Watching movies in the digital age therefore has to and will become part of practices and discourses that make sense of it and that are thereby themselves changed and innovated.

Thus, an important part of the picture is the innovative uses of media. From that perspective, the revolution in media specificities seems to be, on the one hand, negligible to quite a surprising degree. People very smoothly integrate the new digital movable images into their media consumption (and so do I). No one seems to think that the digital images we watch on all the new screens and devices are no longer true moving images. We talk about "movies" and "films" as if that were what we see when we "read" these algorithmically produced data on our more or less portable devices. Their users, it seems, appropriate the new algorithmic images with astonishingly little effort. These movable images on portable devices are taken as a matter of fact to (still) be moving images. Which, conversely, does not mean that practices and discourses are not deeply affected by the social appropriation of technical changes. It just means that what, from a lot of technical and theoretical perspectives, would have to be regarded as a revolution is taken in stride by large parts of the happily prosuming public.

### THE MOUNTAIN COMING TO THE PROPHET

Watching movies nowadays, for me, more often than not is a thing of rather untraditional transport. That is to say: I no longer transport myself to a stationary brick-and-mortar movie theater ten, twenty or thirty minutes away; be it by foot, by bike or the tube (the old tube, not the *YouTube*). I no longer pay for a ticket or wait till the lights go off. There are no ads and trailers to endure, there is no popcorn to smell and there are no noisy people to be hushed. My movie watching goes rather like this: I sit at my desk in front of my laptop, I click on a virtual bookmark up there in my browser (it's the one with the crow) and I enter my username and password. Under the heading "Blue Dawn" I was recently greeted by the following message: The tracker is "now running on a brand new, ultra-fast server with approximately 10 times more processing power and 4 times more memory than the previous server." This is good news, as this will reduce the number of times my movie-theater is basically down (though there are alternatives).

On the left of the screen I am told that, however solitary and single I may feel at my desk, I am the member of quite an impressive community comprising 29,481 users. A few of them are friends and I can identify them by their (fake) names, but most of them I don't know at all: I have no idea where they live, what they do, of what gender or sexual persuasion they are, or what they look like. We say thanks in the form of dancing emoticons, but we never meet—as far as we know—except in the commentary columns below the database information on the films. Still, these are my brothers and sisters in the crime of a very contemporary form of cinephilia. Together we—but mostly they—have built an archive of almost 60,000 movie torrents, i.e., films that we can potentially share as digital files. Having transported myself into this community via a few clicks, and (almost certainly) having found the film I was looking for, I now start transporting the files via BitTorrent from my anonymous friends' hard drive to mine. There are some limitations and rules to be respected, but I won't go into any detail here; if you are interested just send me an email or become my *Facebook* friend (everybody is welcome).

The fact of the matter is this: After an hour or two or, in case my seeder has a slow upload connection, a few days later the movie has arrived as a package of digital data on my own hard drive. I will keep my connection open so that everybody can leech. In most cases I store the digital-data-that-is-a-movie on a USB flash drive and plug it into what is still called my DVD player. From there the data is transported to my very traditional TV screen and my movie experience can begin. This is, admittedly, a bit over-complicated; there are smoother ways via set top boxes and direct Internet-to-TV-streaming. All kinds of (what from here and now looks like) hybrid media will emerge until finally I will be able to watch movies, legally or semi-legally or illegally on a new digital device that encompasses internet and TV, being both and yet neither one exactly: a data machine for processing and transporting the moving image-sound-compound from a server/servers in some or rather no longer a single part of the globe to my senses in another part of the globe.

You can always add a projector and hi-fi Dolby surround loudspeakers to that, and what reemerges is something like a homemade or private replica of the situation formerly known as watching a film in a public movie theater. On the other end of the digital-data-that-is-a-movie experience, let's say, is the iPhone as the ultimate transportable screen that turns virtually every place at any time into a private "movie theater," especially the space of public transport. (Redistribution of aspects of the private and the public, and possibly even redefinitions of what is private and public are very much a part of the picture.) Moving bodies watching moving images in a surrounding that was certainly never built to house a transportable movie-theater-movie-patron configuration like that.

## THE SPECTRUM

There are a lot of questions, not necessarily new ones, to be asked about this (not only) technical reconfiguration of what used to be the movies. Let's even assume, for the sake of argument, that for most of movie history there existed something like a "normal" figuration of what constitutes a film and the experience of watching it: an amalgam of the apparatic (the translucent analog but copyable—"technically reproducible"—medium of the synthetic strip; the projector, virtually unchanged for decades; the screen onto which the images are projected in a cone of light in general darkness), the architectural (a brick-and-mortar building with a box office, open to the paying public, with a stationary projector in a booth) and the social (people gathering at a certain time, creating a spontaneous and mostly silent community of strangers).

This "normal" figuration—coming into existence in the Western sphere in the 1910s with the building of movie theaters that mimicked and outclassed stage theaters—has at all times had its less official and legitimate offspring or countercurrent or anti-establishment: 16mm ciné-clubs, amateur film with its mostly private projections, shady and illegitimate cinemas of the porn or grindhouse or drive-in variety, and traveling movie theaters in less centralized and capitalized regions of the world. (All or most of this still exists, by the way.) What is considered, and often critically so, as the general *dispositif* of watching movies, i.e., the fixation of bodies in a dark place where then spectator and image become a chiastically and subconsciously entwined body-image-affect-mind conglomerate of perception (to take an example of the Merleau-Ponty variety), has, in other words, always been merely one of various practices of watching movies; from watching porn to the far more social event that going to the movies is in certain cultures, especially the tradition of commercial movies in India (Bollywood and its regional cinema brethren). Song and dance and talk are very much a part of the experience there. And even within the dominant paradigm of "the movies" (the ones to which you go) there have always been an enormous variety of spaces and places, of care in projection and luxury in reception, of isolationist versus community practices, etc.

Over time, the moving image has become more and more transportable; first with TV, then with video formats and video recorders and players, with DVD and ultimately the Internet. It has also become easier to copy and less dependent on a specific device and medium. In short: The "normal" social, apparatic and architectural configuration becomes one among different forms in which the reception of moving images takes place—and a more marginal one with every reconfiguration of the *dispositif*. Within their history, the movies (as moving images) have not only developed into dominantly films of color and sound (arguably something that can be described as technical progress), they have also transformed into lines of light in a TV set, projected not onto but from a screen. They have been cropped and distorted and discolored as video copies and now as digital reincarnations in the illegal file-sharing communities of the present (arguably something of a technical degradation), and then turned into shiny and eminently projectable digital high-end data in the Blu-ray and digital cinema era. TV and the videocassette, as media of the diffusion of movie images, could still be regarded as mere supplements of a dominating form (but always beware, cf. Derrida, of the "mereness" of the supplement). In the age of Blu-ray and Dolby surround home cinema installations, it becomes more and more obvious that this is no longer the case.

So this is the diagnosis: We have now reached a state where the movies have evolved into something extraordinarily manifold. Something like the old, traditional "normal configuration" no longer exists as a dominant form—technically, socially, in every respect. In its stead, what used to be clearly identified as "the movies" (with its high point in terms of a unified grand theory and practice in the French, American and other local and national variations of "cinephilia") has turned into a spectrum of more or less equal and equally valid technical and social shapes and forms, having actually become spectral in that respect. This development may be lamented by cultural pessimists and traditionalists of various denominations (old school cinephiles resisting new developments, nostalgically metaphysical cave dwellers of the Schlüpmann variety, etc.), but there can be no doubt that this is the state of things.

It has its corollaries in critical discourse. Jonathan Rosenbaum is the prime example of an old school cinephile critic who regards the changes in cinema culture as a blessing rather than a curse.[3] The new emergence of discussions and passions and communities in blogs, online magazines and all kinds of different digital venues on the Internet certainly is part of the same movement of the digitalization of moving and movable images. These new structures are and will remain—just as cinephilia has been at all times—an altogether niche phenomenon (the new media and discourse conglomerates from the "Huffington Post" to "Spiegel Online" are already well advanced in their formation). But even as such they globalize a discourse that is and will be centered around hubs of aggregation and linking rather than depending on authoritative voices and the distributive forces and structures of print media. Audiences have become far more mobile and fluid themselves, dispersed over the globe, but finding and reconfiguring themselves as passionate interest groups communing on the net. These new structures of cinephilia are rhizomatic rather than centralized, or technically speaking: they consist of communications of addresses in a uniform resource locator system that produce discourses about algorithmically rendered digital data files called movies.

There certainly is a seriousness—sometimes bordering, interestingly enough, on nostalgia—among those hardcore cinephiles in their often fiercely pronounced aesthetic judgments, in their defense of historical knowledge, DVD and Blu-ray image quality, format correctness, and care for the art of projection in the traditional movie theater. It is a culture of knowledgeable amateur experts (with professionals like David Bordwell laudably turning into an amateur with a vengeance), with all the passion and curiosity and width and breadth of interests and critical forms of writing (and video essaying) and—sometimes—with the nerdy *déformations nonprofessionelles* that this implies. This new state so sketchily described here will, undoubtedly, change even faster from here on in, but it seems unimaginable that cinema and the movies and the discourse generated by and

3) See Jonathan Rosenbaum, *Goodbye Cinema, Hello Cinephilia: Film Culture in Transition* (Chicago: University of Chicago Press, 2010) and his contribution to this volume.

around them will ever again be what they used to (seemed to) be for generations of their most ardent interpreters, theorists and plain vanilla movie going audiences: a practice that is to a large degree defined by its dominant brick-and-mortar form with all the consequences this multiple fixation still has.

## REDISTRIBUTIONS: THE NETFLIX ECONOMY

The general globalization—as deterritorialization—of digital image streams, of Internet discourses, of movies and their recipients in the database age is and has been, to put it mildly, a challenge to all forms of and attempts at capitalistically valorizing the production and the distribution of moving images. On the one hand, there is an upswing of niche economies, from crowd funding to *Flattr* to self-distribution (compare, for example, Hal Hartley's "Possible Films") that, however, in its current state leaves little hope of becoming a major part of revenue streams in the general field. There are, on the other hand, immense amounts of files illegally finding their way as uncontrolled—and only partly controllable—copies from one user's hard drive to another, via BitTorrent or one-click hosters. This has produced a whole ecosystem with a disparate culture of software and websites of its own (from *JDownloader* to specialized search engines like *Pirate Bay* or *FilesTube*). The valorization taking place in these dark and hardly legalizable corners unfortunately—but not surprisingly—is never to the benefit of authors and creators but of various intermediaries that offer link and host sites as illegal platforms.

Shadow economies like these can have this kind of success only when there exists no official economy that offers the same product with comparable or better quality and more technical comfort. The huge conglomerates formerly known as Hollywood studios—and to some degree their partly state-funded European equivalents as well—are still having a hard time coming up with business models for the valorization of the online distribution of moving images. One major problem is exactly their tradition of conquering markets by dividing them into geographic units, hence the absurdity of region codes. As far as DVDs go, it actually worked, because borders—which are always an artifice—do not have to be absolute in order to prevent critical amounts of trespassing (cf., the ridiculously surmountable *New York Times* pay wall). As long as the border or wall is reasonably difficult to hurdle for the average user this seems to suffice, sometimes even mere symbolism is enough. With the advent of globally accessible file-sharing and streaming sites this is no longer the case; the newly deterritorialized images and image streams are, to say the least, not easily reterritorializable. This is why the practice of regional blocking—the attempt to (re)introduce regional codes into internet traffic—in general mostly just resulted in the shadow markets we know. Regional blocking is not a globally practical solution to the problem of online valorization, on which the future of the media conglomerates depends, because digital data flows too freely.

It seems useful at this point to look more closely at a model that already works, at least for the North American markets. I am talking, of course, about *Netflix*. The numbers are impressive. It can be argued that *Netflix* has conquered, or rather created, the most important future market of online movie distribution. *Netflix* very recently made an ill-considered move by trying to change from a combined system of cheap DVD and online flat-rate rentals to a model that by dint of its price increase suggests a split in markets; the past (DVD rental, dying a slow death) and a market of the future (video on demand, booming and blooming). After major resistance by its customers and a considerable loss in its stock value, *Netflix* hastily backpedaled. This goes to show that this is an emerging market whose rules and mechanisms are in a constant flux. There is no guarantee that *Netflix* will be the winner in this market, so I should probably add that I use *Netflix* only as the placeholder for "a company or companies like *Netflix*."[4] Already at this moment, data transmissions via the *Netflix* on-demand component, "Watch Instantly," are the single most important part of Internet traffic in North America, accounting for no less than a quarter of the overall traffic.[5] In spite of the recent blunder and in spite of the reluctance by major Hollywood and TV companies to cooperate with *Netflix,* it seems not very likely that any of the existing or potential competitors—from *Hulu* to *Amazon*, from *YouTube* to *Facebook*—will have a chance to beat a market player that has achieved such an almost monopolist status in a mostly emerging market.

The question then is: How and why does *Netflix* "Watch Instantly" work? The answer to this question, which at first sight seems of only local importance, may well be the answer to the question of what the mostly non-cinephile, i.e., general consumers of newly movable images, will look like. For one thing: *Netflix* is a product of North America, which is still the most important global market. By building a quasi-monopoly in online streaming, it has just enough power to force the Hollywood studios into submission. The studios, of course, would have loved to build the market of online distribution themselves. And just like the music industry, they—for structural reasons—missed the boat by insisting on enforcing their own models. *Netflix* may well be what *iTunes* is for the music industry: the successful first mover in a new market whose models and conditions will determine the systems of valorization for the old industries as well as set the benchmarks for emerging competitors.

This is more fundamental than it seems initially. First we have to define what the exact potential forms and prices of commodities in this market of online-streaming are. Will it be something that can be described as en event, like a visit to the movies, or a film festival, or like traditional TV, which by programming

4) See, as one of many instant comments on what may be called the "Qwikster disaster": Peter Kafka, "Qwikster Is Gonester: Netflix Kills Its DVD-Only Business Before Launch," http://allthingsd.com/20111010/qwikster-is-gonester-netflix-kills-its-dvd-only-business-before-launch

5) Devindra Hardawar, "Netflix now accounts for 25% of North American Internet traffic," *Venture Beat*, May 17, 2011, http://venturebeat.com/2011/05/17/netflix-north-america-traffi.

films at specific times created mini-events (but diluted their character as events by promising multiple repetitions)? *Mubi* is actually moving in this direction by creating online events in co-operation with festivals; screening films not so much at fixed hours but coupling the "broadcast" with the offline festival dates. *Netflix* does it completely different—different from *iTunes* as well—by turning a single piece pay-per-view rental system into a flat-rate system. As *Spotify* and comparable services work quite similarly, it seems plausible that this really is the system most perfectly attuned to the new media circumstance of acoustic and optical information as digital data, i.e., a situation where almost all material substrates of the carrier medium have been dissolved—or rather virtualized—into mere digital 1/0 bits of information. However, this changes the game almost completely. Flat-rate rental systems are hardly distinguishable anymore from sale models, at least within environments highly saturated with online access flat-rates—and without the current fluctuations of licensing deals. Flat-rates then seem to be the perfect model of valorization in an "always on" and "always available" culture. This means that the single artifact (be it a film, a track, a book) will become so cheap as to be almost free—which is only logical in an economic system where the incremental costs of a single copy are close to zero. This most certainly does not mean that going to the movies needs to become cheaper or less of an event than it is now, quite the contrary. It seems probable that a sharply divided system of two different markets will take the place of the graded value chains that have existed for decades now all along the changing systems of exploitation, from TV to video and DVD. *Netflix* seems to signal this change in the field of the movies, creating a flat-rate market for always available films at almost zero cost—as opposed to the highly different cinema culture of more and more expensive and lavish movie going experiences.

The costs and consequences will be manifold. Ready availability translates not only into economic devaluation, but also, psycho-dynamically speaking, into de-fetishization of single objects, i.e., into a leveling of the field in film historical terms. Considerable parts of what is traditionally seen as the core of film history will be available via *Netflix* (and even larger parts, for a cinephile niche audience, via illegal sharing communities of the kind described above), but the lack of a lack will have consequences for the libidinal investments into single films, directors and film history in general. Henri Langlois in his cinémathèque practice insisted that a film once projected would go back to the vaults and not be shown for a long time. It is quite unclear at the moment what will and can be the mechanisms of revaluation and re-fetishization of directors, films, etc.—or if this leveling of the field will lead to the fragmentation of the public into smaller and smaller groups as configurations of social graphs. More generally speaking this is a question of redistributing attention. Under the circumstances of pervasive availability, new centers of discourse, advanced mechanisms of filtering and evaluation will have to be found. The creation of new kinds of "events," i.e., of artificial scarcity, and the reorganization of what used to be film criticism will also be necessary. Blogathons, the critical texts commissioned by organizations like the *Museum of the Moving Image,*[6] and aggregatorial endeavors of all kinds are signs that there will be journalistic, curatorial and critical practices and mechanisms to counter the devaluation of (not only) single films in an age of overwhelming choice.

One last note concerning something that looks like a side aspect of the new *Netflix* regime, but is actually one of the major new mechanisms with which attention is created. *Netflix* caused some public (as well as legal[7]) brouhaha with its competition for the 10% improvement of its recommendation algorithms. In 2009, it found a winner called *Pragmatic Chaos*. Already in 2008, about 60 percent of all additions to the *Netflix* users' queue depended on an algorithm that is very much comparable to similar mechanisms used by Amazon, et al. It is the mathematical equivalent of what used to be called taste. These algorithms pretend to know the individual's taste, and obviously quite successfully so. The single user's history is part of the equation, but even more important is the statistical data about preferences by users with similar choices. We are entering into an age where friends whose tastes we share are not only scattered all over the world and come together in anonymous communities of like minds, but where we also learn to trust "friends" who are nothing but aggregated data of equations with learning curves and "taste." Algorithms compute data from databases and thereby teach us to choose which digital data, of movable images formerly and still known as films, we might want to watch. This can go two ways. For skeptics it will be a reason to bemoan the state of things and fear for a future in which everybody becomes enclosed in filter bubbles that blinker the view, in the present and even more so into the past. For others—and I count myself among them—there is much hope and reason to believe that the new communities, algorithmic friends, movable and copyable files of movable images will produce a movie culture that is more variable, resourceful and richer than anything before.

6) These articles are to be found as a separate website at: www.movingimagesource.us.

7) The competition was cancelled in 2010 because of privacy concerns. See Steve Lohr, "Netflix Cancels Contest After Concerns Are Raised About Privacy," *New York Times*, March 12, 2010, www.nytimes.com/2010/03/13/technology/13netflix.html

# Contributors

**RAYMOND BELLOUR,** film and literary theorist, curator and writer, is Director of Research Emeritus at the *Centre National de la Recherche Scientifique* (CNRS), Paris. Since 1972, he has been a visiting professor at numerous universities in the USA and Germany; since 1986, he has taught in the Department for Cinema and Audiovisual Studies at the *Université de Paris III*. Bellour has been the editor of the Complete Works of Henri Michaux in the *Bibliothèque de la Pléiade* (1998–2004). Among his most important book publications are *The Analysis of Film* (1977, English translation 2000), *L'Entre-Images. Photo, film, vidéo* (1990), *L'Entre-Images 2. Mots, Images* (1999), *Le Corps du cinéma. Hypnoses, émotions, animalités* (2009). He is one of the editors of the film magazine *Trafic* which he co-founded with Serge Daney in 1991.

**VICTOR BURGIN** is an artist and writer. He is Professor Emeritus of History of Consciousness at the University of California, Santa Cruz, and Emeritus Professor of Visual Arts at Goldsmiths College, University of London. His academic books include *Situational Aesthetics: Selected Writings* (2009), *The Remembered Film* (2004), *In/Different Spaces: Place and Memory in Visual Culture* (1996), *The End of Art Theory: Criticism and Postmodernity* (1986), and the edited collection *Thinking Photography* (1982). The most recent books devoted to his visual work are *Components of a Practice* (2008), and *Victor Burgin: Objets Temporels* (2007). His most recent book is *Parallel Texts: Interviews and Interventions about Art* (2011). He is currently working on *The Prosthetic Unconscious: Psychoanalysis and Virtual Worlds*, for Polity books.

**TOM GUNNING** is the Edwin A. and Betty L. Bergman Distinguished Service Professor in the Department of Cinema and Media Studies at the University of Chicago. He is the author of *D.W. Griffith and the Origins of American Narrative Film* (1994) and *The Films of Fritz Lang: Allegories of Vision and Modernity* (2000), and of over one-hundred articles on early cinema, film history and theory, avant-garde film, film genre, and cinema and modernism. With André Gaudreault he originated the influential theory of the "Cinema of Attractions." In 2009 he was awarded an Andrew A. Mellon Distinguished Achievement Award, the first film scholar to receive one, and in 2010 was elected to the American Academy of Arts and Sciences. He is currently working on a book on the invention of the moving image.

**MIRIAM BRATU HANSEN** (1949–2011) was Professor in the Humanities at the University of Chicago and the founding chair of what is now the Department of Cinema and Media Studies. Her publications include books on Ezra Pound and *Babel and Babylon: Spectatorship in American Silent Film* (1991). The last book she finished is *Cinema and Experience. Siegfried Kracauer, Walter Benjamin, and Theodor W. Adorno*, published posthumously by University of California Press in September 2011. Her numerous essays on film, cinema and the public sphere were highly influential for the rise of film theory.

**VINZENZ HEDIGER** is Professor of Film at Goethe University, Frankfurt am Main. He is one of the co-founders of NECS, the *European Network for Cinema and Media Studies*. He is an editor of *Montage AV* (www.montage-av.de) and was the founding editor of *Zeitschrift für Medienwissenschaft* (www.zfmedienwissenschaft.de). His publications include *Films that Work. Industrial Films and the Productivity of Media* (2009) and *Nostalgia for the Coming Attractions. American Movie Trailers and the Culture of Film Consumption* (Columbia University Press, forthcoming).

**UTE HOLL** is Professor of Media Aesthetics in Basel, Switzerland. Her main focuses of research are the history of perception in technical media, the history of the audiovisual in scientific knowledge, and the media history of acoustics and electro-acoustics. She has also published widely on experimental and ethnographic film. Book publications include *Kino, Trance & Kybernetik* (2002) and *Suchbilder. Visuelle Kultur zwischen Algorithmen und Archiven* (co-editor, 2003).

**EKKEHARD KNÖRER** is a film critic and cultural studies scholar. He is the editor of *Merkur. Deutsche Zeitschrift für europäisches Denken* and co-founder of *CARGO. Film/Medien/Kultur*. Publications in English: "The Pleasures of the 'Not-Quite-Movie'," in Bernd Herzogenrath (ed.), *Edgar G. Ulmer* (2009); "On Signs and Money in Robert Bresson's

*L'Argent*," in Fiona Cox / Hans-Walter Schmidt-Hannisa (eds.), *Money and Culture* (2008); and "Undoing Make-Believe," in Bernd Herzogenrath (ed.), *The Cinema of Tod Browning* (2008).

**GERTRUD KOCH** is Professor of Film Studies at the Free University in Berlin. She was visiting professor and scholar at Columbia University, New York University, Washington University, the University of California Irvine, University of Pennsylvania, the Getty Research Center and other US research institutions. Her many publications deal with aesthetic theory, feminist film theory and with questions of historical representation. She has also written books on Herbert Marcuse and Siegfried Kracauer (English translation, 2000) and edited volumes on the visual representation of the Holocaust, the aesthetics of illusion and problems of mimesis. She is co-editor and board member of several German and international journals such as *Babylon*, *Frauen und Film*, *October*, *Constellations*, *Philosophy & Social Criticism*. She is currently working on a book about the aesthetics of illusion in film and the other arts.

**THOMAS MORSCH,** Associate Professor of Film Studies at the Free University Berlin. Head of a research project on the aesthetics of television series within the framework of the Collaborative Research Center "Aesthetic Experience and the Dissolution of Artistic Limits." Author of *Medienästhetik des Films. Verkörperte Wahrnehmung und ästhetische Erfahrung im Kino* (2011). An edited volume on genre and series as regulatory systems in film and television is in preparation for 2012.

**VOLKER PANTENBURG** is Assistant Professor of Moving Images at the Bauhaus University Weimar and Junior Director of the *Internationales Kolleg für Medienphilosophie und Kulturtechnikforschung (IKKM)*. His book publications include *Film als Theorie. Bildforschung bei Harun Farocki und Jean-Luc Godard* (2006) and *Ränder des Kinos. Godard – Benning – Wiseman – Costa* (2010).

**JONATHAN ROSENBAUM** was film critic for the Chicago Reader from 1987 to 2008. His books include *Goodbye Cinema, Hello Cinephilia: Film Culture in Transition* (2010), *The Unquiet American: Transgressive Comedies from the U.S.* (2009), *Discovering Orson Welles* (2007), *Essential Cinema: On the Necessity of Film Canons* (2004), *Abbas Kiarostami* (2003, with Mehrnaz Saeed-Vafa), *Dead Man* (2000), *Placing Movies: The Practice of Film Criticism* (1995), *Greed* (1993), *Midnight Movies* (1991, with J. Hoberman), and *Moving Places: A Life at the Movies* (1980). He has also edited *This is Orson Welles* (1992) and co-edited, with Adrian Martin, *Movie Mutations: The Changing Face of World Cinephilia* (2003). Since 2008, he has maintained a web site at jonathanrosenbaum.com and has taught film courses in Chicago and Richmond, Virginia.

**SIMON ROTHÖHLER** is a research fellow at the Collaborative Research Center "Aesthetic Experience and the Dissolution of Artistic Limits" of the Free University Berlin. In 2010 he completed a doctorate which examines the intersection between film theory and theories of historiography (*Amateur der Weltgeschichte. Historiographische Praktiken im Kino der Gegenwart*; 2011). He is a co-founder and co-editor of the magazine *CARGO. Film/Medien/Kultur*.

# Acknowledgments

The editors would like to thank Clemens von Wedemeyer for providing the photograph of his *Sun Cinema* for the cover of this book; Sara VanDerBeek for generously allowing us to use the image of her father's *Movie-Drome*; Wendy Dorsett & John Mhiripiri (Anthology Film Archives) for providing stills of the original Invisible Cinema and Roland Fischer-Briand & Barbara Vockenhuber (Österreichisches Filmmuseum) for the still of Ernie Gehr's *Eureka;* Douglas Gordon for the installation view of his *24 Hour Psycho;* David N. Rodowick for slightly revising an earlier version of "The Film Spectator. A Special Memory," written by Raymond Bellour in English; Duke University Press for the permission to reprint Tom Gunning's text; Judith Galka and Susanne Wagner for helping with references and footnotes.

Alexander Horwath has been a meticulous reader of the manuscript and helped tremendously with critical remarks and suggestions.

A special thanks goes to Michael Geyer for making it possible to publish Miriam Hansen's essay in this volume.

Tom Gunning's essay, "Moving Away from the Index: Cinema and the Impression of Reality," has been previously published in: *differences*, Vol. 18, Issue 1 (2007), pp. 29–52.

# Illustrations

Cover: *Sun Cinema*, Mardin, Turkey, 2010
The project *Sun Cinema* by Clemens von Wedemeyer was commissioned by *My City*, an initiative of the British Council Istanbul; Photo: Clemens von Wedemeyer © VG Bild-Kunst, Bonn

Page 71: Richard Estes, American (b. 1932). *Central Savings*, 1975. Oil on canvas, 36 × 48 inches; The Nelson-Atkins Museum of Art, Kansas City, Missouri. Gift of the Friends of Art, F75-13. Photo: Jamison Miller

Page 81: Stan VanDerBeek, *Movie-Drome* interior; Sara VanDerBeek Collection

Page 83: Invisible Cinema, Anthology Film Archives, Stills Collection

Page 89: Douglas Gordon, *24 Hour Psycho;* Video Installation, Dimensions Variable, Installation view Akademie der bildenden Künste Vienna, 1996. Photo: Angelika Krinzinger

Page 89: Ernie Gehr, *Eureka,* Österreichisches Filmmuseum, Stills Collection

# FilmmuseumSynemaPublikationen

Volume 14
**WAS IST FILM. PETER KUBELKAS ZYKLISCHES PROGRAMM IM ÖSTERREICHISCHEN FILMMUSEUM**
*Edited by Stefan Grissemann, Alexander Horwath, and Regina Schlagnitweit*
*Vienna 2010, 208 pages. ISBN 978-3-901644-36-8*
*In German*

Volume 13
**ROMUALD KARMAKAR**
*Edited by Olaf Möller and Michael Omasta*
*Vienna 2010, 256 pages, ISBN 978-3-901644-34-4*
*In German*

Volume 12
**APICHATPONG WEERASETHAKUL**
*Edited by James Quandt*
*Vienna 2009, 256 pages. ISBN 978-3-901644-31-3*
*In English*
Apichatpong Weerasethakul is widely praised as one of *the* central figures in contemporary cinema. This first English-language volume on the Thai filmmaker looks at his works from a variety of angles and is extensively illustrated. With contributions by James Quandt, Benedict Anderson, Mark Cousins, Karen Newman, Tony Rayns, Kong Rithdee, and Tilda Swinton. With two interviews and personal essays the filmmaker's own voice is also a strong presence in the book.

Volume 11
**GUSTAV DEUTSCH**
*Edited by Wilbirg Brainin-Donnenberg and Michael Loebenstein*
*Vienna 2009, 252 pages. ISBN 978-3-901644-30-6*
*In English and German*
According to Viennese filmmaker Gustav Deutsch, "film is more than film." His own career proves that point. In addition to being an internationally acclaimed creator of found footage films, he is also a visual artist, an architect, a researcher, an educator, an archaeologist, and a traveler. This volume traces the way in which the cinema of Gustav Deutsch transcends our common notion of film. Essays by Nico de Klerk, Stefan Grissemann, Tom Gunning, Beate Hofstadler, Alexander Horwath, Wolfgang Kos, Scott MacDonald, Burkhard Stangl, and the editors.

Volume 10
**MICHAEL PILZ. AUGE KAMERA HERZ**
*Edited by Olaf Möller and Michael Omasta*
*Vienna 2008, 288 pages, ISBN 978-3-901644-29-0*
*In German*

Volume 9
**FILM CURATORSHIP ARCHIVES, MUSEUMS, AND THE DIGITAL MARKETPLACE**
*Edited by Paolo Cherchi Usai, David Francis, Alexander Horwath, and Michael Loebenstein*
*Vienna 2008, 240 pages. ISBN 978-3-901644-24-5*
*In English*
This volume deals with the rarely-discussed discipline of film curatorship and with the major issues and challenges that film museums and cinémathèques are bound to face in the Digital Age. *Film Curatorship* is an experiment: a collective text, a montage of dialogues, conversations, and exchanges among four professionals representing three generations of film archivists and curators.

Volume 8
**LACHENDE KÖRPER. KOMIKERINNEN IM KINO DER 1910ER JAHRE**
*Claudia Preschl*
*Vienna 2008, 208 pages, ISBN 978-3-901644-27-6*
*In German*

Volume 7
**JEAN EPSTEIN**
**BONJOUR CINÉMA UND ANDERE SCHRIFTEN ZUM KINO**
*Edited by Nicole Brenez and Ralph Eue, translated from French by Ralph Eue*
*Vienna 2008, 160 pages, ISBN 978-3-901644-25-2*
*In German*

Volume 6

**JAMES BENNING**

*Edited by Barbara Pichler and Claudia Slanar*

*Vienna 2007, 264 pages. ISBN 978-3-901644-23-8*

*In English*

James Benning's films are among the most fascinating works in American cinema. He explores the relationship between image, text and sound while paying expansive attention to the "vernacular landscapes" of American life. This volume traces Benning's artistic career as well as his biographical journey through the United States. With contributions by James Benning, Sharon Lockhart, Allan Sekula, Dick Hebdige, Scott MacDonald, Volker Pantenburg, Nils Plath, Michael Pisaro, Amanda Yates, Sadie Benning, Julie Ault, Claudia Slanar and Barbara Pichler.

Volume 5

**JOSEF VON STERNBERG**
**THE CASE OF LENA SMITH**

*Edited by Alexander Horwath and Michael Omasta*

*Vienna 2007, 304 pages. ISBN 978-3-901644-22-1*

*In English and German*

*The Case of Lena Smith,* directed by Josef von Sternberg, is one of the legendary lost masterpieces of the American cinema. Assembling 150 original stills and set designs, numerous script and production documents as well as essays by eminent film historians, the book reconstructs Sternberg's dramatic film about a young woman fighting the oppressive class system of Imperial Vienna. The book also includes essays by Janet Bergstrom, Gero Gandert, Franz Grafl, Alexander Horwath, Hiroshi Komatsu and Michael Omasta, a preface by Meri von Sternberg, as well as contemporary reviews and excerpts from Viennese literature of the era.

Volume 4

**DZIGA VERTOV. DIE VERTOV-SAMMLUNG IM ÖSTERREICHISCHEN FILMMUSEUM**
**THE VERTOV COLLECTION AT THE AUSTRIAN FILM MUSEUM**

*Edited by the Austrian Film Museum, Thomas Tode, and Barbara Wurm*

*Vienna 2006, 288 pages. ISBN 3-901644-19-9*

*In English and German*

For the Russian filmmaker and film theorist Dziga Vertov *KINO* was both a bold aesthetic experiment and a document of contemporary life. This book presents the Austrian Film Museum's comprehensive Vertov Collection: films, photographs, posters, letters as well as a large number of previously unpublished sketches, drawings and writings by Vertov including his extensive autobiographical "Calling Card" from 1947.

Volume 3

**JOHN COOK. VIENNESE BY CHOICE, FILMEMACHER VON BERUF**

*Edited by Michael Omasta and Olaf Möller*

*Vienna 2006, 252 pages. ISBN 3-901644-17-2*

*In German (part 1) and English (part 2).* OUT OF PRINT

Volume 2

**PETER TSCHERKASSKY**

*Edited by Alexander Horwath and Michael Loebenstein*

*Vienna 2005, 256 pages. ISBN 3-901644-16-4*

*In English and German.* OUT OF PRINT

Volume 1

**CLAIRE DENIS. TROUBLE EVERY DAY**

*Edited by Michael Omasta and Isabella Reicher*

*Vienna 2005, 160 pages. ISBN 3-901644-15-6*

*In German.* OUT OF PRINT

---

All bilingual or English-language publications produced by the Austrian Film Museum are distributed internationally by Columbia University Press (**cup.columbia.edu**). For German-language titles please see **www.filmmuseum.at** or **www.synema.at**.